THE MARKED BODY

The Marked Body

Domestic Violence in Mid-Nineteenth-Century Literature

Kate Lawson and
Lynn Shakinovsky

State University of New York Press

Published by
State University of New York Press, Albany

Printed in the United States of America

For information, address State University of New York Press,
90 State Street, Suite 700, Albany, NY 12207

Production by Kelli Williams
Marketing by Patrick Durocher

Library of Congress Cataloging-in-Publication Data

Lawson, Kate, 1958–
The marked body : domestic violence in mid-nineteenth-century literature / Kate Lawson and Lynn Shakinovsky.
p. cm.
Includes index.
ISBN 0-7914-5375-8 (alk. paper)—ISBN 0-7914-5376-6 (pbk. : alk. paper)
1. English fiction—19th century—History and criticism. 2. Family violence in literature.
3. Browning, Elizabeth Barrett, 1806–1861. Aurora Leigh. 4. Domestic fiction, English—History and criticism. 5. Hawthorne, Nathaniel, 1804–1864. Birthmark. 6. Body, Human in literature. I. Shakinovsky, Lynn, 1955– II. Title

PR878.F29 L39 2002
823'.809355—dc21 2002021056

10 9 8 7 6 5 4 3 2 1

Contents

With love and gratitude to Hilda and Leo Shakinovsky,
and in loving memory of Jean Macdonald Lawson and Francis Lawson

Acknowledgments

We are indebted to the friends, colleagues, institutions, and families who supported the writing of this book in a variety of ways.

We gratefully acknowledge the generous and invaluable support of the Social Sciences and Humanities Research Council of Canada and also Wilfrid Laurier University. The Wilfrid Laurier University Course Remission Grant and Book Preparation Grant provided invaluable time to write in the early stages of the book and much needed financial assistance in its final stages.

We are deeply indebted to Michael Ross for his generous and careful reading of an early version of this manuscript and also appreciative of the constructive and encouraging advice of the anonymous readers at SUNY Press; their suggestions for revisions have made this a better book.

We have been fortunate to have the advice and assistance of friends and colleagues at both Wilfrid Laurier University and University of Northern British Columbia. We particularly appreciate the council, wisdom, and friendship of Viviana Comensoli, Eleanor Ty, and Maria di Cenzo; the book has benefited greatly from their guidance. Thanks also to Stan Beeler, Gary Boire, Jane Campbell, Jodey Castricano, Joel Faflak, Paul Tiessen, and Lorraine York who have been supportive and caring colleagues. Lynn Shakinovsky also thanks Peter Elder for his unwavering loyalty, support, and belief in the project throughout its long years.

We are grateful to our fine research assistants: Sarah Brophy, Carolyn Findlayson, and Jennifer Bell did excellent work; Deirdre Kwiatek kept us in touch with a good research library; and Darlene Shatford's meticulous work made the final preparations of the manuscript a pleasure.

Finally, our greatest debt is to our families. Martin Shakinovsky, Bertha Shakinovsky, Keith Lawson, Christy Luckyj, John Lawson, and Sue Campbell have been supportive and caring throughout the writing of the book. Kate Lawson deeply thanks Emma, Ariel, Sonia, and Trystan Wyse for constantly reminding her about what is truly important in a loving domestic sphere. She also thanks Bruce Wyse for his unfailing generosity of heart and mind; his largesse in ideas, in books, in argument, and in good food and wine were and are invaluable. Lynn Shakinovsky thanks her son Ben with all her heart. His loving presence, his generosity of spirit, his sweetness of heart and mind make everything possible. And finally, also Terry Shakinovsky, her earliest and dearest sharer of books.

❧

An earlier version of Chapter 1, "'A frightful object': Romance, Obsession, and Death in Nathaniel Hawthorne's 'The Birth-Mark'" was published under the title "The Return of the Repressed: Illiteracy and the Death of the Narrative in Hawthorne's "'The Birth-mark'" in *ATQ,* Volume 9, No. 4, December 1995. Reprinted by permission of The University of Rhode Island.

An earlier version of Chapter 2, "Domestic Violence, Abjection, and the Comic Novel: Anthony Trollope's *Barchester Towers,*" was published as "Abject and Defiled: Signora Neroni's Body and the Question of Domestic Violence" in *Victorian Review,* Volume 21, No. 4, Summer 1995. Reprinted by permission.

Cover photo (c. 1857–1864) by Clementina, Lady Hawarden, of Lady and Lord Hawarden, courtesy of the Trustees of the Victoria & Albert Museum.

Introduction

THE BODY

In Tolstoy's epic novel *War and Peace,* readers are provided with a piece of passing information about a character, Dolohov. In a discussion between two of his commanding officers about the wildness of his temper, one tells the other that "in Poland, if you please, he all but killed a Jew." The response of the other is a mollifying "yes, yes. . . . Still one must be easy on a young man in misfortune" (133). The reference to anti-Semitic violence is at once mundane and startling; the tone of the conversation informs the reader that this event, although culpable, is commonplace. Yet in the vast social, political, and emotional tapestry of the novel, in its glittering and compelling portrait of the Russian aristocracy, the "all but killed" Jew is an anomaly, a signifier of the kind of violent experience that is *not* part of the novel's representational field. The "all but killed" Jew is the realist text's marker of the violence and moral degradation of the character Dolohov, but at the same time this single Jewish body also functions as a kind of tear in the fabric of the narrative, momentarily rendering the invisible visible, reminding us of what is *not* represented in this realist text, and opening to us briefly the universe of discarded, excluded, and persecuted bodies.

This book is a study of discarded and violated bodies of middle-class women in selected texts of mid-nineteenth-century fiction and poetry. Like *War and Peace*, most of these texts do not urgently explore the violence visited upon these bodies as pressing social, political, or moral problems, and even in those that focus on these questions, such as George Eliot's "Janet's Repentance" where the beaten wife is at the center of the plot, the implications of these questions finally tend to be evaded, or set aside. These bodies thus partake in some measure of the liminality of the "all but killed" Jew. At the same time, however, what makes the violence explored in these texts startling is that the violence does not take place in the space of a largely unrepresented other, as is the case in Tolstoy's text where it occurs in the space of the ethnic other, the Jew in Poland; rather, violence takes place in the home, in the privileged sphere of bourgeois women's lives, and at the hands of their husbands and fathers. Domestic violence is thus itself a rupture in a cultural order that stressed the home as a woman's sphere, as the place of her security and her rule.[1]

"Domestic violence" has of course a specific idiomatic meaning in current discourse; Kathleen J. Ferraro's claim that the term originated in the early 1970s as "a code for physical and emotional brutality within intimate relations, usually heterosexual" (78, 77) suggests that it may be an anachronism in a discussion of mid-nineteenth-century literary texts. The equivalent nineteenth-century terms would be "marital cruelty" as a legal description or "wife beating" as a colloquial one.[2] Although we have wrestled with the connotations of the term *domestic violence,* we have chosen to employ it since the ongoing critical analysis of nineteenth-century bourgeois women's lives in relation to the *domestic* sphere provides the critical backdrop for our interest in texts in which *violence*—actual or threatened—challenges the integrity of that domestic sphere from within. Whether in accounts of a brutal husband, such as in George Eliot's novella, or of a brutal father, as in Elizabeth Gaskell's short story, we believe we have identified texts in which the representation of bourgeois women fades into blankness, liminality, ghostliness, or instability as the safety of their domestic sphere is threatened. We have thus chosen to use the term *domestic violence* to signify the rupturing of the privileged sphere of nineteenth-century women's lives by threats of, or more particularly, actual physical violence.

Feminist criticism has, of course, been intimately involved with tracing the experience of both the real and fantasized bodies of women; it has frequently taken as its starting point for analysis the visibility and invisibility of the female body and of female experience. When Virginia Woolf in *A Room of One's Own* wants to understand "why no woman wrote a word of that extraordinary literature" of the Elizabethan period, she says she first needs to know "[w]hat were the conditions in which women lived" (53). Taking down Trevelyn's *History of England* from the shelf, Woolf confronts the reality of domestic violence:

> Once more I looked up Women, found "position of" and turned to the pages indicated. "Wife-beating," I read, "was a recognized

> right of man, and was practised without shame by high as well as low. . . . Similarly," the historian goes on, "the daughter who refused to marry the gentleman of her parents' choice was liable to be locked up, beaten and flung about the room, without any shock being inflicted on public opinion." (54)

The brutalized bodies Trevelyn describes form one of the main strands of Woolf's work, reappearing, for instance, in the imagined story of Shakespeare's sister.

Faced with a history that records the violent reality of women's lives or nothing of their lives at all, Woolf turns to the power of imagination to probe other aspects of female experience. Imagining "a very ancient lady crossing the street," Woolf longs to interrogate her about her personal history even as she knows that the woman "could remember nothing": "For all the dinners are cooked; the plates and cups washed; the children sent to school and gone out into the world. Nothing remains of it all. All has vanished. No biography or history has a word to say about it" (116). Woolf argues that although the "ancient lady" has a direct lived experience of nineteenth-century social and cultural history, the concrete particulars of that experience have vanished; female experience is absorbed by, and lost in, the fleeting and the routine, the invisible and silent domestic sphere.[3] Woolf's sense of women's absorption into the fleeting and the routine is captured almost eighty years earlier by Florence Nightingale in "Cassandra," a work that describes women who "sink to living from breakfast till dinner, from dinner till tea, with a little worsted work, and to looking forward to nothing but bed":

> Women dream till they have no longer the strength to dream. . . . All their plans and visions seem vanished, and they know not where; gone, and they cannot recall them. They do not even remember them. And they are left without the food of reality or of hope. (qtd. in Helsinger, Sheets, and Veeder 2:145, 146)

Nightingale's despairing language encapsulates a feminine experience that is both fleeting and doomed. Set against the violence that is described by Trevelyn or experienced by Shakespeare's sister are these vanished domestic lives, felt only as "the pressure of dumbness, the accumulation of unrecorded life" (Woolf, *Room* 117). The invisibility of women's domestic life is thus compounded by a decorous muteness. Woolf's foray into women's bodily experience opens her into two modes: a sense of the violence inflicted on the female body, and a sense of the vanished and dumb lives to which she must give voice. Our study can, by analogy, also be situated between these two points, between a reading of the bourgeois female body as marked by violence and of that same body as a site of unspeaking and invisible experience.

The intimate relation between bourgeois women and a secure domestic sphere in nineteenth-century culture has frequently been embodied in the figure of "the angel in the house." Taken from Coventry Patmore's 1854–1856 long poem sequence of that title, the angel is the feminine presiding spirit of purity, sympathy, and self-sacrifice in domestic life. Patmore only briefly alludes to the potential for what he calls "The Wife's Tragedy" (Book 1: Canto 9) in his poem, the tragedy being a husband who is merely neglectful and impatient, certainly not cruel or violent. In this case, the wife nevertheless "casts her best, . . . flings herself" at her husband's cold and unresponsive heart: "How often flings for nought! and yokes / Her heart to an icicle or whim" (778–80). If a husband's remorse is not forthcoming—the worst case that Patmore's poem envisions—then the husband's indifference is still met by the wife's unchanging love: "And when, ah woe, she loves alone, / Through passionate duty love flames higher, / As grass grows taller round a stone" (796–98). Although Patmore's metaphor pictures the angel as enveloping a stony, unresponsive male place, Mary Jacobus comments that "woman" more frequently marks the silent and pure space *within* patriarchy; "[Woman] is the term by which patriarchy creates a reserve of purity and silence in the materiality of its traffic with the world and its noisy discourse" (10–11). The woman's literal space is of course the home, so that, as Nina Auerbach notes, through a "convenient shorthand . . . '[a]ngel' and 'house' become virtual synonyms" (67–69). The angel is able to "spiritualize space" through her maternal, sequestered warmth, making the home an image of her own body, and then through a reciprocal motion, "the house in turn could spiritualize the woman" (Dickerson xv–xvi). The stultifying passivity of this feminine role, as well as its capacity for deception and self-deception, leads Virginia Woolf in "Professions for Women" to call for the killing of this phantasmic angel; since the angel can never tell "the truth about human relations, morality, sex" (238), this remnant of Victorian domestic relations must be extinguished.

The angel has remained a compelling prism through which to view women's place in the bourgeois domestic sphere. Sandra M. Gilbert and Susan Gubar in *The Madwoman in the Attic* note the angel's extreme "alienation from ordinary fleshly life," which makes her in a sense already dead, an "Angel of Death" (24); their book carefully reveals the extent to which the domestic bourgeois angel thus also embodies a "repressed (but therefore all the more frightening) capacity for explosive rage" (26). Perhaps their clearest example of this doubled angel/monster figure is the relationship of Jane Eyre to Bertha Mason Rochester: the latter is figuratively "Jane's truest and darkest double" (360). Although Gilbert and Gubar do not explicitly examine tropes of domestic violence, their analysis of the demonic Bertha Mason indicates one of the moments in which violence may enter the bourgeois nineteenth-century home—when the Victorian man is confronted by a "monstrous" wife. Yet it is important to note that Rochester himself, the bourgeois gentleman, claims that he is in fact not cruel but exhibiting a commendable "restraint" in his dealings with Bertha Mason: "[H]er vices," he says, "were so strong, only cruelty could check them, and I would not use cruelty" (Brontë 333–34). Even Jane, sensibly appalled by Bertha Mason's violence, is also seemingly impressed by Rochester's self-control: "He could have settled her with a well-planted blow; but he would not strike: he would only wrestle" (321). Gilbert and Gubar's analysis of the Janus-faced angel in the house thus invites readers to pay close attention to the moment when the bourgeois angel may resolve into a monster, a point taken up by Auerbach who notes that the angel's "revolutionary ardor and . . . dangerous mobility" allow her an "otherworldly power [which] translates itself imperceptibly into a demonism that destroys all families and all houses" (4). *Jane Eyre*'s gothicism is also a reminder that the haunted castle and the predatory male villain may be read as distorted yet psychologically "true" portraits of the domestic hearth and the violent husband.[4]

More recent historians of the novel have also examined the centrality of the home in the creation of specifically feminine middle-class power and values. Nancy Armstrong in *Desire and Domestic Fiction* and Elizabeth Langland in *Nobody's Angels* argue that nineteenth-century bourgeois women had far more real political power than Patmore's passive heroine could possibly acknowledge. Armstrong links "the history of British fiction to the empowering of the middle-classes in England through the dissemination of a new female ideal" (9); in this new ideal, the "domestic woman" established "her dominance over all those objects and practices we associate with private life" (3). This power is not cut off from but, rather, essentially linked to power in the public sphere. Thus, she argues that the brutality and violence that enter the private worlds of such novels as *Wuthering Heights, Jane Eyre,* and *Vanity Fair* emerge in the first instance from political suppression of radical movements, which instigates tropes of "unjustified punishment generat[ing] tremendous outrage on behalf of the powerless": "In one form or another, history has intruded upon the household and disrupted its traditional order" (177), whether that history intervened in the shape of the Napoleonic wars, as in *Vanity Fair*, or British colonialism, as in *Jane Eyre*. Such "social disorder" is however inscribed in the novels as "sexual scandal" (177), so that "monstrous women" such as Catherine in *Wuthering Heights* and Becky in *Vanity Fair* represent an "illicit desire" which is "the secret cause of all the disruptive events" in these novels (178); closure can come in these fictions only through a "revealing display of social redemption through the domestication of desire" (185). However, for Armstrong it seems crucial that "the monstrous women" who fuel these plots typically have "other than middle-class origins" (183), so that the bourgeois home remains unchallenged from within in its domestication of disruptive desires.

For Langland, the supposed angel in the house is in reality "Nobody's Angel" since she performs "a more significant and extensive economic and political function than is usually perceived," in that she has a role in "the active management of class power" (8). Langland notes that *public* violence against women is an explicit part of the plot of such eighteenth-century novels as Fanny Burney's *Evelina;* by the mid-nineteenth century, "[s]o powerful had social semiotics become in establishing and disciplining class behaviour . . . that an Esther Summerson is free to roam through brickmaker's slums surrounding Bleak House, . . . [and] a Margaret Hale to visit the slums of Manchester: and no one will touch a hair on their heads" (224). As Langland notes, "[C]ertain plots become non-narratable in a particular historical moment" (4); *public* violence against bourgeois women seems to be one of the "non-narratable" plots of mid-nineteenth-century culture. As this study hopes to show, domestic violence with an origin *inside* the bourgeois home verges on the edge of the non-narratable, and is thus replete with manifest evasions, silences, and distortions in its representations of both the woman's body and the domestic sphere it inhabits.

Violence made domestic gives the broken and marked bodies of bourgeois women and of the domestic sphere itself both an invisibility and a certain suggestiveness. In Anne Brontë's *Tenant of Wildfell Hall,* as the drunken Hattersley pulls his wife Millicent onto his knees and begins "remorselessly crushing her slight arms in the gripe of his powerful fingers," she implores: "Do let me alone, Ralph! remember we are not at home" (289). Their life "at home" is never represented in the novel, but Millicent's plea is both indirect and highly suggestive in its evocation of that life. By way of analogy, one can consider Nicole Loraux's examination of women's deaths in Greek tragedy; she points out that unlike male characters in Greek tragedy, the female character inevitably dies offstage, "in the depths of her house" (ix). The narration rather than the spectacle of women's deaths, argues Loraux, suggests that "female death could be entrusted only to words" (ix), and yet the richness of description in "[d]eath by report lends itself to conjecture vastly more than does violence exposed to the public view" (x). The bourgeois domestic world of the nineteenth century is of course neither invisible nor silent in the period's literature; its representation is central to most if not all nineteenth-century fictions. Yet even in a political analysis of the function of the bourgeois home, such as that undertaken by Elizabeth Ermarth in *The English Novel in History,* the home has a liminal status; since the home as ideological function simultaneously "operates as a refuge from the marketplace" and "*as* a market for improving its fortunes by selling its marriageable children for money or status," Ermarth concludes that "[t]he private refuge—'home'—provides a liminal space, a kind of bracket, for containing unresolved conflicts between these two incompatible social definitions" (189). Vanessa Dickerson comments that the home's "interiority, though ostensibly valued, was still based in negation and separation and ultimately associated with subordination if not out-and-out inferiority: the home was 'other' " (xiv).

This otherness and liminality become all the more pronounced as one looks for evidence of domestic violence and cruelty. As in Greek tragedy, violence against bourgeois women is rarely exposed to public view; rather, a certain invisibility and silence is attached to the violated bodies of these women and to the space in which the violations occur. Yet as William A. Cohen notes, silence itself "composes a strategic form, not an absence, of representation" (2); thus, concealed or invisible marks and bruises, like "[d]eath by report," far from being an absence of representation, serve to arouse "conjecture" as to the scene of violence and cruelty, and to the experiences of the suffering and marked body.

DOMESTIC VIOLENCE IN THE WORKING CLASSES

The marks of domestic violence were not invisible in one crucial sphere of mid-nineteenth-century discourse. Stories, novels, and essays proliferate that relate incidents of violence against working-class women, prostitutes, and "fallen women," whether publicly in the streets, or domestically in their squalid homes, an aspect of women's lives that has been examined by critics such as Judith Walkowitz, Deborah Epstein Nord, and Barbara Leah Harman. Locating violence against women in the poor and working classes seems to have been an attempt by bourgeois society to quarantine the pestilence of violence to the "lower orders." The presumption that domestic violence and cruelty were endemic in the working classes is clear in essays such as Harriet Taylor's "The Enfranchisement of Women," published in the *Westminster Review* in 1851:

> The truly horrible effects of the present state of the law [regarding marital property rights] among the lowest of the working population, is exhibited in those cases of hideous maltreatment of their wives by working men, with which every newspaper, every police report, teems. Wretches unfit to have the smallest authority over any living thing, have a helpless woman for their household slave. (Taylor 16n.)

Even such an enlightened writer as Frances Power Cobbe, in "Wife-Torture in England" (1878), exempts bourgeois men, if only for pragmatic reasons, from the class of wife beaters: "In his apparently most ungovernable rage, the gentleman or tradesman somehow manages to bear in mind the disgrace he will incur if his outbreak be betrayed by his wife's black eye or broken arm, and he regulates his cuffs or kicks accordingly" (Cobbe 134).[5] For Cobbe, not only is "wife-torture" depressingly common among the poor and working classes, but the female victims themselves are clearly recognizable types. Describing the "localities wherein Wife-torture flourishes in England," she writes:

> Wages are usually high though fluctuating. Facilities for drink and vice abound, but those for cleanliness and decency are scarcely obtainable. The men are rude, coarse, and brutal in their manners and habits, and the women devoid, in an extraordinary degree, of all the higher natural attractions and influences of their sex. . . . Throughout the whole of this inquiry I think it very necessary, in justice to all parties, and in mitigation of too vehement judge-

> ment of the cases only known from printed reports, to bear in mind that the women of the class concerned are, some of them woefully unwomanly, slatternly, coarse, foul-mouthed—sometimes loose in behaviour, sometimes madly addicted to drink. There ought to be no idealizing of them, *as a class*, into refined and suffering angels if we wish to be just. (Cobbe 136–37)

Cobbe's and Taylor's class prejudices manifest themselves in the matter of fact language of these passages. Descriptions such as "helpless women," and "woefully unwomanly, slatternly, coarse" indicate that the writers expect their bourgeois readers to recognize the victim "type"[6] but not themselves to identify with her misfortune.

This discourse is quite naturally carried over to fictional representations of poor and working-class women's bodies, representations that make violence visible in a spectacular manner. For instance, Sikes's murder of Nancy in Dickens's *Oliver Twist,* grotesque and horrific as it is, is true to the "type" bourgeois readers are to expect from such degraded characters. Led on by Fagin, Sikes's intention to murder is always clear, but it is Nancy's description of a life away from the sin and degradation of poverty and prostitution that indirectly precipitates his violence. Nancy tells Bill of her desire to find "a home in some foreign country where I could end my days in solitude and peace" and urges that they henceforth live separately and "repent" of their sinful lives (303); this home will not be a middle-class one, but will be constructed in emulation of that ideal. Dickens's "Appeal to Fallen Women" (1847) describes the life of former prostitutes in such a retreat:

> In this Home they will be taught all household work that would be useful to them in a home of their own, and enable them to make it comfortable and happy. In this Home, which stands in a pleasant country lane, and where each may have her little flower-garden, if she pleases, they will be treated with the greatest kindness; will lead an active, cheerful, healthy life; will learn many things it is profitable and good to know; and, being entirely removed from all who have any knowledge of their past career, will begin life afresh, and be able to win a good name and character. (382–83)

The "pleasant country lane," the "little flower-garden," and the "active, cheerful, healthy life" sound as wholesome as the life of the exemplary Rose Maylie; it is Nancy's stated desire for this life lived in imitation of bourgeois values that seals her death warrant, making her a traitor to the degraded and degrading code of Bill and his gang. Bill's reaction to her suggestion is instantaneous:

> The housebreaker freed one arm, and grasped his pistol. The certainty of immediate detection if he fired, flashed across his mind even in the midst of his fury; and he beat it twice with all the force he could summon, upon the upturned face that almost touched his own. . . .
>
> It was a ghastly figure to look upon. The murderer staggering backward to the wall, and shutting out the sight with his hand, seized a heavy club and struck her down. (303)

Bill is true to the violent code of his class. Nancy's attempt to move beyond the "woefully unwomanly, slatternly, coarse, foul-mouthed" existence that Cobbe describes precipitates her death. Although Rose Maylie's handkerchief grasped in the dying Nancy's hand may act as a metonymy for the well-intentioned intervention of the middle-class angel into the scene of lower-class depravity, the unsullied purity of the always "white handkerchief" could equally well be said to signify Rose Maylie's distance from it.

Sikes in *Oliver Twist,* like Jerry Cruncher ("crunch her") in *A Tale of Two Cities* and the brutal brick makers in *Bleak House*, is thus an example of how Dickens, in spite of the subtlety and complexity of his social analyses, still attempts to sequester domestic violence within the poor and working classes.[7] Similarly, when Thackeray notes in *Vanity Fair* that Becky Sharp's father "used to beat his wife and daughter" (15–16) when he was drunk, he is using an accepted shorthand to indicate the squalor and poverty of her upbringing.

However, such a segregation of degradation and contamination away from the middle classes could not ultimately be successful in Victorian discourse. Deborah Epstein Nord, for example, points out that the contagion associated with poverty and degradation *could* cross the boundary from the working to the middle classes (9), when, for example, bourgeois men visited prostitutes and carried venereal diseases home to their wives.[8] Similarly, middle-class men entering into association with the working classes could adopt their violent code. Thackeray's degraded Sir Pitt, whose appearance leads Becky Sharp at first to believe that he is a porter not a baronet, behaves according to a working-class "type." He beats his second wife, Rose, significantly the daughter of the local ironmonger: "He had his pretty Rose, and what more need a man require than to please himself? So he used to get drunk every night: to beat his pretty Rose sometimes: to leave her in Hampshire when he went to London for the parliamentary session, without a single friend in the wide world" (97).

By contrast, Thackeray is careful to note that the "gentlemen" of *Vanity Fair*—George Osborne, Rawdon Crawley, Lord Steyne—whatever their defects as husbands, do not resort to violence against their wives. Rawdon strikes Lord Steyne when he finds him philandering with Becky, but he does not touch his wife. He is like the aggrieved husband in George Meredith's "Modern Love" (1862), whose "most ungovernable rage" is indeed governable if its object is a woman, and who thus resists the temptation to strike the false wife:

> The love is here; it has but changed its aim.
> O bitter barren woman! what's the name?
> The name, the name, the new name thou hast won?
> Behold me striking the coward stroke!
> That will I not do, though the sting is dire.
> —Beneath the surface this, while by the fire,
> They sat, she laughing at a quiet joke. (6: 10–16)

The awkwardness of Meredith's redundancy in verb and object—"striking the coward stroke"—functions as an avoidance of even the suggestion that a gentleman might be "striking a woman." Lord Steyne in *Vanity Fair* adopts this gentlemanly code even as he flaunts his most belligerent impulses. When his family objects to having the interloper Becky introduced into their company, Lord Steyne retorts maliciously to his childless daughter-in-law, Lady Gaunt, that her sister-in-law (whose son stands to inherit the peerage) "is the only person in the family who doesn't wish you were dead." The scene continues:

> "You may strike me if you like, sir, or hit any cruel blow," Lady Gaunt said. To see his wife and daughter suffering always put his lordship into a good humour.
>
> "My sweet Blanche," he said, "I am a gentleman and never lay my hand upon a woman, save in the way of kindness." (Thackeray 613)

Lady Gaunt would seemingly prefer outright violence, but Lord Steyne is true to the code of his class: "I am a gentleman and never lay my hand upon a woman." His suave brutality is unexceptionable; his "coward stroke" is gloved in velvet. With its withering examination of class codes and scorn for the marriage marketplace, *Vanity Fair* views male predators and female victims as part of the inevitable order of society: "[I]f Henry the Eighth or Bluebeard were alive now, and wanted a tenth wife, do you suppose he could not get the prettiest girl that shall be presented this season?" (Thackeray 98) One of the most remarkable features of works such as Meredith's and Thackeray's is their ability to suggest the depths of aggression that lie "[b]eneath the surface" of polite middle-class society.

Nevertheless, outright physical violence is consistently *seen* throughout the century in the working classes, and seen not merely as *typical* of the class, but in such a way as to be foregrounded and sensationalized. As Harriet Taylor notes, "every newspaper, every police report, teems" with reports of the "hideous maltreatment of their wives by working men." By contrast, as we will argue, domestic violence aimed at *bourgeois* women in mid-nineteenth-century representations partakes of the same liminality as the "all but killed" Jew in Tolstoy's novel. The violent markings on the bodies of bourgeois women are not the result of a spectacular depravity, but of that which is unspeakable, evaded, deferred, denied.

THE BODY AS EVIDENCE

The status of the body in law, its apparent potential to function straightforwardly as evidence, would seem to provide a remedy for the uncertainty created by the concealed or occluded representations of bourgeois women and domestic violence. But as historicist criticism demonstrates, law and visibility are themselves culturally and discursively constructed. Marie-Christine Leps argues in her analysis of the discourse of deviance in the nineteenth century that "[r]elations of knowledge establish fields of visibility" (210); Michel Foucault points out in *Discipline and Punish* that "a legal decision . . . bears within it an assessment of normality and a technical prescription for a possible normalization" (20–21). Thus, legal assessments function not so much to describe as to prescribe the "visible" limits of "normal" marital behavior.

The attempt throughout the nineteenth century to define the term "marital cruelty" is a good example of the complex social, legal, political, and ethical field into which the body of evidence is thrown. A finding of marital cruelty was crucial for anyone seeking legal protection from a violent spouse throughout the century, since "cruelty" was the operative word in law to describe a state that would allow for a legal separation of a husband and wife—divorce *a mensa et thoro*—and eventually, after 1857, to qualify (in part) for a divorce.[9] Given the overwhelming social, legal, and religious importance of marriage, one can understand the insistence of Sir William Scott (later Lord Stowell), in his 1790 case *Evans v. Evans*, that "great caution" be used in making a finding of cruelty:

> What merely wounds the mental feelings is in few cases to be admitted where they are not accompanied with bodily injury, either actual or menaced. Mere austerity of temper, petulance of manners, rudeness of language, a want of civil attention and accommodation, even occasional sallies of passion, if they do not threaten bodily harm, do not amount to legal cruelty: they are high moral offences in the marriage state undoubtedly, not innocent surely in any state of life, but still they are not that cruelty against which the law can relieve. Under such misconduct of either of the parties, for it may exist on one side as well as the other, the suffering party must bear in some degree the consequences of an injudicious connection; must subdue by decent resistance or by prudent conciliation; and if this cannot be done, both must suffer in silence. (161 *English Reports* 467, qtd. in Hammerton, "Victorian Marriage" 273).

Scott's judgment was frequently cited throughout the nineteenth century. Although his definition—"bodily injury, either actual or menaced"—suggests that threats and mental sufferings may prove cruelty, in practice the body of a woman normally had to be able to provide clear and compelling evidence of physical violence if a verdict of "marital cruelty" were to be supported.[10] (Even then, the cruelty might have been "condoned" by a wife, which would negate its force in law.[11]) If evidence in a case suggested injured "mental feelings" rather than "bodily injury" then the "suffering party" had to bear with the situation or decently resist it, *or* "both must suffer in silence." Rhetorically, Scott's shift between what the "suffering party must bear" and what *both* parties must "suffer" is masterful. The assertion that "both must suffer in silence" restores the idea of mutuality and symmetry so desirable in a marriage, ignoring the power structures that render that kind of mutuality impossible, and the fact that if there is one "suffering party" then there may well be another who inflicts that suffering.

The status of the body as the site of visible evidence of violence is complicated by J. W. Kaye in his May 1856 essay in the *North British Review*, "Outrages on Women." The range and ferocity of the cruelty that Kaye describes underscore the Victorian gentleman's own sense of anxiety and unease with regard to his broader aggressive impulses, and signal an entry into the liminal realm. In contrast to accounts such as Taylor's and Cobbe's, which claim that marital cruelty is by and large a working-class phenomenon, Kaye insists that his middle-class brothers are to be condemned, not for "bodily injury, either actual or menaced," but for a more subtle, and to his mind, a more cruel barbarity toward their wives:

> Men of education and refinement do not strike women; neither do they strike one another. This is not their mode of expressing resentment. They may utter words more cutting than sharp knives; they may do things more stunning in their effects on the victim than the blows of pokers or hammers; they may kill their wives by the process of slow torture—unkindness, infidelity, whatever shape it may assume—and society will forgive them. The Law, too, has nothing to say to them. They are not guilty of what is recognised as an assault, because they only assail the affections—only lacerate the heart. (235)

Thus far, Kaye's essay is a challenge to contentions such as Scott's that mental sufferings cannot be relieved by law; lacerations to the heart are metaphoric, and thus cannot be "recognised as an assault." Yet the next step in his argument throws into question what kind of evidence of lacerations, of cruelty, can be seen and thus can be admitted as evidence:

> If we would see the worst type of man's cruelty to woman, we must not go into the police courts, where women with dishevelled hair and disfigured faces give painful evidence against their husbands, but into the best streets of London after night-fall, where the unspeaking and unspeakable evidence meets us at every turn. (235)

Kaye claims that although poor and working-class women's bodies with "dishevelled hair and disfigured faces" may figure as visible "painful evidence" of *a* cruelty, the *worst* cruelty is both "unspeakable"—beyond representation—and "unspeaking"—unable to give the necessary evidence in police courts, either in words or in the tangible form of "disfigured faces." Yet if "unspeakable" cruelty is not *marked* on the bourgeois body, is not *voiced* anywhere, how can "evidence" of that cruelty meet us "at every turn" in "the best streets of London after night-fall"? In mapping the interstices of physical violence and mental cruelty, Kaye is brought to confront "unspeaking" and invisible evidence, a spectral evidence which is *not* of the body, yet evidence that meets us "at every turn," and points to a cruelly "unspeakable" experience.

In turning to mid-nineteenth-century fictional representations of physical violence against women, we find that Kaye's problem of invisible, "unspeaking and unspeakable evidence" still obtains. As Loraux suggests about dead women in Greek tragedy, the invisibility and silence that attaches itself to the female body, and to intimate domestic experience generally, ensures that even physical violence yields evidence that is "suggestive" but not definitive. This book argues that mid-nineteenth-century representations of bourgeois domestic violence do not always in fact offer the intelligible or clear "evidence" which Scott demands or which Kaye insists belongs to physical violence. Disfigured faces or bodies, viewed obliquely, may be unable to *prove* domestic violence, and may simultaneously suggest something *more* than or *different* from a blow or a slap. Thus, not only does the marked body of the woman yield equivocal evidence, it constantly pushes against the limits of what Kaye calls the "unspeaking and unspeakable."

By late in the century, female misery in bourgeois marriages was, arguably, no longer shrouded from view. Mona Caird's 1888 exposé of nineteenth-century marriage is literally that, a making visible of the misery which she claims is, or ought to be, apparent to any onlooker:

> Suffice it to say that the cruelties, indignities, and insults to which women were exposed are (as every student of history knows) hideous beyond description. In Mongolia there are large cages in the market-place wherein condemned prisoners are kept and starved to death. The people collect in front of these cages to taunt and insult the victims as they die slowly day by day before their eyes. In reading the history of the past, and even the literature of our own day, it is difficult to avoid seeing in that Mongolian market-place a symbol of our own society, with its iron cage, wherein women are held in bondage, suffering moral starvation, while the thoughtless gather round to taunt and insult their lingering misery. (278–79)

In this ringing denunciation of the bourgeois ideals of domesticity and of women's place in the home that dominated midcentury ideology,

Caird's cage metaphor portrays the home as neither a private sphere, protecting women from the gaze of the world, nor a gilded cage, a domestic domain of delicacy and refinement. The market of Caird's essay is not even masked by the deceptive shimmer of a Vanity Fair, where men sell their daughters to the highest bidder; rather, it is an exposed prison, displaying women held in the iron cages of marriage, women who "die slowly day by day" from a lingering "moral starvation." While such a critique of bourgeois marriage is available in the 1890s, in the primarily midcentury texts that this book examines—*Barchester Towers*, "Janet's Repentance," "The Poor Clare," and *Aurora Leigh* (all published in the 1850s)—cruelty in the domestic sphere is still veiled, is still negatively inscribed, not subject to the scathing exposure of a Mona Caird.

READING THE MARKED BODY

This book is neither encyclopaedic nor exhaustive in its choice of texts. As one begins to look for evidence of bourgeois domestic violence in mid-nineteenth-century literature, one quickly begins to see that it is endemic even as it is obscured. It is this obscurity surrounding the representation of the scene of violence that demands the close attention to detail which the individual readings in this book attempt to provide. We have chosen our texts as exemplary of a broad range of possibilities in mid-nineteenth-century literature and culture, including prose and poetry, male and female writers, canonical and less canonical texts, realist, comic, and sensational works, and texts that range from the 1840s to the 1870s, but which are clustered in the 1850s, the decade when the reform of marriage laws and the introduction of the Divorce Court in England made the miseries of marriage an object of widespread interest.[12] Most importantly, we have chosen texts that best illustrate the range of theoretical, cultural, and social problems raised by representations of domestic violence. The earliest selection, and the only American text, is Nathaniel Hawthorne's "The Birthmark" (1843), a story fundamentally concerned with the ethical and aesthetic problems of marking and representation. The final novel we have chosen, Wilkie Collins's *Man and Wife* (1870), is the most polemical in its call for a reform of marriage laws that are seen as responsible for victimizing women, and yet is a novel that still employs the same silence and indirection characteristic of texts of the 1850s in representing the misery of bourgeois women.

While the chapters that follow use, at times, broadly divergent psychoanalytical and theoretical approaches—Freud, Lacan, Kristeva, Abraham and Torok, Lyotard—each begins with a text where a woman's bruised body is a compelling presence but paradoxically and simultaneously a haunting absence. While a historicist approach would ask why certain narratives are, in Langland's words, "non-narratable" at a particular political-historical moment (a question taken up by critics such as Langland, Leps, and Cohen), we hope that our psychoanalytic approach, while not ignoring historicist questions, will unveil other aspects of mid-nineteenth-century culture—its characteristic repressions, evasions, and alternative constructions—and will thus focus on why signification and direct representation have become inaccessible. Esther Rashkin points out that this reading strategy "entails showing how the processes by which coherence is obstructed can themselves be interpreted in certain texts to reveal unspeakable dramas concealed within the narratives" (6). Paraphrasing Rashkin, we would say that the psychoanalytic approach which we employ throughout asks why and how "coherence is obstructed" in the barely narratable stories of domestic violence against bourgeois women, in order to expose the "unspeakable dramas" buried within them. Cohen notes that the word *unspeakable* "usefully condenses two meanings: something *incapable* of being articulated as well as something *prohibited* from articulation" (3); the realm of prohibition is the point at which psychoanalysis can uniquely offer a mode of interrogating that which is "registered *negatively* in speech" (Copjec 14).[13]

Thus, while our study does not neglect the political matrices through which Armstrong, Langland, and other critics view the bourgeois woman, we are more centrally concerned with tracing the perpetual movement in these texts away from realist representation into repression, into a phantasmic realm of report, rumor, and conjecture. In privileging a psychoanalytic approach, we examine narrations of domestic violence and the peculiar figurations of the wounds or marks on bourgeois women's bodies in order to reveal a discursive realm of aggression, desire, and fear, which exists in spite of or in the midst of a certain silence and invisibility. This reading strategy will unmask the matrices of Victorian social life that discursively produce the unspoken and unspeakable sources of trauma: the bourgeois home, the parental relationship (both maternal and paternal), the intimacy of marriage, and, perhaps most disturbingly, the self who may be complicit in the violence she experiences. At the same time, our readings will suggest that mid-nineteenth-century literature itself functions as an important precursor to psychoanalysis in its interrogation of unspoken familial and psychological structures.

The realist enterprise, it has long been recognized, is already fraught with contradictions. Helena Michie's subtle and wide-ranging exploration in *The Flesh Made Word* of how women's bodies in Victorian culture become "both metaphors for the unknowable, and metaphors for metaphor, their bodies figures of figuration" (7) is an important foundation for our analyses; in particular her inquiry into the "representational taboos" (9) that make women's bodies oscillate between absence and presence grounds many of our readings. Trauma theory also provides an important substructure for our analysis, since the history of trauma is based precisely on a paradox of inaccessibility. Cathy Caruth argues that a history of trauma is "referential precisely to the extent that it is not fully perceived as it occurs" (*Trauma* 8). The subject who has experienced trauma is unable either to remember the experience (because one can never fully assimilate it), or to forget it (because one is possessed by it): "[H]istory can be grasped only in the very inaccessibility of its occurrence," says Caruth (*Trauma* 8); the subject therefore carries "an impossible history within" (*Trauma* 5). Dori Laub agrees that the history of the trauma is inaccessible, having

> no beginning, no ending, no before, no during and no after. This absence of categories that define it lends it a quality of "otherness," a salience, a timelessness and a ubiquity that puts it outside the range of associatively linked experiences, outside the range of comprehension, of recounting and of mastery. (Felman and Laub 69)

Laub's state of "otherness," like Caruth's notion of being "possessed," points to the tendency of trauma narratives to create a liminal state of instability, indeterminacy, and hauntings. Caruth and Laub thus both employ a symptomatic reading of narratives, a mode we have found useful, since it provides a model for interpreting what seem to be failures and gaps in representation.

THE DENIGRATED BODY

Having read Trevelyn's *History of England*, Virginia Woolf tries to make sense of a culture in which women are virtually absent from history and yet which creates a literature of strong and eloquent women:

"Clytemnestra, Antigone, Cleopatra, Lady Macbeth, Phèdre, Cressida, Rosalind, Desdemona, the Duchess of Malfi" (55). She concludes:

> A very queer, composite being . . . emerges. Imaginatively she is of the highest importance; practically she is completely insignificant. She pervades poetry from cover to cover; she is all but absent from history. . . .
>
> It was certainly an odd monster that one made up by reading the historians first and the poets afterwards—a worm winged like an eagle; the spirit of life and beauty in a kitchen chopping up suet. (*Room* 56)

The contradictions Woolf finds are, of course, not merely the result of reading historians first and poets afterward; the contradictions in the social construction of woman are to be found at the very foundation of culture.

J. W. Kaye, in "Outrages on Women," begins his essay by pointing out an analogous contradiction at the heart of Victorian culture. Where Woolf finds a "worm winged like an eagle," Kaye discovers in his own culture the pampered "invalid" who is simultaneously spurned as an "inferior animal":

> Tender, considerate, self-sacrificing, caressing, on the one hand; violent, selfish, brutal, on the other, Man treats his helpmate as a child or an invalid, incapable of self-assertion and self-defence, indeed, of all independent action,—and therefore an object of deference and attention, to be humoured and indulged, to be aided and supported; or else, as an inferior animal, strong in endurance, to be buffeted, and persecuted, and outraged, and humiliated, and made to suffer every kind of wrong. (233)

Having noted this contradiction, Kaye tries to probe its source:

> Now all this, doubtless, arises from the one common feeling, that woman is the "weaker vessel." As is man's conception of the purposes and uses of strength, so is his treatment of woman either of a defensive or an offensive character. In either case there is an overweening sense of his own superiority, the practical expression of which, whatever its intent, is degrading to the other sex. We are very far from any disposition to assert, that the two extremes of defensiveness and offensiveness are equal evils. . . . But they are evils, which, though differing in degree, as they arise from the same cause, tend also to the same result. Both indicate and perpetuate

> the weakness of woman. To start from one's seat, or rush across the room to pick up a woman's pocket-handkerchief, or to open the door for her, is a very different thing from knocking her down and stamping upon her; but both acts originate in the same sense of man's superiority, and tend to perpetuate woman's weakness. The one is a blunder, the other is a crime. (233)

Kaye's analysis acutely recognizes woman's "weakness" to be the result of man's action; both the "offensiveness" and "defensiveness" of man "*indicate* and *perpetuate* the weakness of woman" (our emphasis). Kaye's analysis suggests that female subjectivity is constructed by male desires and fears; a man's desire to protect and his impulse to attack are both rooted in "the same cause, and tend also to the same result." Like Woolf, he is vitally concerned with the woman as she is perceived and formed by and in culture, and more specifically, by and in patriarchy.

Jacques Lacan also investigates the simultaneous elevation and degradation of woman in culture; he discusses the elevation of the woman in a trope such as courtly love, an elevation that is simultaneously a kind of elegant subjection. In the courtly love tradition, says Lacan, the "lady was entirely, in the most servile sense of the term, his [the man's] female subject" (*Feminine Sexuality* 141). Lacan, according to Jacqueline Rose, understands "courtly love as the elevation of the woman into the place where her absence or inaccessibility stands in for male lack, . . . just as he sees her denigration as the precondition for man's belief in his own soul" ("Introduction II" 49). Lack projected onto the woman can lead to what Kaye calls man's "defensiveness," while the *disavowal* of lack by the man leads to a very inelegant defamation, or what Kaye calls man's "offensiveness." Lacan states:

> For the soul to come into being, she, the woman, is differentiated from it, and this has always been the case. Called woman *[dit-femme]* and defamed *[diffâme]*. The most famous things that have been handed down in history about women have been strictly speaking the most defamatory that could be said of them. (*Feminine Sexuality* 156)

It is this radical contradiction in the male apprehension of the woman—elevation/denigration, existence/nonexistence—which is of central concern to this study.

Lacan has (in)famously argued that "*the* woman does not exist"; rather, she is a "symptom" for the man (*Feminine Sexuality* 167, 168). This book returns to cultural representations of women's bodies and claims that the degraded and scarred woman's body is a central symptom, not for man, but for mid-nineteenth-century culture itself. The task Woolf set herself in *A Room of One's Own* was to find or to imagine a more authentic woman than the one she found (un)represented in history or in art; the task of this book is perhaps the opposite, to turn back to the contradictions Woolf notes in the literary representation of women, contradictions underscored most compellingly in the bourgeois female body marked by violence.

We will thus argue in this study that domestic violence is a crucible in which the female body is placed, where it becomes marked by scars, disfigurement, even erasure; yet these marks point beyond the violence that begets them to broader areas of female experience, sexuality, and consciousness. As Elizabeth Bronfen argues in *Over her Dead Body,* "[W]hat is plainly visible . . . also stands in for something else" (xi);[14] as Lacan says of the project of psychoanalysis, the analyst must "read beyond what [he has] incited the subject to say" (*Seminar XX* 26). Representations of the bourgeois female body and female experience in mid-nineteenth-century literature foreground this need to "read beyond"; the method for our analysis of the female body battered by domestic violence is thus to "read beyond" realism, to probe the "something else" disclosed by representation. The exquisite perfection of Georgiana's murdered body in "The Birth-Mark"; the almost naked, discarded body of Janet in "Janet's Repentance"; the crippled body of Signora Neroni in *Barchester Towers;* the uncannily doubled body of Lucy in "The Poor Clare"; the raped body of Marian Erle in *Aurora Leigh;* and the mute body of Hester Dethridge, sealed by "terrible past suffering" in *Man and Wife* (113)—all provide a form of overstated, fascinating visibility that simultaneously comes to stand for that which is occluded or unspoken. Thus, overstated visibility signals the disruption attendant upon repression; in each case the peculiar exhibitionism that is consequent upon representations of the injured bourgeois body is inextricably bound up with that which is secret, hidden, denied. The marked body is an exteriority that indicates an inexpressible interiority. The female body, already the site of alterity, is inscribed here with something that cannot quite be expressed; it thus becomes that which is culturally and psychically denied, the place that is not.

1

"A Frightful Object"

Romance, Obsession, and Death in Nathaniel Hawthorne's "The Birth-Mark"

Domestic violence manifests itself peculiarly in Nathaniel Hawthorne's "The Birth-Mark," a story that first appeared in *Pioneer Magazine* in 1843. Published earlier than many of the texts under discussion in this book, "The Birth-Mark" is a narrative that obscures its subject matter from itself. Representing itself as a tale of brilliant scientific investigation and research, "The Birth-Mark" turns out to be the story of a marked body and a murder. Aylmer, an illustrious scientist, becomes obsessed with a mark on his wife's cheek, determines to eradicate it, and in doing so kills her. The story thus concerns itself with the marking and representation of the woman's body—a body that appears at first to be noted for its stunning beauty, but turns out instead to be a body marked merely for destruction.

"The Birth-Mark" is distinct from the other texts discussed in this book; not only was it published earlier, it is the only American text and is also a romance. There is a laconic, guarded quality in the narration of events; the narrative style is arguably not only brief and succinct but cursory. The generic features of romance—the lack of a detailed social context, the stylized, allegorized quality of the characters, and the strange, pervasive air of distance—release both the reader and the characters into a world unconstrained by the realist expectations of social actuality. In this story, unlike most of the other texts explored in this book, little explanation or context is offered for the violence and destruction that occur and Aylmer's destructive desires are not narratively placed in a psychological or social or cultural context. "The Birth-Mark" may therefore appear to be a strange starting point for a book that principally considers mid-nineteenth-century realist texts.

Paradoxically, however, it is precisely the absence of context that works to illuminate the perversity and distortion of the violence that is portrayed in the story.

For Henry James, the lack of context, of detail, of explanation, or of actuality is the defining quality of the romance and functions to free the imagination from constraint:

> The only *general* attribute of projected romance that I can see . . . is the fact of the kind of experience with which it deals—experience liberated, so to speak; experience disengaged, disembroiled, disencumbered, exempt from the conditions that we usually know to attach to it. (Preface, *The American* xvii)

For James, then, the lack of realist constraints in the romance has the paradoxical effect of enhancing and intensifying its capacities for human investigation. This notion is elaborated upon by a number of theorists of the genre, all of whom perceive the denuded, simplified world of the romance as exposing that which is partially excluded by the realist text—the world of the unconscious, of dreams, fantasies, nightmares, and of the private, the hidden, the dark. Gillian Beer states that "the romance gives repetitive form to . . . those desires which cannot find controlled expression within a society" (13); Northrop Frye discusses the "subjective intensity" of romance and the way in which something "nihilistic and untameable is likely to keep breaking out of [its] pages" (304–05); and Richard Chase argues that the romance embodies the "aesthetic possibilities of radical forms of alienation, contradiction, and disorder" (2).

For Hawthorne himself, romance, both because of and in spite of this instability, is fully committed to "the truth of the human heart" (Preface, *House* 1). "Nihilism," lack of control, outbreak, "contradiction," and "disorder" all seethe beneath the stylized veneer of "The Birth-Mark" allowing it to reveal aspects of the psyche and "human heart" that might be less accessible in the detailed, contextualized world of the realist text.

The principal "context" of the story is markedly unreal: when Aylmer takes his wife into the artificially created space that he has constructed for her and in which he will kill her, he feels as though "he could draw a magic circle round her, within which no evil might intrude" (44). While, on the one hand, the figuration of this "magic circle" highlights the essential liminality of the domestic sphere (an important aspect of all the domestic spaces this book examines), on the other hand, its magical unreality foregrounds the fact that the evil from which Aylmer ostensibly wishes to protect his wife comes from within rather than without, from *inside* the "magic circle," inside the domestic sphere. Thus, the tale's lack of context and of realist detail functions not only to isolate the violence (thereby intensifying it) but to point directly to its source.

Ironically then, the absence of explanation or narrative detail allows for a strangely direct intervention into the traumatic moment. Dori Laub's statement that trauma has "no beginning, no ending, no before, no during and no after" (Felman and Laub 69) aptly sums up the compelling atmosphere of timelessness that is so prevalent in "The Birth-Mark." The story exhibits or embodies what Laub describes as quintessential to the traumatic moment, namely an "absence of categories that define it [which] lends it a quality of 'otherness,' a salience, a timelessness and a ubiquity that puts it outside the range of associatively linked experiences, outside the range of comprehension, of recounting and of mastery" (Felman and Laub 69). As the narrator and Aylmer collude to create the impression that the story is merely one of a scientific experiment unfortunately gone awry, the story's hints about and oblique references to the experience of Georgiana suggest that everything that happens to her in her marriage is infected by an " 'otherness,' a salience, a timelessness and a ubiquity" quite beyond the realm of mastery. In fact, it is by relying on the comprehension, recounting, and mastery of Aylmer, and by abandoning her own, that Georgiana is left open to his scientific depredations.

The one context the story does provide in detail is the story of Aylmer, "a man of science—an eminent proficient in every branch of natural philosophy" (36); yet in spite of his amazing proficiency his "most splendid successes were almost invariably failures" (49). "Mastery" in the narrative appears to belong to a failed scientist; when science fails again at the end of the story, the events are subject merely to the banal moralizing of the narrator rather than to any sense of effective "comprehension . . . [or] mastery." The experiences of Georgiana are left unnarrated, and assumed to be unnarratable. Thus this short story about a mark and an extraordinary act of violence inside the domestic sphere encapsulates and highlights the major concerns of the investigations that follow.

SIGNIFICATION AND THE FEMALE BODY

The progression of the narrative in "The Birth-Mark" might be said to be the inverse of the other narratives under consideration in this book. In all the other texts, the plot develops around the violent marking of the female body; in this text the identifying mark is present at the beginning of the story and the tale is about the protagonist's attempts to eradicate the mark. The act of violence perpetrated against the female subject consists of the unmarking of her body; the removal of the mark becomes the apparent key to power, triumph, and happiness. The "meaning" of this mark, the way in which it is read, is thus central to the unfolding of "The Birth-Mark."

The mark on Georgiana's face, as the subject around which the entire narrative revolves, is quite obviously of central thematic and structural concern in the story but, from the outset, what is regarded as most interesting about it is its signifying quality. Its capacity for different readings by different readers is presented to us as one of its first and major characteristics:

> It must not be concealed, however, that the impression wrought by this fairy sign-manual varied exceedingly, according to the difference of temperament in the beholders. Some fastidious persons—but they were exclusively of her own sex—affirmed that the Bloody Hand, as they chose to call it, quite destroyed the effect of Georgiana's beauty, and rendered her countenance even hideous. But it would be as reasonable to say, that one of those small blue stains, which sometimes occur in the purest statuary marble, would convert the Eve of Powers to a monster. Masculine observers, if the birth-mark did not heighten their admiration, contented themselves with wishing it away, that the world might possess one living specimen of ideal loveliness, without the semblance of a flaw. After his marriage—for he thought little or nothing of the matter before—Aylmer discovered that this was the case with himself. (38)

In calling the mark a "manual," the narrator suggests its readability and openness to interpretation, again foregrounding the notion of its textuality.[1] His focus on conflicting ways of reading the mark reveals various social and cultural responses to it. He reveals Aylmer's attitude to the mark—the one "flaw" in "ideal loveliness"—an attitude that is in strong contrast to Georgiana's, which, up until this opening point in the story, has been to regard it as a "charm" (37). Most significantly, and seemingly inadvertently, the narrator, under the guise of offering us ordered, reasonable, normative comments, reveals his own attitudes to the mark. Although he argues that "reason" should correct the vision of "some fastidious persons," it is clear that the narrator is not as objective or as reasonable as he considers himself to be. His response manifests ambiguities and biases of which he is completely unaware, for while he disagrees with the unreasonable assumptions of those of Georgiana's "own sex," he avoids deconstructing the assumptions of "masculine observers" in general, and of Aylmer in particular. From the story's commencement then, the ambiguities of reading are built into the narrative itself, which, as Steven Youra points out, "thematizes the act of reading" (43).[2]

Much critical attention has been focused on the mark; clearly, the way in which the mark is "read" is fundamental to any interpretation of the story.[3] One of the most crucial readers of the mark is Aylmer himself; the story's plot revolves around the way in which he chooses to interpret the mark. But Aylmer cannot see his own response of disgust as an interpretation; it is precisely the mark's capacity for polysemous signification, highlighted by the narrator, that Aylmer is incapable of apprehending. Trapped in an obsessional, fixed world view he reduces the mark of many significations to a single signification; his relationship to the mark is a commitment always and only to its literal removal. Thus, although Aylmer may be said to *see* the mark, he really cannot read it at all.[4]

But the ambiguities surrounding the mark's capacity for figuration extend beyond the limitations created by Aylmer's (murderous) illiteracy. Not only are Aylmer's distortions perfectly mirrored by Georgiana's—the two of them collude in her destruction—but the "deeply impressive moral" (37) which the narrator promises at the beginning of the story and delivers at its conclusion—that Aylmer "failed to look beyond the shadowy scope of Time, and living once for all in Eternity, to find the perfect Future in the present" (56)—is filled with enough bizarre ambiguities and incongruities to throw the narrator's own capacity to read severely into question.

The explanation for the increasing unreadability of the readable mark lies in the nature of the body to which it is attached. The comparison of the mark to a stain of blood serves to associate or designate the mark with the aura of femininity:

> But if any shifting motion caused her to turn pale there was the mark again, a crimson stain upon the snow, in which Aylmer sometimes deemed an almost fearful distinctness. Its shape bore not a little similarity to the human hand, though of the smallest pygmy size. (37–38)

That the mark is in the shape of a hand is, in itself, significant since as Peter Brooks comments, any special sign marked on a body looks "suspiciously like a linguistic signifier" (*Body* 3). In this story, the shape of the mark invites a particular association with the world of writing, foregrounding its signifying quality. This in conjunction with the notion that it is a "bloody hand," a "crimson stain" (38) announces it as a kind of women's writing. It is the femininity of the mark that Aylmer cannot tolerate; the female signed body creates such havoc that Aylmer feels compelled to erase it. Its signification—its very capacity to signify—is so disruptive that only annihilation would appear to restore the prevailing order.

The mark's utter determination to exist offends Aylmer; the story describes repeatedly how it refuses to subject itself to his vision. Its autonomy emerges most clearly in the description of the mark's relationship to its background:

> [I]n the centre of Georgiana's left cheek, there was a singular mark, deeply interwoven, as it were, with the texture and substance of her face. In the usual state of her complexion,—a healthy, though delicate bloom,—the mark wore a tint of deeper crimson, which imperfectly defined its shape amid the surrounding rosiness. When she blushed, it gradually became more indistinct, and finally vanished amid the triumphant rush of blood, that bathed the whole cheek with its brilliant glow. But, if any shifting motion caused her to turn pale, there was the mark again, a crimson stain upon the snow. (37–38)

Barbara Johnson, commenting upon the mark's relation to its background in the story, sees it as the "mark of intersubjectivity; it is interpreted differently by different beholders, and it interprets *them* in response. . . . [W]hat Aylmer wishes to do in erasing the mark is to erase the difference—to erase sexual difference—by reducing woman to 'all,' to ground, to blankness" (259). Since Aylmer cannot read (a female body entered into writing), he cannot see the mark is "one of Georgiana's givens, in fact equivalent to her" (Fetterley 25). It is a metaphor for her identity, her sexuality, her being. As he cannot read the mark in its metaphoric and metonymic capacity as associated with (and representative of) the whole, Aylmer (at least consciously) refuses the realization that in removing the mark, he removes all there is of her. The story reminds us repeatedly, and through each of its characters, of the indissoluble connection between Georgiana and her mark. The narrator tells us that the mark is "deeply interwoven . . . with the texture and substance of her face" (37); Aminadab comments: "If she were my wife, I'd never part with that birth-mark" (43); Georgiana, herself, tells us that "the stain goes as deep as life itself" (41). Aylmer, in his turn, provides Georgiana with his "scientific findings":

> "Know, then, that this Crimson Hand, superficial as it seems, has clutched its grasp into your being, with a strength of which I had no previous conception. I have already administered agents powerful enough to do aught except to change your entire physical system." (51–52)

The emotional implications of these scientific findings surface in his nightmare when he dreams that "the deeper went the knife, the deeper sank the Hand, until at length its tiny grasp appeared to have caught hold of Georgiana's heart" (40). But in no matter what form knowledge occurs—social, scientific, or emotional—he represses it. All of the characters in the story—Aylmer, Georgiana, Aminadab, and the narrator—know (and evade the fact) that the mark cannot be removed because it cannot be separated from Georgiana, or she from it. The mark is Aylmer's object and since, as the sign of her subjectivity, it represents Georgiana, it becomes she who is his object. The corollary is also true; since Georgiana (together with her mark) is already an object (of his scientific and sexual attention and scrutiny), her subjectivity is unbearable to him and must be destroyed.

THE OBJECT, THE NARRATOR, AND THE GAZE

The notion of scrutiny, the act of looking, is crucial in this tale; Aylmer cannot take his eyes from Georgiana's mark. The gaze is, as always in Western culture, the privilege of the male subject with the woman constituted as the object "of representation, of discourse, of desire" (Irigaray 133). In "The Birth-Mark," Aylmer's stare is not only indicative of his social and sexual power over Georgiana, but also of his scientific power. In the second sentence of the story, we are told that Aylmer "persuaded a beautiful woman to become his wife" (36) and the use of the indefinite article emphasises visual beauty as the crucial element in his choice. That Georgiana's physical beauty is stressed as a vital aspect of Aylmer's attraction toward her turns out to be as important for his scientific concerns as for his sexual ones. The motif of looking is reiterated again and again throughout the tale. We are told that "very soon after their marriage, Aylmer sat gazing at his wife, with a trouble in his countenance" (37) and that his obsession with the mark comes to dominate their whole relationship:

> [I]t became the central point of all. With the morning twilight, Aylmer opened his eyes upon his wife's face, and recognized the symbol of imperfection; and when they sat together at the evening hearth, his eyes wandered stealthily to her cheek, and beheld, flickering with the blaze of the wood fire, the spectral Hand that wrote mortality, where he would fain have worshipped. (39)

Even when Aylmer is working to remove the mark, he cannot refrain from either his staring or his revulsion. "While thus employed, he failed not to gaze often at the fatal Hand, and not without a shudder," the narrator remarks (54).

But as Aylmer's growing obsession turns Georgiana into a hateful object destined for destruction, she, in equal measure, turns her own self into that object and colludes entirely with her own destruction. Thus, while we are told early on in the story that "Georgiana soon learned to shudder at his gaze" and that it "needed but a glance, with the peculiar expression that his face often wore" to prompt her response (39), toward the end, we learn that "she place[s] her hand over her cheek, to hide the terrible mark from her husband's eyes" (44) with no prompting from him at all.

Her progressive deterioration is carefully plotted. Her response to his comments at the beginning of the story demonstrates an insight and power that vanishes as the tale develops. Thus at the beginning of the story, she is able to confront Aylmer with "momentary anger":

> "Shocks you, my husband!" cried Georgiana, deeply hurt; at first reddening with momentary anger, but then bursting into tears.

> "Then why did you take me from my mother's side? You cannot love what shocks you!" (37)

By the end of the narrative, this insight (as well as her capacity for rage) has been entirely lost and she wants to die: "life—while this hateful mark makes me the object of your horror and disgust—life is a burthen which I would fling down with joy," she states (41).

The significant symptom of her deterioration is her loss of capacity to read the mark. The sense of play present in her initial response to the mark where she regards it as a "charm" with all the overtones of attractiveness, luck, and delight gives way to a fixed sense of herself (as obsessional as Aylmer's) as an object of horror and disgust. After her first angry response at the beginning of the story, Georgiana never really questions Aylmer's judgments about her body. If anything, once she begins to perceive the mark upon her cheek in his terms, she desires to make her body and self a gift to him, to enslave herself absolutely, to become his object. The bizarre distortions that this entails are encapsulated in her desperate plea to her husband: "Cannot you remove this little, little mark, which I cover with the tips of two small fingers?" (41). The repetition—"little, little . . . small"—foregrounds her urgency and intensity at the same time that it emphasizes the thorough absurdity of her desire.

Indeed, the duality and splitting that such a psychological stance entails is demonstrated in her newly learned illiteracy when she reads Aylmer's carefully maintained record of his work. She refuses to grasp the implications of her reading, unconsciously obscuring her own perceptions from herself. Thus, although she notes that the record is a record of failure, we are told that as she reads, she "reverenced Aylmer, and loved him more profoundly than ever, but with a less entire dependence on his judgement than heretofore" (49). As this text—the record of Aylmer's failures—is precisely the text in which her own story (his most devastating failure) is being written, it is her own story (her own mark) that becomes illegible and incomprehensible to her. This is inevitable since in giving up her own subjectivity, she gives up her own story.

What would happen, Luce Irigaray asks, "if the 'object' started to speak? Which also means beginning to 'see,' etc. What disaggregation of the subject would that entail?" (135). But Georgiana never speaks, never fractures Aylmer's vision of the world. She mirrors Aylmer's hatred of the mark with her own, eventually almost delighting in his psychotic view. Significantly, the one time that we see Georgiana looking is when she sees herself in a mirror, that is, she sees herself seeing herself (and is the object of her own gaze):

> Still, whenever she dared to look into the mirror, there she beheld herself, pale as a white rose, and with the crimson birth-mark stamped upon her cheek. Not even Aylmer now hated it as much as she. (48)

Irigaray comments:

> Once imagine that woman imagines and the object loses its fixed, obsessional character. As a bench mark that is ultimately more crucial than the subject, for he can sustain himself only by bouncing back off against some objectiveness, some objective. If there is no more "earth" to press down/repress, to work, to represent . . . then what pedestal remains for the ex-sistence of the "subject"? (133)

Georgiana joins in creating herself as the object for Aylmer to "work." Not wishing to interrupt the fixedness of his gaze, she never reconstitutes herself as subject. The removal of the mark that results in her death is therefore as much a product of Georgiana's vision as Aylmer's. For Georgiana as well as for Aylmer, the mark is all there is.

The perversity of the bond between Aylmer and Georgiana manifests itself in the bizarre language of sexual ecstasy that pervades all their conversations about the mark. The first words of love and tenderness that we hear Aylmer utter toward Georgiana are after she asks him to remove the mark: "'Noblest—dearest—tenderest wife!' cried Aylmer, rapturously" (41). This ecstasy pervades all their discussions about the removal of the mark: "Do not shrink from me! Believe me, Georgiana, I even rejoice in this single imperfection, since it will be such rapture to remove it" (44). The sense for both of them of satisfaction obtained, of repleted desire, is clear in the drinking of the fatal potion: "It allays a feverish thirst, that had parched me for many days," Georgiana says (53–54), while for Aylmer the operation is accompanied by "almost irrepressible ecstasy" (55). The eroticism of Georgiana's death brings together the unacknowledged arousal, revulsion, and murderousness present in both of them. Death is the only possible end to Georgiana's story. Her being and subjectivity simply disappear; they are incorporated into Aylmer's vision, the dominant and only available version of the world. By the time the birth-mark disappears, there is simply nothing left of her.

It is not only Aylmer, however, who reduces Georgiana to "nothing." The narrator of the story colludes entirely with Aylmer's world view; beneath the tone of studied indifference lies a collusiveness and an involvement with the progression of events of which the narrator seems entirely unaware. Like Aylmer, the narrator is centrally concerned with looking and, like Aylmer, he turns Georgiana into an object of art. Having described the different ways in which the mark might be viewed according to the temperament of the observer, he goes on to provide us with his own point of view, significantly explained in the language of looking:

> But it would be as reasonable to say, that one of those small blue stains, which sometimes occur in the purest statuary marble, would convert the Eve of Powers to a monster. (38)

The narrator announces himself to be in disagreement with Aylmer here, beginning argumentatively with "But it would be as reasonable to say." But the fundamental analogy on which his argument depends—the comparison of Georgiana to a marble statue of Eve—is suggestive. Not only is Georgiana once again the object of the gaze, but the narrator's imagery anticipates Aylmer's later triumphant comparison of himself to Pygmalion and the implied transformation of Georgiana into a marble statue. His use of the word *monster* also possesses an intensity that belies his laconic tone. Like Aylmer, the narrator regards the mark as a blemish, shifting his perspective only slightly from Aylmer's. The mark, for the narrator, is a sign of Georgiana's earthliness and therefore implies her true perfection. In all essentials, he is just like Aylmer and Georgiana; he cannot ultimately grasp the mark's symbolizing quality, its capacity for multiple significations or play. In this sense, the narrative is as obsessive as the tale it recounts.[5] Georgiana and Aylmer see their actions as the actions of idealism; the narrator shifts this view only in that he tells a story of misguided idealism.

Finally, the narrator's own peculiar biases are particularly evident in the bizarrely evasive moral that he draws at the end of the story, a moral that replaces and represses its true end, the death of Georgiana:

> Yet, had Aylmer reached a profounder wisdom, he need not thus have flung away the happiness, which would have woven his mortal life of the self-same texture with the celestial. . . . [H]e failed to look beyond the shadowy scope of Time, and living once for all in Eternity, to find the perfect Future in the present. (56)

Like Georgiana and Aylmer, he reads the story as a story of failure rather than, in Judith Fetterley's words, "the success story it really is—

the demonstration of how to murder your wife and get away with it" (22). We never learn of Aylmer's response to Georgiana's final comment to him that she is dying—almost the only time since the very beginning of the story that she feels free to correct his perception. His silence, which mirrors here a textual silence or gap, is replaced by the narrator's "interpretation" of events, an interpretation that in fact appears thoroughly contradicted by the events of the story itself. Alan Lloyd Smith comments on the ending: "The story pretends to the conclusion: She is perfect, but alas, she is dead! It secretly concludes: She is dead but [therefore] she is perfect!" (100).[6] In this sense, the narrator is as cruel as the protagonist whose tale he tells. The point of view of the narrator (a concept expressed significantly in terms of the language of looking) is closer to Aylmer's than he cares to reveal.

The narrator's collusion with Aylmer profoundly furthers the sense that is so prevalent in the story as a whole—that there is no space in which Georgiana could independently function. In his discussion of "trauma as the Real" (*Plague* 215), Slavoj Žižek addresses the question of the (redeeming) space that might be provided by "the Other." Since the traumatic event constitutes itself as "a stain which blurs our clear perception of it,"

> a trauma is always redoubled into the traumatic event "in itself," and into the trauma of its symbolic inscription. That is to say: when one is caught in a trauma (a concentration camp, a torture chamber . . .), what keeps one alive is the notion of bearing witness—"I must survive in order to tell the others (the Other) what really went on here. . . . " The second trauma takes place when this recognition of the first trauma through its symbolic integration necessarily fails (my pain can never be fully shared by the other): it then appears to the victim that he or she has survived in vain, that their survival was meaningless. . . . (*Plague* 215–16; ellipses in original)

In "The Birth-Mark" this double aspect of trauma is collapsed for Georgiana into a single experience. There is no "Other" in the enclosed world Aylmer has created and the possible alternative (to Aylmer's vision) that might have been provided by the narrative framework does not exist. The absence of this alternative other (narrative) space accounts for the overwhelming sense of claustrophobia that dominates the story. Since no world is represented as being outside the metaphoric "torture chamber" Aylmer has created, the possibility of "bearing witness" is foreclosed. The "symbolic integration" of trauma does not succeed in this narrative because it is never attempted; rather, it becomes evident from the start that, for Georgiana, "survival was meaningless." In this sense, Georgiana can only join with Aylmer (and the narrator) and comply with her own destruction; she can only surrender to the traumatic "Real." What looks like Georgiana's collusion in her own death is thus in reality "the denial of [the] symbolic recognition" of trauma (*Plague* 216), a denial that functions throughout the tale as a symptom of the unspeakable narrative of Georgiana's short and tragic married life.

Thus, the unexpressed bond between the narrator and Aylmer powerfully exacerbates the silence that surrounds the trauma of Georgiana's marriage and death. Since the narrative framework allows no space for the expression of her trauma, it is figured in the narrative only by its lack, existing only through suggestion and by conjecture. The tone of laconic indifference that so characterizes the narrative voice also intensifies the atmosphere of timelessness that Laub describes as being fundamental to the experience of trauma and that prevails over the story in so peculiar a fashion. There is no "other" space in which Georgiana can exist and function.

THE HOME AS DOMESTIC LABORATORY

The absence of narrative space (for Georgiana) is uncannily matched by the domestic physical space of the story as the couple move from their first marital home to their second in Aylmer's laboratory. The home in which Aylmer and Georgiana first live is almost undescribed in the narrative; its only remarkable feature is the light it is able to throw onto the birth-mark: "[W]hen they sat together at the evening hearth, his eyes wandered stealthily to her cheek, and beheld, flickering with the blaze of the wood fire, the spectral Hand that wrote mortality, where he would fain have worshipped" (39); and again, "the lights were growing dim, so as hardly to betray the stain on the poor wife's cheek" (39). The insistent visibility of the mark in this first home demands its excision, leading Aylmer and Georgiana to leave this space and instead take up residence in his laboratory, since the experiment that is to effect its excision demands "constant watchfulness" (42).

When Aylmer takes Georgiana to their new home, the narrator states that "he led her over the threshold of the laboratory" (43). The home as laboratory, as the experimental space in which the marriage of Aylmer and Georgiana is to be played out, has at least two important implications. First, the image brings together the two spheres of mid-nineteenth-century life—the public and the private. The public world of male activity and power, rather than being separate from the central concerns of domestic fiction, is brought not merely into intimate connection with the private realm, but is, indeed, inseparable from it. Although the "boudoir"—the "beautiful apartments, not unfit to be the secluded abode of a lovely woman" (44)—is separated from the laboratory by rich hangings, Georgiana need only follow Aylmer from her rooms to enter into the laboratory with its "furnace," "retorts, tubes, cylinders, crucibles," and "electrical machine" (50). If, as Elizabeth Langland argues, the angel in the house performs "a more significant and extensive economic and political function than is usually perceived" (8), it seems in Hawthorne's story that the reverse is equally true: the public man plays the essential role in constructing a domestic economy. The public realm as engulfing private space leads to the second point, that is, that Aylmer's marriage with Georgiana is nothing other than an experiment undertaken by Aylmer, and the domestic sphere is nothing other than the laboratory in which this murderous experiment will be played out. The scientific questing after power not merely invades the domestic sphere, it completely absorbs it into its own project.

Science is conceived of in the story as a "faith in man's ultimate control over nature" (36). Thus, Aylmer's project throughout his scientific career has been the obsessional attempt to master "the secret of creative force" (36), such a force being figured in the narrative as a female body. All of his experiments are attempts to "fathom the very process by which Nature assimilates all her precious influences from earth and air, and from the spiritual world, to create and foster Man, her masterpiece"; up to the point of his marriage to Georgiana, however, these ventures have all failed, since "our great creative Mother, while she amuses us with apparently working in the broadest sunshine, is yet severely careful to keep her own secrets, and, in spite of her pretended openness, shows us nothing but results" (42). Having failed to "fathom" the "secrets" of the "Mother," having indeed nothing but a series of "mortifying failures" (46) to show as the result of his scientific career, he turns instead to a domestic experiment—to marriage, to the home, and to the woman—as the place where his preeminence will be established.

His marriage to Georgiana is explicitly a part of his scientific quest for mastery since, the narrator states, Aylmer "has devoted himself . . . too unreservedly to scientific studies, ever to be weaned from them by any second passion" (36). Thus, his love for Georgiana can only flourish "by intertwining itself with his love of science, and uniting the strength of the latter to its own" (37). When the narrator concludes, "Such a union accordingly took place" (37), he is referring as much to the unequal union of science and love as the union of Aylmer with Georgiana. Once married to Georgiana, Aylmer is again obsessed by the ineluctable manifestation of the "Mother" apparent on her body, for although she "came so nearly perfect from the hand of Nature," she bears "the visible mark of earthly imperfection" (37). "Mother" Nature has again left its unreadable mark.

Georgiana is, however, fatally open to Aylmer's depredations in a manner in which Nature is not. The "Mother" can "keep her own secrets" from science but the individual body of Georgiana can be fatally injured in the attempt to plumb them. Georgiana's plaintive cry—"why did you take me from my mother's side?"—can be read allegorically as her belated knowledge of the safety that resided on the "side" of the Mother. In the laboratory/home, the preserving mother is nowhere to be found.

In figuring the home as an experimental space, Hawthorne's story is able to describe Georgiana's everyday life as, unbeknownst to her, the experiment itself. It is only as Aylmer "made minute inquiries as to her sensations" (47) that Georgiana is made aware that the experiment is already in progress: "Georgiana began to conjecture that she was already subjected to certain physical influences, either breathed in with the fragrant air, or taken with her food" (48). Thus, for Georgiana, life itself, with its mere acts of breathing and eating, constitutes an experimental procedure undertaken by the man in the domain of his power. These "minute inquiries" are also the only moments of intimacy that readers ever witness between the couple. Otherwise they seem never to converse—except, of course, about the mark.

Aylmer's conception of himself as the scientist is matched by Aylmer's vision of himself as the artist. He compares himself to Pygmalion: "[W]hat will be my triumph," he exclaims, "when I shall have corrected what Nature left imperfect, in her fairest work! Even Pygmalion, when his sculptured woman assumed life, felt not greater ecstasy than mine will be" (41).[7] Aylmer, in his comparison of his work to Pygmalion's, ignores some crucial differences, the most significant being that his efforts result, not in the creation of a being, but in its destruction. Indeed, the notion of the metamorphosis of a human being into marble constantly recurs in the imagery of the story:

> It needed but a glance, with the peculiar expression that his face often wore, to change the roses of her cheek into a deathlike paleness, amid which the Crimson Hand was brought strongly out, like a bas-relief of ruby on the whitest marble. (39)

Similarly, we hear of Georgiana's "marble paleness" (54) after she has drunk the draught given her by her husband. The metaphoric comparison in the first quotation (indicated by the use of a simile) is replaced by a description in the second, which eventually becomes entirely literal. Aylmer takes a living human being and converts her into dead marble. By contrast, Ovid's description of Orpheus's narration of the story of Pygmalion and Galatea in Book 10 of the *Metamorphoses* conveys most movingly the transformation of dead marble into living flesh:

> The lover stood, amazed, afraid of being mistaken, his joy tempered with doubt, and again and again stroked the object of his prayers. It was indeed a human body! The veins throbbed as he pressed them with his thumb. (232)

In Ovid's story the play of hands, the repetitive, loving human touch, registers the moment of Galatea's coming alive, of her veins beginning to throb. In "The Birth-Mark," the imprint of Aylmer's thumb on Georgiana's arm carries precisely the opposite implications: "He rushed towards her, and seized her arm with a gripe that left the print of his fingers upon it" (51). The marking of her body here (which in itself echoes the hand-shaped mark) is indicative of Aylmer's violent determination to do away with Georgiana. Significantly, in an echo of his transformation of her into marble, he is "pale as death" through this encounter (50).[8]

Aylmer's perverted artistic endeavor functions as a metaphor for his failed scientific experiment as he produces his final, perfect, dead object. The domestic space in which Georgiana's marriage takes place is Aylmer's laboratory. From the unspoken point of view that might have been Georgiana's, this space is no space; it exists only to announce a lack of context or possibility in which a life or a narrative might have taken shape. The lack of defining detail or context so endemic to the genre of romance here speaks to the absent story that is the life and death of Georgiana.

Thus, Hawthorne precipitates the reader into a world of psychic darkness, of hidden obsessions and private desires; he creates a space in which the radical impulses in human experience might be acted out. Although the conventions of the genre might account, at least in part, for the lack of explanation, or cause, or context, these absences possess a further psychological function. Hawthorne's tale does reveal "the truth of the human heart." Both Aylmer's destructiveness and Georgiana's compliance with it appear peculiarly motiveless; man's murderous desires, Hawthorne appears to be saying, defy explanation.

In the chapters that follow, the question of destructiveness or motive for evil is confronted again and again. The specific social and psychological opacity of Hawthorne's tale differentiates it generically from some of the texts that follow, but the blank or incomprehensibility that surrounds the marked female body emerges as a pattern of cultural and representational recurrence. Aylmer's attempts to unwrite Georgiana, to reduce her to blankness, functions as a useful figuration for the "blank" that we find at the heart of all of the texts that we investigate. The complexities that accrue around the marked female body are exquisitely illuminated in Hawthorne's tale of bizarre love and distorted desires.

2

Domestic Violence, Abjection, and the Comic Novel

Anthony Trollope's Barchester Towers

Anthony Trollope's *Barchester Towers,* with its gentle satire, careful romance, and polished and witty scenes of bourgeois domestic life, may seem to be a complete departure from the mad and obsessional world of "The Birth-Mark." Similarly, the grotesquely marked body of Signora Neroni in Trollope's novel could seemingly find no point of comparison with the body of Georgiana in "The Birth-Mark," for to compare the tiny mark on Georgiana's cheek with Signora Neroni's "hunchback" gait (Trollope 66) is to contrast a minute flaw in otherwise "ideal loveliness" with flamboyantly displayed and grotesque disabilities. Yet the deformed body beneath Signora Neroni's beautiful robes, like the tiny mark on Georgiana's cheek, is a textual mark whose meaning is obsessively gazed at and interpreted by the fiction's various readers. The "flaw" in Georgiana's perfection is not the same as the "filth" with which Signora Neroni is associated, but both point to a crisis of representation attached to the female body. The presence of the marked female bodies in both texts produces an upheaval of personal and social relations—in Aylmer's marriage to Georgiana, in Eleanor Bold's relations with Mr. Arabin—which precipitates a crisis in the texts' closures.

The crucial difference between the two texts is that *Barchester Towers* is a comic novel, "The Birth-Mark" a dark story of insane compulsion. While the removal of the mark in Hawthorne's story results in the death of Georgiana, the presence of the marked body of Signora Neroni in *Barchester Towers* creates a comic and romantic crisis which is resolved through the expulsion of the Signora from the domestic world of Barchester. In this sense the comedy centered on Signora Neroni in Trollope's novel repeats the disruptive power of festive misrule in Renaissance comedy; the Signora's interventions into Barchester society provide the "release for impulses which run counter to decency and decorum, and the clarification about limits which comes from going beyond the limit" (Barber 13). As U. C. Knoepflmacher says in *Laughter and Despair,* "Trollope welcomes chaos because, through the mock-heroic and burlesque, he can reduce it and laugh it away" (26). At the same time, this analogy to comic ritual and Shakespearean comedy is a reminder of how destructive and dark comedy can be; the expulsion of Signora Neroni at the end of Trollope's novel may recall the scapegoating of a perhaps ultimately tragic figure such as Shylock at the end of *The Merchant of Venice*, another character who can find no place in the world of the text. Between them, "The Birth-Mark" and *Barchester Towers* embody what Elizabeth Ermarth in *The English Novel in History* calls the "Catch 22" of women's domestic life in nineteenth-century fiction: "[I]t is not possible for [women] to live outside social time because there is nothing outside it beyond a narrow domestic ledge; but inside it her function is to die" (221). Thus, although the tone of Trollope's novel differs markedly from that of Hawthorne's story, and although Signora Neroni does not suffer a literal death, as Georgiana does inside the "narrow domestic ledge," her exclusion from the Barchester world indicates a kind of social death, the worst tragedy of which comedy can conceive.

VULGARITY, FILTH, AND WAR

Henry James's devastating comment, "Life is vulgar, but we know not how vulgar it is till we see it set down in [Trollope's] pages" ("Trollope" 1865: 44), is a useful reminder of the nature of Trollope's concerns. In spite of his keen sense of propriety, he is a writer fascinated by the common, the coarse, the quotidian aspects of everyday life, including the coarseness of bourgeois domestic relations. As P. D. Edwards points out, Trollope's "unexcitable levelness of tone, his lumbering, strictly sequential unfolding of plot, his sameness of style in novel after novel have blinded most readers to the variety of his subject-matter and especially to his fondness for the sensational, the morally macabre, the exotic" (3). Yet it is important to note that James acquits Trollope of a meaner level of baseness, what he calls the "morbid" and the "polluting."[1] In describing the single slap which Eleanor Bold inflicts upon the repugnant Mr. Slope, the cautious Trollope expresses his fear that such a graphic description of violence will induce "every well-bred reader of these pages [to] lay down the book with disgust" (384). And yet Trollope sets himself the much harder task of describing Signora Neroni, an abused wife and the victim of unspecified enormities. Trollope's depiction of violence, according to James's dictum, must thus tread a fine line between an acceptable vulgarity and commonness on the one hand, and a repellent pollution and morbidity on the other. As this chapter will argue, Trollope accomplishes this by identifying and isolating a female body—that of Signora Neroni—as the source of pollution and defilement in the Barchester community and eventually expelling it from the community's midst.

To analyze the novel's presentation of domestic violence inevitably calls for a focus on the domestic romance plot of *Barchester Towers;* however there are important analogies that must be drawn between the representation of violence and degradation in the domestic sphere and the "battle" and "rubbish" in the public world of ecclesiastical politics that dominates the novel. Unlike the enclosed, almost hermetic world of "The Birth-Mark," *Barchester Towers,* like all of Trollope's fiction, is fundamentally concerned with bourgeois social relations and public life. The explicit language of violence is not used in relation to the domestic world of the novel; rather, it provides the governing metaphor for the civil war in the Church between the Tory "high and dry" party and the Evangelicals. It is this that becomes the great "civil war" in *Barchester Towers*. What seems to be at the center of this battle is the worth of tradition; where the current clergy of Barchester are content "to confine themselves to such ceremonial observances as had been in vogue for the last hundred years" (40), the Evangelicals, who are gaining power and prestige in the church, believe in innovation. Mr. Slope casts himself as a "new man" who is doing the unpleasant but necessary task of "carting away the useless *rubbish* of past centuries" (99, our emphasis). For their part, Mr. Grantly and his faction have for many years "exercised [their] ministry without schism" (51), but the arrival of the Proudies and Mr. Slope makes it clear that the true enemies of the church are internal: "It is not the dissenters or the papists that we should fear, but the set of canting, low-bred hypocrites who are wriggling their way in among us" (39). Although the schism that threatens the integrity of the Church of England concerns the relative merits of the new and the traditional, the *content* of the debate focuses on issues of purity and impurity—of deciding what the "rubbish" is that must be discarded. Is Sunday travel an impure practise or not? Is chanting in the cathedral a mark of holiness or of defilement? Is questioning the worth of tradition from the pulpit a cleansing of the temple, or the sign of, as Mr. Harding says, "disrespect to the ministration of God's services, as conducted in conformity with the rules of the Church of England" (60)? The text chosen by Mr. Slope when, to the horror of Mr. Grantly and his party, he preaches in the cathedral is not surprisingly concerned with making these distinctions: "Study to shew thyself approved unto God, a workman that needeth not to be ashamed, rightly dividing the word of truth" (2 Timothy 2: 15; 43). Slope and Grantly each believes that he can "divide the word of truth" correctly, and what is at stake in the ecclesiastical "war" that the novel records is precisely the line of division or demarcation between purity and defilement.

However, as Knoepflmacher argues, "[t]he real battle fought in Barchester is not the short-lived struggle between 'Proudieism' and 'Grantlyism' but rather the more elementary contest waged between men and women" (*Laughter and Despair* 35). The central interest of this chapter is the transposition of this public battle into the private sphere.[2] The household of the Bishop of Barchester, with its ongoing power struggles between Mrs. Proudie and Mr. Slope, is one clear example of a public battle made domestic. However, the novel's depiction of seemingly real acts of violence against women underlines the nature of the battle waged in *Barchester Towers*; it is a battle for purity and cleanliness in the private as well as in the public sphere. The woman most affected by male violence, Signora Neroni, arouses an intense sexual interest in all of the male characters in the novel, but her impure associations mean that she is not, as the upright Miss Thorne remarks, a woman whom many men "would be glad to take . . . to their hearths" (462). Whereas Aylmer's efforts are directed toward producing within the domestic space a laboratory in which his murderous intentions can be played out, *Barchester Towers* is concerned with the construction of a pure and safe domestic realm, one in which a man may safely take a woman to his hearth. The splitting that this entails is played out through the expulsion of what is considered to be impure and polluting from that safe domestic realm.

DOMESTIC SCANDAL

Two women occupy antithetical poles of the domestic romance plot of the novel: the pure if slightly tedious heroine, Eleanor Bold, and her foil, the maimed and abandoned seductress, Signora Madeline Stanhope Neroni. At the end of the novel preceding *Barchester Towers, The Warden,* Eleanor Harding married John Bold. Their marriage is portrayed as the ideal of domestic felicity, although not, of course, without some ironic undertones: "As the parasite plant will follow even the defects of the trunk which it embraces, so did Eleanor cling to and love the very faults of her husband" (13). At the opening of *Barchester Towers,* however, John Bold is dead, and the security of Eleanor's domestic sphere is disrupted:

> She wept as for the loss of the most perfect treasure with which mortal women had ever been endowed; for weeks after he was gone the idea of future happiness in this world was hateful to her; consolation, as it is called, was insupportable, and tears and sleep were her only relief. (13)

Eleanor cannot retreat to her parental home since her father, Mr. Harding, has lost it through the machinations of various political enemies, including, ironically, those of her late husband. The novel records Eleanor Bold's quest to reestablish a secure domestic realm for herself and her young son by choosing one of her three suitors: Mr. Arabin, Mr. Slope, or Bertie Stanhope. Quest is perhaps the wrong word, however, for Eleanor Bold is only reluctantly drawn away from the memory of her late husband and the demands of her son, and much of the novel's plot depends upon her not realizing the extent to which she is being wooed, particularly by Mr. Slope.

Signora Neroni is an obvious foil for Eleanor Bold. Her husband is also missing, though it seems likely that Paulo Neroni has not died but abandoned her. Like Eleanor Bold she has one child, but unlike the doted-upon little Johnny Bold, her splendidly attired daughter is generally neglected unless a display of maternal affection serves some selfish purpose. Signora Neroni also has admirers, indeed almost every man in the novel is drawn to her almost irresistibly, though she seemingly has neither an interest in remarriage nor the ability to remarry. She has retreated to her parental home for the seeming social and financial security it offers; however, as readers we know that her presence there is only one more destabilizing influence in a family in imminent danger of disintegration.

Madeline Stanhope Neroni's married life is also represented as antithetical to Eleanor Bold's lost domestic paradise. If Eleanor Bold is a domestic angel, Signora Neroni is, as Jane Nardin suggests, a parody of the angel in the house:

> Madeline represents the ornamental aspect of the angel figure, who should, in some versions at least, be beautiful and useless, existing solely to amuse and charm men. Certainly Madeline, witty and beautiful, but so badly crippled as to be completely unfitted for all practical purposes, is an angel in this sense. (42)

That Madeline is an angel in any sense makes her complex figuration that much more compelling for readers. The narrator tells us that although her great beauty had attracted many suitors:

> As is so often the case, she married the very worst of those who sought her hand. Why she had chosen Paulo Neroni, a man of no birth and no property, a mere captain in the Pope's guard, one who had come up to Milan either simply as an adventurer or else as a spy, a man of harsh temper and oily manners, mean in figure, swarthy in face, and so false in words as to be hourly detected, need not now be told. When the moment for doing so came, she had probably no alternative. . . . Six months afterwards she arrived at her father's house a cripple, and a mother. (65–66)

The narrator is both ambivalent and reticent about the reasons for her hasty marriage. On the one hand he indicates that "Why [they married] . . . need not now be told," but on the other hand states clearly that her child is born no later than six months after the marriage. The implication is clear, and one can attribute the narrator's reticence to a keen sense of where, for the bourgeois Victorian reader, the scales might tip from vulgarity—the fact of a premarital pregnancy—toward "pollution"—a candid disclosure of it. The description of her crippled state that follows is, however, almost clinically accurate:

> She had fallen, she said, in ascending a ruin, and had fatally injured the sinews of her knee; so fatally, that when she stood she

> lost eight inches of her accustomed height; so fatally, that when she essayed to move, she could only drag herself painfully along, with protruded hip and extended foot, in a manner less graceful than that of a hunchback. (66)

In a novel that seems to range between sentimental comedy and bold satire, this description of Madeline Neroni's disability is a rather shocking one for the reader. Where Eleanor Bold's widowed state merited a fond apostrophe from the narrator—"Poor Eleanor Bold! How well does that widow's cap become her . . . Poor Eleanor!" (12)—Madeline Neroni's grotesque disfigurement evokes an account that is strikingly precise—"she lost eight inches of her accustomed height"; a "protruded hip and extended foot"—and unsentimental—"a manner less graceful than that of a hunchback."

The cause of Madeline's infirmity again calls for the narrator's equivocation. Her explanation, a fall ascending a ruin, may be a partial truth (and even metaphorically apt), but it veils the full story. The narrator's interest in unveiling the real cause is limited:

> Stories were not slow to follow her, averring that she had been cruelly ill-used by Neroni, and that to his violence had she owed her accident. Be that as it may, little had been said about her husband, but that little had made it clearly intelligible to the family that Signor Neroni was to be seen and heard of no more. (66)

The very neat dismissal—"Be that as it may . . ."—puts the question of domestic violence clearly beyond the proper bounds of narrative interest. Like premarital pregnancy, domestic violence is a real but, one assumes, "morbid" topic and, as James says, the morbid and polluting are beneath the notice of Trollope the novelist. An oblique reference is all that Trollope can risk in the interests of middle-class propriety. At the same time, this and following scenes involving Signora Neroni keep the image of the maimed body before us, the tantalizing yet repellent reminder of the grotesque possibility of domestic violence. Her disfigurement is both a source of continual fascination, of curiosity, and of continual repulsion.[3]

The ambivalences hovering around Trollope's representation are evocative of both Dickens and Thackeray. Like those two authors he is content to isolate the English middle classes from the contamination of spectacular domestic violence. However, while Dickens and Thackeray, as the Introduction argued, typically confine domestic violence to the poor and working classes, Trollope here employs another equally effective if crude marker, ethnicity. Trollope makes Paulo Neroni an Italian, not an English gentleman, the same xenophobic gesture used by Dickens in his portrait of the wife-murdering Rigaud in *Little Dorrit.*

But Trollope's ambivalence is also a refusal to admit clear evidence of the harm that may be done to women in a patriarchal society. Like the narrator of "The Birth-Mark," the narrator of *Barchester Towers* seems content to leave the question of harm to the woman unexamined. The omniscient realist narrator's obfuscatory "be that as it may" is a disavowal of what such a narrator ought in fact to "know." As it stands, the critic who wishes to "try" Paulo Neroni *in absentia* on the charge of domestic assault will certainly encounter a difficulty since a lack of specific evidence may constitute "reasonable doubt" leading to an acquittal. Yet what is precisely fascinating in the novel, as in Hawthorne's story, is the nature of the "evidence" before us, for the evidence *is* the woman's body, what Hélène Cixous calls the "dark continent" within the male "economy" (68).

The critic as jurist, righting the ills of the past, is a not unfashionable critical position. There are good reasons for this, since, as Robin West points out in her feminist phenomenological critique of legal theory and practice, "women's injuries are often not recognized or compensated *as injuries* by the legal culture. The dismissal of women's gender-specific suffering comes in various forms, but the outcome is always the same: women's suffering for one reason or another is outside the scope of legal redress" (82). What is striking about Signora Neroni's injuries, however, is that on the one hand they are not gender specific at all; she has been crippled in a way that makes her injuries wholly visible: the "protruded hip and extended foot." On the other hand, the representation of those injuries in the novel is always oblique, teasing, and our vision of them is always partially occluded. Gaze as we might at the evidence of these injuries, their exact nature eludes us, or is suggestive of something more than a mere injured foot or hip; as with Georgiana's mark, the body becomes textual, demanding reading and interpretation. As Helena Michie points out in *The Flesh Made Word,* there are "inherent limitations" to realism; first is "its inability to tell one everything one wants to know," and second is the more specific limitation caused by "the taboos that governed both the perception and representation of women's bodies in the Victorian era and beyond"

(82). Thus, commenting on Trollope's description of Lily in *The Small House at Allington,* Michie concludes that realism "is governed by a series of representational taboos—rhetorical codes that conceal in the very act of depiction" (82).[4] In the case of *Barchester Towers,* most critics agree that the marked body of Signora Neroni is inflected by such "representational taboos," and that what is concealed in Trollope's realism is a particular articulation of female sexuality.[5] Thus, a woman's hidden injury signifies something *more* than the fact of the physical disability; realism ensures that the fact of an injury is strikingly clear, but its exact nature distressingly unclear.

Luce Irigaray places this distress in a larger context: "[T]he woman, supposedly has *nothing* you can see. She exposes, exhibits the possibility of *a nothing to see*. . . . This is the odd, the uncanny thing, as far as the eye can see, this nothing around which lingers in horror, now and forever, an overcathexis of the eye, of appropriation by the gaze" (47). The male gaze is both attracted to and repelled by the female body; the injury, castration, cannot be seen directly because there is "nothing to be seen," yet an injury has occurred. "Legal redress" for injury, in West's words, would entail distinguishing these "injuries" from each other—which injury constitutes the woman proper, and which is super-added, not "natural." Indeed, this impasse is precisely symbolized in "The Birth-Mark" where the attempt to separate Georgiana from her mark—in Aylmer's gaze, from her "injury"—quite literally kills her. Thus, the woman's body can "testify" to its injury, we can gaze at its "deformity," and yet the marks defy any simple reading, and certainly any easy "redress."

The visibility of Signora Neroni's body, its function as "spectacle" or "exhibit," is insisted upon in the novel. In her grand entrance in the novel, she is carried into Mrs. Proudie's reception by a "*cortège*" of five people and put on display on a sofa especially prepared for her. We are told that "[s]he had sent a servant beforehand to learn whether it was a right- or a left-handed sofa, for it required that she should dress accordingly, particularly as regarded her bracelets" (81). The effect *is* spectacular:

> On the one arm which her position required her to expose she wore three magnificent bracelets, each of different stones. Beneath her on the sofa, and over the cushion and head of it, was spread a crimson silk mantle or shawl, which went under her whole body and concealed her feet. Dressed as she was and

> looking as she did, so beautiful and yet so motionless, with the pure brilliancy of her white dress brought out and strengthened by the colour beneath it, with that lovely head, and those large, bold, bright, staring eyes, it was impossible that either man or woman should do other than look at her. (81)

The specifics of the description are clear enough: she must remain motionless, otherwise the gait "less graceful than that of a hunchback" would be obvious. Parts of the body must be hidden—the feet, one arm—and others on display—the arm with the bracelets, the eyes. The exhibition is compelling for two reasons: first there is the "brilliancy" of the effect, the splendor of the façade. Secondly, there is the mystery of what must lie beneath the façade. We cannot "do other than look at her" because we want to see *and* see beneath. Just as the mark on Georgiana's cheek refuses to subject itself to Aylmer's vision, so readers are baffled by the intolerable indeterminacy of Signora Neroni's injuries. We cannot see the disfigurement, for there is nothing of it to be seen, but our gaze is compelled to look and look again, to probe for the certain injury which she bears. She is later called a "noxious siren" (250), and while the allusion is not so elaborately developed by Trollope as it is by Thackeray with reference to Becky Sharpe in *Vanity Fair* (ch. 64), it is clear that while the visible parts of her body are enticing and seductive, the hidden body is unimaginably deformed and defiled—and defiling. On this woman's body—simultaneously inviting, demanding our gaze, and veiled, rigorously hidden—is a margin between the beautiful and the disgusting, the visible and the unimaginable. She is, like so many of the violated women studied in this book, "abject."

Julia Kristeva's discussion of abjection, purity, and impurity in *Powers of Horror: An Essay on Abjection* resonates with the representation of the marked female body within the social world of *Barchester Towers*. Kristeva reads certain psychological episodes, religious and cultural practices, and literary texts as fundamentally concerned with establishing the boundaries between what is acceptable within a psyche or a community and what is not. The boundary separates the pure and the impure, the outside and the inside, attraction and repulsion.[6] She reads *Oedipus Rex*, for example, as a play that records the purification of a community; it is tragic because the central character Oedipus is at once the defiler—through murder and incest—and the purifier—through his unrelenting search for the source of defilement: "[P]rohibition and ideal are joined in a single character in order to signify that the speaking being has no space of his own but stands on a fragile threshold as if stranded on account of an impossible demarcation" (84–85). Our reading of "The Birth-Mark" suggests that Georgiana's body is also an "impossible demarcation" which joins "prohibition and ideal." In this sense Aylmer's efforts may be seen as an attempt at "purification," at cleansing the "defiled" object, at eradicating a taboo. The inherent failure of his project arises precisely from the fact that he attempts to separate the inseparable.

One can also read *Barchester Towers* as a novel of social purification (as Robert Polhemus does in his suggestion that the novel depicts the "comic reformation" of the community). It is tempting to read the novel, not as a tragedy that mixes the pure with the impure, but as a simple comedy where the defiler of the domestic realm—Signora Neroni—and its purifier—Eleanor Bold—are quite separate. The comic resolution of the novel is in fact achieved through such a separation. However, as Réné Girard says in his discussion of Oedipus as "scapegoat," the assignation of guilt and innocence is often arbitrary, so that purifier and defiler may well be "twins" or "doubles" rather than opposites (79). Arguably the marking of a woman's body by violence in the novel is the marking of the same "fragile threshold" as in Oedipus, the drawing of an uncertain boundary between pure and impure elements of the psyche, and of society. As the Church of England is a body riven by schism, by a putative separation of pure and impure practises, so the body of woman in the novel is similarly marked, with the body of Signora Neroni itself indicating the margin. In this sense the ills of the culture are inscribed on the woman's body.

Fundamental to the drawing of boundaries between purity and impurity is the experience of abjection and the ensuing rejection of the maternal body. For Kristeva, the pre-symbolic state is one of idyllic union with the "mother," but even in this ideal and desired state there are moments of repulsion or horror—abjection. The "mother" comes to stand in as the "object" for this abjection even though she is still also the lost object of desire; "the 'mother' is gradually rejected through becoming, at the pre-symbolic level, the prototype of what the drives expel" (Lechte 159). According to John Lechte, Kristeva, differing from Lacan, asserts that "the symbolic is not, of its own accord, strong enough to ensure separation [of the subject from the mother]; it depends on the mother becoming abjected" (159). The abject maternal body thus comes to mark the boundary between the self and the not-self: "There, I am at the border of my condition as a living being. My body extricates itself, as being alive, from that border" (Kristeva 3).

The subject, as a part of the symbolic realm, thus comes into being as that which is not abject.

The experience of abjection is a curious mixture of disgust and fascination. Kristeva writes:

> There looms, within abjection, one of those violent, dark revolts of being, directed against a threat that seems to emanate from an exorbitant outside or inside, ejected beyond the scope of the possible, the tolerable, the thinkable. . . . Apprehensive, desire turns aside; sickened, it rejects. . . . But simultaneously, just the same, that impetus, that spasm, that leap is drawn toward an elsewhere as tempting as it is condemned. Unflaggingly, like an inescapable boomerang, a vortex of summons and repulsion places the one haunted by it literally beside himself. (1)

Abjection is thus the precondition for the experience of separation from the maternal—at once sickening and desirable, threatening and constitutive of the subject itself.

Moments of abjection permeate many of the representations of violated female bodies in the texts studied in this book, as well as in other novels by Trollope. In "The Birth-Mark," attraction, repulsion, and compulsion are inextricably bound up with one another. Alymer finds himself compelled "to gaze often at the fatal hand [on Georgiana's cheek], and not without a shudder." In Trollope's *He Knew He Was Right* (1868–1869), Trevelyn is driven into madness by his (ungrounded) fears of his wife's faithlessness: "Could it be that she was so base as this—so vile a thing, so abject, such dirt, pollution, filth? But there were such cases. Nay, were they not almost numberless?" (289) However, one would be hard pressed to find a more exact and visceral representation of the experience of abjection than Mr. Slope's relationship with Madeline Neroni.[7] Slope finds himself powerfully drawn to the Signora, much as he despises himself for it; he visits her privately at her house, even though he knows that public exposure of such visits might lose him his chance of professional advancement:

> Mr Slope tried hard within himself to cast off the pollution with which he felt that he was defiling his soul. . . . He had come across the fruit of the Dead Sea, so sweet and delicious to the eye, so bitter and nauseous to the taste. He had put the apple to his mouth, and it had turned to ashes between his teeth. Yet he could not tear himself away. (250)

Although, as Christopher Herbert argues, Slope's dilemma results in part merely from his "unnatural suppression of [his] own cravings for pleasure" (170), his strong attraction to Signora Neroni combined with his disgust and nausea suggests that it is also a more primitive reaction, one recalling the early associations of abjection with the maternal body. In Kristevan terms, what Mr. Slope finds in the violated frame of Signora Neroni is a representation of the mother's body as it was before the coming of the symbolic order, a call to the place where desire found its first object, its entire satisfaction, and the place that was expelled and cast out as abject and defiled. He desires her and he must repel her; he is forced into an admission of his love for her and a simultaneous admission that he will not "lower" himself to win her.

Having reached this impasse, Signora Neroni has no further use for Mr. Slope. She has enjoyed her prey, but now weary, publicly humiliates him, and initiates the movement of expulsion that will gain momentum at the hands of Mrs. Proudie and eventually propel Mr. Slope from Barchester. Mr. Slope's humiliation, however warranted, is a warning to the reader. Mr. Slope desires to gaze at the female body, to maintain his desire for it, to take possession of it, and yet at the same time to hold himself above the impurity he is sure resides there (in James's terms, to hold himself above the level of the morbid and the polluting). Such a relationship to the female body is impossible. Irigaray argues that however much the male gaze attempts to unveil the "woman-object" (207), "the desire of the mystery remains": "For even if the place of origin, the original dwelling, even if not only the woman but the mother can be unveiled to his sight, what will he make of the exploration of this mine? Except usurp even more of the right to look at everything, at the whole thing, thus reinforcing the erosion of his desire in the very place where he firmly believes he is working to reduce an illusion" (145). At stake in Trollope's representation of the woman's body, and in Mr. Slope's relationship with Signora Neroni, is the desire to expose the marked body, to investigate it, even metaphorically to violate it, and yet simultaneously to demonstrate that such an exposure necessarily fails since the "illusion" cannot be unmasked, the "mystery" never plumbed. Rather than seeking to expose the hidden markings of the female body, then, the narrative of *Barchester Towers* directs us to make do with the forever veiled, forever unveiling female body, with the fact of its "injury" and its impurity known but with their exact nature unfathomed; in James's terms, we are to content ourselves with the vulgar, not the morbid. To do otherwise, as Mr. Slope discovers, is to court humiliation.

Mr. Slope is the only character who takes his obsession with Signora Neroni to such an extreme; however, he is not the only one who feels a complex attraction and repulsion toward her. Mr. Thorne, for example, believes her to be dangerous and coarse, but falls in love with her at first sight. "Messrs Browne, Jones and Robinson" (366), "Rev. Messrs Grey and Green" (447) are all numbered among the "lady's squires" (441), and all compete for her attention. Even Mr. Arabin, the man who will wed Eleanor Bold and satisfy the romance demands of the plot, finds her "charm" (364) compelling. At the Ullathorne social gathering, Arabin first tried to resist "temptation" in the shape of Signora Neroni, but then "he yielded himself up to the basilisk, and allowed himself to be made prey of" (363). She does not prey on him as fiercely as she does on Slope; nevertheless, he experiences her impure presence as an intimate, psychological intrusion: "Who was this woman that thus read the secrets of his heart, and re-uttered to him the unwelcome bodings of his own soul? . . . It seemed to him as though he were being interrogated by some inner spirit of his own, to whom he could not refuse an answer, and to whom he did not dare to give a false reply" (365–66). Signora Neroni's basilisk gaze thus occasions introspection rather than recoil.

The interrogation she prompts in part concerns his feelings toward Eleanor Bold, and makes Arabin (and the reader) question whether impurity resides only in the female body. We have already learned that while Mr. Arabin has admitted to himself that he loves Mrs. Bold, he has not acquitted himself of "impure motives." Her wealth makes her an attractive bride, and Arabin fears that this fact colors his thoughts about her; the narrator comments: "It was and ever had been his weakness to look for impure motives for his own conduct" (317). In this interview, Signora Neroni urges him to risk impurity to win Mrs. Bold. She points out to him that his scruples prevent him from acting at all, while a man such as Mr. Slope, with few scruples, wields his sword to "sever the everyday Gordian knots of the world's struggle, and win wealth and renown"—and matrimony (365). Arabin, she insists, must risk impurity if he is to attain his desire.

In directing Arabin's erotic interest back to Eleanor Bold, and thereby directing the narrative itself back to the question of what constitutes a safe hearth and home, Signora Neroni is ironically hurrying her own expulsion from the narrative. The comic plot of the novel is in fact resolved in the projected marriage of Eleanor and Mr. Arabin, and the dangerously impure Signora Neroni, like Slope, is expelled.[8] The end of the novel thus refocuses attention on the domestic realm and on the body soon to be given in marriage to Arabin, the body of Eleanor Bold.

What is the status of the woman's body in this comic resolution? The narrator seems to figure the body of Eleanor Bold as pure, pliant and submissive. The metaphor of the married woman as a pliant parasite plant is recollected by the narrator as he describes the "glory" of Eleanor Bold's love for Mr. Arabin:

> When the ivy has found its tower, when the delicate creeper has found its strong wall, we know how the parasite plants grow and prosper. . . . Alone they but spread themselves on the ground, and cower unseen in the dingy shade. But when they have found their firm supporters, how wonderful is their beauty; how all pervading and victorious! (470)

The metaphor of married woman as clinging parasite suggests on the one hand her pliancy and faithfulness, but on the other hand implies that she has a dangerous grasp, since a parasite may well strangle that which supports it. Further, her surname—albeit "parasitically" acquired from her late husband—does suggest a newly acquired boldness of character, and certainly her determination to defy her family and friends in her wary friendship with Mr. Slope indicates an independence of mind not usually associated with a "delicate creeper" cowering in the shade.

The most signal example of her strength of character comes when Mr. Slope makes his unwelcome romantic advances to *her*. Alone in the shrubbery at Ullathorne, he addresses her by her first name and "contrived to pass his arm round her waist":

> She sprang from him as she would have jumped from an adder, but she did not spring far; not, indeed, beyond arm's length; and then, quick as thought, she raised her little hand and dealt him a box on the ear with such right good will, that it sounded among the trees like a miniature thunder-clap. (384)

A slap!—it is the only act of physical violence the novel actually represents and it is delivered with a Zeus-like power (albeit in miniature).[9] The slap precipitates two pages of (partly) earnest reflections by the narrator.

Where responsibility for the terrible injury inflicted on Signora Neroni was waved aside by the narrator—"be that as it may"—this slap calls forth all his fears of arousing the readers' repulsion. Impurity—"pollution" is James's word—has threatened the pages of the novel itself:

> And now it is to be feared that every well-bred reader of these pages will lay down the book with disgust, feeling that, after all, the heroine is unworthy of our sympathy. She is a hoyden, one will say. At any rate she is not a lady, another will exclaim. I have suspected her all through, a third will declare; she has no idea of the dignity of a matron; or of the peculiar propriety which her position demands. At one moment she is romping with young Stanhope; then she is making eyes at Mr Arabin; anon she comes to fisty-cuffs with a third lover; and all before she is yet a widow of two years' standing. (384–85)

The comic tone is of course evident, yet the narrator feels keenly the need to defend Eleanor, even if he cannot exonerate her completely: "It were to be wished devoutly that she had not struck Mr Slope in the face" (385). At fault, according to the narrator, is Eleanor's overly developed "feeling of independence, a feeling dangerous for a young woman" (385), and a feeling obviously inimical with her future role as a pliant parasite plant dependent on Mr. Arabin's stony strength. As Sheila Burgar notes in her analysis of women's choices in Trollope's novels, Trollope frequently presents women caught between "the opposing forces of social duty and spontaneous emotion" (37). Readers, of course, may well have been longing for any "joke" (385) against the pomposity of Mr. Slope, and while the narrator acknowledges that Eleanor's spontaneous act is the "fittest rebuke" (385) that she could deliver, it is also clearly a contravention of her moral duty. Eleanor's action is, in comic terms, unequivocally condemned.

What is most interesting in the passage following the slap, however, is the suggestion that Eleanor is a woman whose independence of mind and violent action may bring a threat of impurity, not on the same scale as Madeline Neroni, of course, yet who as a woman opens the possibility of defilement, of the abject. The idea of defilement is specifically invoked by the narrator as he discusses the effect of Eleanor Bold's slap on Mr. Slope:

> There are such men; men who can endure no taint on their personal self-respect, even from a woman; men whose bodies are to themselves such sacred temples, that a joke against them is desecration, and a rough touch downright sacrilege. Mr Slope was such a man. . . . (385)

The metaphor here is extremely suggestive once again connecting the domestic romance plot to the realm of ecclesiastical politics. The male body—at least Mr. Slope's body—is figured as a sacred temple. Any joke against such a body is a "desecration" of the temple, and a woman's act of violence—perhaps especially a woman's act of violence, a slap—is "downright sacrilege." Like the grip of Aylmer's thumb, which imprints itself on Georgiana's arm, Eleanor's violence seemingly marks Mr. Slope's body with signs of defilement that others may read: "His cheek was stinging with the weight of Eleanor's fingers, and he fancied that everyone who looked at him would be able to see on his face the traces of what he had endured" (386). Indeed, when Signora Neroni verbally humiliates him a few chapters later, the force of the blow is renewed: "He felt on his cheek the sharp points of Eleanor's fingers, and did not know who might have seen the blow, who might have told the tale to this pestilent woman" (447). For readers of the body, such "traces" are evidence that he has "endured" something; the marked body does speak its injury. In this case the slap signifies a culpable female violence which has desecrated the pure male body. Mr. Arabin should beware of the delicate parasite he is to marry.

It is too simple to read *Barchester Towers* as a novel that depicts a female body as abject and the male body as sacred; female violence—a slap—as "unspeakable" sacrilege, and male violence as a topic to be delicately avoided. Certainly the novel's humor should at least temper any such strong reading. Also Mr. Arabin's anxiety over his own possible impurity of motive indicates that purity and impurity are not strictly gendered categories. Finally, Mr. Slope is himself expelled from the world of the novel as firmly as Signora Neroni is—sacred body or not. James Kincaid reads both *The Warden* and *Barchester Towers* as shaped by "patterns of disruption and consequent expulsion. Bold [in *The Warden*] does not really have a 'case,' nor does Slope. It is not that their positions are bad but that they are irrelevant. Their assumptions about life and morality are so askew that they must be admitted only to be expelled" (98). However much Slope may regard his body as a sacred temple, in the Barchester community he and Madeline Neroni are much alike; they are both outsiders who threaten the purity of communal life, and who must be expelled in the novel's resolution. Both are marked as unclean by an act of violence: he by a slap, she by an unspecified enormity.

Still, the language of the sacred and the profane extends from the religious and ecclesiastical plot of the novel into the sphere of domestic and sexual relations which the novel depicts. Sexual difference is related to purity and impurity; it is not that male and female are marked as pure and impure, but gender does seem to determine the depth and type of impurity and its effects. The allegorical, symbolizing mode of "The Birth-Mark" allows these distinctions to manifest themselves that much more starkly than does the comic realist world of *Barchester Towers*. Slope's *ideas* are intellectually impure, but the tingling marks of Eleanor's small hand merely expel Mr. Slope into the greener fields of London and into the arms of a rich widow. Madeline Neroni's *body,* complexly figured as it is, carries the weight of her impurity, and is ineluctable. Her body, like Georgiana's, is marked by a femininity that is both intolerable (in its refusal to subject itself to male vision) and inescapable.

Drawing on the work of cultural anthropologists such as James Frazer and Mary Douglas, Kristeva points out:

> In a number of primitive societies religious rites are purification rites whose function is to separate this or that social, sexual, or age group from another one, by means of prohibiting a filthy, defiling element. It is as if dividing lines were built up between society and a certain nature . . . on the basis of the simple logic of *excluding filth,* which, promoted to the ritual level of *defilement,* founded the "self and clean" of each social group if not of each subject.
>
> The purification rite appears then as that essential ridge, which, prohibiting the filthy object, extracts it from the secular order and lines it at once with a sacred facet. Because it is excluded as a possible object, asserted to be a non-object of desire, abominated as ab-ject, as abjection, filth becomes defilement and founds on the henceforth released side of the "self and clean" the order that is thus only (and therefore, always already) sacred. (65)

Barchester Towers is a novel that depicts the rejuvenation, or "reformation," of a community through a redefining of this ridge, through a separation of the sacred and profane. The ecclesiastical questions that pervade this book essentially concern the institutionalization of this ridge or margin, and the expulsion of Mr. Slope at the novel's conclusion is a sign of the success of this communal purification rite. In a parallel movement, the novel also defines a ridge in the domestic realm, inscribes a border on the female body which marks it as abject, both desired and reviled. The resolution of the novel is achieved through a facile separation of the female body into the clean and the unclean. Signora Neroni's marked body comes to act as the "other"—for Girard, the "double," "twin," or "scapegoat"—which, when expelled, allows Eleanor Bold's body to be figured (albeit ambiguously) as pliable, submissive, and pure.

3

Violence, Causality, and the "Shock of History"

George Eliot's "Janet's Repentance"

Of Trollope's style, Richard Barickman, Susan MacDonald and Myra Stark claim, "[w]e do not have in Trollope . . . a wise, controlling, exploring, and synthesizing narrative voice; readers instead are forced to do the exploring and synthesizing for themselves" (199). The "wise, controlling, exploring, and synthesizing narrative voice" has often been said to belong instead to George Eliot who, in each of her fictions, faces questions of the reality of domestic life directly and unsparingly. "Janet's Repentance," the third story in *Scenes of Clerical Life,* presents perhaps the most realist depiction of bourgeois domestic violence of any text examined in this book. Published in *Blackwood's Magazine* in 1857, the novella can be seen in part as a response to the new Divorce Law of that same year, a law that includes cruelty, in combination with adultery, as grounds for granting a woman's request for divorce.[1] Eliot asks in this novella the question "The Birth-Mark" chooses not to ask, and the question that is evaded by Trollope in *Barchester Towers,* that is, *why* domestic violence takes place, why a man abuses a woman. Aylmer's impulses in Hawthorne's story are taken as given by the narrator. Trollope simply avoids the hard question of why or even whether actual violence was inflicted on Signora Neroni's body; if violence has been done, Trollope assumes that bourgeois English readers will accept an unseen foreigner,

Neroni, as a simple brute: "a man of harsh temper and oily manners, mean in figure, swarthy in face, and . . . false in words." This chapter will argue that George Eliot's typical preoccupation with tracing the intricacies of character and motivation is here applied to the question of Janet's suffering. Unsatisfied by evasions, Eliot tackles directly the ethical questions raised by the representation and the reality of violence. Given George Eliot's prominence as a realist, the acts of domestic violence, and their context and results, are represented in the story with the terrible faithfulness we would expect in a newspaper report or a sociology text;[2] given Eliot's distinction as a moralist, the story is able to depict the dreadful dilemmas faced by the battered woman as she tries to remain true to her own sense of ethical imperatives; and finally, given Eliot's unerring sense of human complexity, the narrative attempts to plumb the psychological depths of a marriage gone wrong, particularly of the lost world of love and erotic attraction that initially brought the wretched couple together. This domestic plot is not developed in isolation, but is deeply embedded within a complex set of social relations in the small town of Milby; the various discursive realms of this small town—the religious, the medical, and the legal—each generates its own paradigm of understanding, a paradigm that is then brought back into play with the dynamics of the domestic plot.

Critics have not always treated "Janet's Repentance" generously.[3] Sandra M. Gilbert and Susan Gubar, perhaps the first critics to pay due attention to the domestic, as opposed to the political and religious plots of *Scenes of Clerical Life,* note that Eliot may have chosen clerical characters for her first work of fiction because clergymen are "profoundly aware of what goes on behind the veil, and they invite confessions from all who 'tremble to let in the daylight on a chamber of relics which we have never visited except in curtained silence' (chap.18)" (488). In spite of the powerful unveiling that takes place, however, Gilbert and Gubar claim that the domestic plots of all of the *Scenes of Clerical Life* "are almost embarrassingly melodramatic" (484).[4] Andrew Dowling, on the other hand, suggests that the "curtained silence" of matrimonial conflict is probed in such a way as to draw the stories beyond melodrama and sentimentality. Reading "Janet's Repentance," *Daniel Deronda,* and *Middlemarch* in the context of the new Divorce Court in England, Dowling argues that

> her emphasis on silence as a *literal* symptom of oppression reflects the wider cultural concern about those forms of marital conflict that

> are not obviously physical. At the same time, however, silence functions as a rhetorical device that, by suggesting more than it openly states, addresses a readership increasingly interested in the "unspeakable" details of married life. (323)

As indicated in our introduction, the liminal world of domestic violence in the mid-nineteenth century is situated on realism's borders, constantly shifting into the realm of the unspeakable. This chapter thus argues that Eliot's portrayal of the "curtained silence" of the Dempster marriage is not an evasion (of representation) but rather a blankness which nevertheless speaks the appalling history of Janet's abuse.

In the novella Dempster and his wife play out depressing (and by the late twentieth century familiar) patterns of domestic violence: its hallmarks are male aggression, female passivity and lack of self-esteem, and the willful inaction of the surrounding community. The precipitating causes of male violence portrayed in the story are trivial; on the occasion that provokes the story's crisis, Janet refuses to pick up clothes that Dempster, in a rage, has thrown on the floor. Nonetheless, Janet blames herself for her husband's violence, believing that she must "try to make up for what has been wrong in me" (274). Even after she has been forced from her home by her husband at midnight, clothed only in a light nightdress, she believes it to be her "duty" to return to him (274). She will not seek legal protection, perhaps not surprising given that her husband is a lawyer who has always been able to manipulate the law to suit his own and his clients' best interests. (The futility of seeking any type of legal protection, indeed the harm done in the name of the law, is addressed more explicitly by Collins in *Man and Wife*.) Janet can thus seek no avenue of rescue: "[S]he shrank utterly, as she had always done, from any active, public resistance or vengeance: she felt too crushed, too faulty, too liable to reproach, to have the courage, even if she had had the wish, to put herself openly in the position of a wronged woman seeking redress" (251). Conventional community opinion, mouthed by Dempster's mother, Mamsey, reinforces the view that it is Janet who is open to "reproach"; Mamsey Dempster believes that "the true beginning of it all [was] in Janet's want of housekeeping skill and exactness" (239). Other women in the story, such as Janet's servant, reasonably assert that *they* would not put up with such treatment: "I wouldn't stan' bein' mauled as she is by no husband, not if he was the biggest lord i' the land" (266). Finally, alcohol plays a key role in the story, loosening the inhibitions and feeding the temper of Dempster, contributing to his brutal acts. Janet Dempster herself also drinks in order to avoid the pain inflicted by her husband, and to escape the violent and unpredictable reality around her.[5]

In examining the unspeakable aspects of Janet's experience, this chapter addresses one problem in particular: the question of causality. In spite of the "curtained silence" and evasions offered in the novella, can a cause for domestic violence be discovered? Can a source for this all too common human misery be identified?

THE "SEED" OF VIOLENCE

Among the enduring and repeated topics addressed by George Eliot's fiction is the question of what makes, and in some cases, breaks a marriage; the other two tales in *Scenes of Clerical Life,* "The Lifted Veil," *Silas Marner, Felix Holt, Romola, Middlemarch,* and *Daniel Deronda* all address this problem. Eliot's interest in marital violence in "Janet's Repentance" should thus not be viewed in isolation, but as part of her larger concern with destructive marriages as a whole. What is striking in the case of "Janet's Repentance" is that the Dempster marriage seemingly begins in harmony and content. Whereas the reader of *Middlemarch* senses the immediate distress of Dorothea during her wedding trip to Rome, and the reader of *Daniel Deronda*—and Gwendolen herself—fully understand Grandcourt's cold immorality even before the marriage, the narrator of "Janet's Repentance" is insistent upon the initial happiness of Janet Raynor and Robert Dempster. The mystery, or as Janet calls it the "riddle," is why a terrible contrast has developed between her early happiness as a bride and her misery after fifteen years of marriage. After Dempster thrusts her out of the house into the cold at midnight, Janet despairingly muses that:

> All her early gladness, all her bright hopes and illusions, all her gifts of beauty and affection, served only to darken the riddle of her life; they were the betraying promises of a cruel destiny which had brought out those sweet blossoms only that the winds and storms might have a greater work of desolation, which had nursed her like a pet fawn into tenderness and fond expectation, only that she might feel a keener terror in the clutch of the panther. (246-47)

Her life, and her marriage, were not cruel and bitter from their inception; the "riddle" that puzzles her is how they have both gone so dreadfully wrong.

Gilbert and Gubar's answer to the riddle—that Janet married Dempster only because of economic necessity (487)—neglects the fact that the scenes of domestic violence depicted in the story contrast strongly with Janet's memories of her early married life, when physical experience was not cruel and violent but loving and erotic: "I loved my husband dearly when we were married" (256), Janet asserts; "I loved him once better than all the world" (265). We learn of her "trembling joy" (246) as a bride, of her "sweet wedded love and hope" (238) which was shown in "caressing playful affection" (239–40). Most clear is

> her ever-living remembrance of the too short years of love that went before; and the thought that her husband would ever put her hand to his lips again, and recall the days when they sat on the grass together, and he laid scarlet poppies on her black hair, and called her his gypsy queen, seemed to send a tide of loving oblivion over all the harsh and stony space they had traversed since. (279)

Now that world of erotic fulfilment and "trembling joy" is only the source of bitter irony: "He had no pity on her tender flesh; he could strike the soft neck he had once asked to kiss" (240). A relationship once characterized by Dempster's seeking of permission to bring erotic pleasure has been transformed into a relationship of unapologetic brutality.

The narrator carefully considers the question of what has turned this marriage from love to cruelty:

> Do you wonder how it was that things had come to this pass—what offence Janet had committed in the early years of marriage to rouse the brutal hatred of this man? The seeds of things are very small: the hours that lie between sunrise and the gloom of midnight are travelled through by tiniest markings of the clock: and Janet, looking back along the fifteen years of her married life, hardly knew how or where this total misery began; hardly knew when the sweet wedded love and hope that had set for ever had ceased to make a twilight of memory and relenting, before the oncoming of utter dark. (238–39)

The image of the seed, frequently used in Eliot's fiction, here suggests that a moment of "offence" can be located—a hostile incident, a chilly word, a thoughtless remark—which grew and flourished like a noxious plant, a moment that turned love to cruelty, erotic fulfilment to sadism. The image also explains the disproportion between cause and effect: a small, seemingly insignificant cause, like the mustard seed in Christ's parable,[6] brings about an incalculably large effect.

Yet having used the metaphor of the seed, the narrator offers no direct mode of interpreting it. The narrator proffers Mamsey Dempster's simplistic interpretation—"the true beginning of it all [was] in Janet's want of housekeeping skill and exactness" (239)—but then dismisses it by asserting:

> But do not believe that it was anything either present or wanting in poor Janet that formed the motive of her husband's cruelty. Cruelty, like every other vice, requires no motive outside itself—it only requires opportunity. You do not suppose Dempster had any motive for drinking beyond the craving for drink; the presence of brandy was the only necessary condition. And an unloving, tyrannous, brutal man needs no motive to prompt his cruelty; he needs only the perpetual presence of a woman he can call his own. (239)

The only motive for human cruelty is cruelty; it is like the craving for drink, a significant simile in this story soaked with alcohol. Cruelty's only precondition for Dempster is having a "woman he can call his own," a possession that indicates both Dempster's intoxication with power (as well as with alcohol and violence) and the inability of the law to protect women who are regarded as property. Yet the explanation that Dempster is cruel because he is cruel is really no explanation at all. Dempster once asked to kiss Janet's soft neck; now he is "unloving, tyrannous, brutal." The image of the "seed" of violence raises the question of the cause of this transformation, but then the question is seemingly left suspended and unanswered.

The succeeding sections of this chapter will argue that the novella offers a series of discursive paradigms—medical, hermeneutic, religious—each one of which provides its own method of understanding the relation of cause to effect, of interpreting the cause of suffering and violence. Each paradigm will be tested for the power of explanation it offers of the "seed" or the dark riddle, that is, each paradigm will be tested for its ability to make sense of the appalling transformation of the Dempster marriage from love to violence.[7]

MEDICINE AND CAUSALITY

In a lengthy digression from the main plot, readers are asked to understand the various types of medical diagnostic procedures current in the town of Milby. There are two doctors in Milby, Mr. Pratt and Mr. Pilgrim; they divide the town between them, so that all inhabitants have a strong allegiance to the practice of one or the other. The difference between the two doctors is described succinctly:

> Pratt elegantly referred all diseases to debility, and with a proper contempt for symptomatic treatment, went to the root of the matter with port wine and bark; Pilgrim was persuaded that the evil principle in the human system was plethora, and he made war against it with cupping, blistering, and cathartics. (179)

Although the narrator does not champion either Pilgrim's or Pratt's diagnostic method, it is clear that both are deterministic models of interpretation. Disease is caused by one of two principles: either there is an inherent "debility"—a feebleness, a lack of strength—or there is "plethora"—an excess of red corpuscles. "Debility" is treated through systemic stimulants;[8] "plethora" is treated symptomatically through the practices of "cupping, blistering, and cathartics." "Debility" demands a strengthening regime; "plethora" requires a "lowering," "active treatment" (179, 180). The two theories of cause are left to stand as an example of an irreconcilable yet amicable dispute. The two men in question have a "friendly contempt for each other" which dissolves into a "perfect unanimity" (179) the moment a third medical practitioner has the temerity to appear in Milby. The only certainty for the town of Milby is that disease must be caused by plethora or debility, not a third element.[9]

However disputed the particulars, the medical model of diagnosis and its theory of causality appear to offer a straightforward deterministic model for understanding the human condition. Although the precise seed of disease may be disputed, the correct model for identifying potential seeds is resolved.

This same deterministic model of interpretation was carried over into Victorian discourse on the causes of domestic violence. Frances Power Cobbe is voicing a Victorian truism when, in "Wife-torture in England," she states that alcohol is the first of the "principal incitements to . . . outbursts of [men's] savage fury" against their wives: "The seas of brandy and gin, and the oceans of beer, imbibed annually in England [especially when adulterated] . . . literally sting the wretched drinkers into cruelty, perhaps quite foreign to their natural temperaments" (140). Alcohol, Cobbe asserts, is a direct cause of domestic cruelty.

Eliot invokes this commonplace in her portrait of the brutal alcoholic Dempster in order to expose its limitations. The weakness of the medical deterministic model of cause and effect is immediately evident in the story itself. Although Mr. Pratt and Mr. Pilgrim hold clear views on the causes of disease, their treatments are unavailing; both of their patients, Tryan and Dempster, die. Furthermore, the story itself explicitly states that alcohol does not inevitably cause Dempster to be brutal; we learn that he can drink a bottle of brandy and retain a clear head (173), and that he can exercise self-restraint when it suits him (254). If the seed of domestic violence is "one of the mysteries of alcoholism" (Bennett 60), medical investigation has failed to reveal anything beyond what was already clear to Janet—that the causes of Dempster's violence are mysterious, a riddle.[10] In one of the most striking scenes in the novella, our sense of the gap between what medicine can explain and what in fact demands explanation is extreme. Janet, who has just begun to fear that her husband is ill, rushes into the bedroom she shares with her husband and finds him in the midst of full-fledged hallucinations:

> "Let me go, let me go," he said in a loud, hoarse whisper; "she's coming . . . . she's cold . . . . she's dead . . . . she'll strangle me with her black hair. Ah!" he shrieked aloud, "her hair is all serpents . . . . they're black serpents . . . . they hiss . . . . they hiss . . . . let me go . . . . let me go . . . . she wants to drag me with her cold arms . . . . her arms are serpents . . . . they are great white serpents . . . . they'll twine around me . . . . she wants to drag me into the cold water . . . . her bosom is cold . . . . it is black . . . . it is all serpents . . . ." (276; ellipses in original)

The description of the hallucination continues for two pages, as the horrified Janet tries to assure Dempster that she is not dead, and that she forgives him for shutting her out of the house. The delirium persists with threats of revenge and denials of guilt, hallucinations that his bed is covered with lice and toads (leading him to implore Janet to come and take them away), another vision of Janet herself as dead, coming out of the iron closet with hair of black serpents and arms of white serpents, and finally the delusion that he is beating his horse and threatening a devilish revenge on his religious enemies.

In response to this terrifying scene, the doctor takes Janet by the arm and attempts to draw her from the room. He reassures her that "We shall soon relieve these symptoms, I hope; it is nothing but the delirium that ordinarily attends such cases" (278). Having made the correct diagnosis, Pilgrim is content to believe that the work of explanation is done: sudden withdrawal of alcohol leading to delirium tremens. Dempster's behavior, for Pilgrim, is explained.

What the diagnosis does not explain, and presumably what arouses Janet's (and the reader's) horror, however, is the *content* of Dempster's delirium. The medical notion of causality is uninterested in content; "Crying, calls for help, cursing, muttering, moaning, and other vocal productions" ("Delirium," *DSM-III-R*) are symptoms that in themselves call for no further explanation. The content of the hallucination, however, is arguably crucial to our understanding of Dempster's character and Janet's misery. It is here that we can see clearly the limitations of the medical or positivist model of interpretation.

The narrator of "Janet's Repentance" offers a very clear explanation as to why deterministic methods of understanding causality may very well fail:

> Do not philosophic doctors tell us that we are unable to discern so much as a tree, except by an unconscious cunning which combines many past and separate sensations; that no one sense is independent of another, so that in the dark we can hardly taste a fricassee, or tell whether our pipe is alight or not, and the most intelligent boy, if accommodated with claws or hoofs instead of fingers, would be likely to remain on the lowest form? If so, it is easy to understand that our discernment of men's motives must depend on the completeness of the elements we can bring from our own susceptibility and our own experience. See to it, friend, before you pronounce a too hasty judgment, that your own moral sensibilities are not of a hoofed or clawed character. The keenest eye will not serve, unless you have the delicate fingers, with their subtle nerve filaments, which elude scientific lenses, and lose themselves in the invisible world of human sensations. (230–31)

The narrator's musings here are a warning to all interpreters of "men's motives" and should give pause to any reader who considers leaping to a "hasty judgment." Nevertheless, it is clear that the mere power of observation—"the keenest eye"—will not explain motive; "scientific lenses" will not open to us "the invisible world of human sensations." Positivist or deterministic models of human behavior fall short of being fully satisfactory because all our powers of observation are finally of the "hoofed or clawed character," unable to approach the "invisible" and the silent. Thus, readers need at least to test other ways of approaching an investigation into "men's motives," into the cause of Dempster's violence.

CAUSE AND HERMENEUTICS

A more metaphoric approach to the seed or riddle of domestic violence involves not a deterministic account of cause leading to effect, but a hermeneutic effort directed at interpreting the seed, unpacking the riddle. In *The Metastases of Enjoyment*, Slavoj Žižek offers a useful way of contrasting deterministic and hermeneutic models of explanation in contemporary Lacanian psychoanalysis. Although Žižek examines the extent to which psychoanalysis itself rests on a deterministic model of drives and "energies," he also points out that psychoanalysis offers an "in-depth hermeneutics" which demonstrate that "even in the case of (what appear to be) purely physiological corporeal disturbances, we are still dealing with a dialectic of meaning, with the subject's distorted communication with himself and his Other" (8). Psychoanalysis thus offers a model for analyzing the *content* of Dempster's hallucination; however much Dempster's delirium is the result of "purely physiological corporeal disturbances"—withdrawal from alcohol—it also partakes of a "dialectic of meaning" that opens itself to hermeneutic rather than to medical analysis.

Dempster's hallucination, like dreams and other psychic events, is profoundly determined, indeed overdetermined, by his inner world. Some of the elements of the hallucination are clearly the product of biblical and classical mythology. The lice and the frogs recall two of the plagues visited upon Egypt; as the one who suffers from the plagues, Dempster is cast into the role of the cruel but suffering Pharaoh who refuses to let God's chosen people go. The serpents of hair of course recall the Medusa, the horrific figure of classical mythology whose glance turns man to stone, and who can be seen as a repulsive image of the female genitalia. That the white serpentine arms are dragging Dempster down into the water suggests that the female figure is also a Siren, who lures men to their destruction through beautiful music. Other elements of the hallucination clearly relate to incidents in Dempster's life: the "psalm-singing maggots" and the "sneaking idiots" who "think they've outwitted me" (277) refer to the Evangelical faction in the novella which has won the battle of the Sunday evening lecture series against Dempster's heated opposition. The beating of the bedclothes with his arm, and the sound "—sc—sc—sc!" is in imitation of his habitual driving and beating of his horse, and the "iron chest" in which he believes Janet is buried is the one in his bedroom to which only he has the key, and in which he locked Janet's clothes in order to deceive the servants as to her whereabouts. The meaning of still other elements of the hallucination can only be conjectured. When he demands, "prove that I took the money . . . prove it . . . you can prove nothing" (277), he is presumably referring to some clever theft that he has committed but which cannot be proved against him. The threat "I'll have every drop of yellow blood out of your veins if you come questioning me" (277) may refer to Dempster's fear that Janet is dead and he will be questioned by the authorities, or that questions will be raised about his legal dishonesty. One may also assume that Dempster himself has a personal dread of vermin such as lice, frogs, and maggots, and that their reiterated presence is a signal of this dread.

Dempster's manifold hallucination thus exposes his complex inner world of delusions of grandeur, of violence, and, most significantly, his dread and loathing of women. Although the figures in Dempster's hallucination do shift, the most recurrent is Janet herself. Janet certainly believes that she is the female figure he refers to: "'No, Robert,' Janet cried, . . . 'no, here is Janet. She is not dead—she forgives you'" (276). In Dempster's hallucination, Janet is the Medusa and the Siren: loathsome, dangerous, and beautiful. As Gilbert and Gubar argue, Janet is "[n]othing less than a female monster to her husband's sickened imagination" (489). Although she may be a helper, called on to exterminate the loathsome lice and frogs that torment him, she may at the same time be the Moses-figure who invokes the plagues as punishment. Dempster is then a Pharaoh; keeping Janet captive and enslaved, he deserves chastisement. Finally, the beating of his horse in the hallucination reflects his real behavior toward that animal, and of course toward Janet herself.[11]

The Janet whom we as readers see through the sympathetic gaze of the narrator is obviously quite a different creature from the Janet of Dempster's delirium. Rather than the pitiful, loving, and abused creature readers have become familiar with throughout the narrative, this fantasized Janet is an object of horror, fear, and repulsion. The memories of past happiness in the Dempster marriage, which Janet treasures, play no part in his hallucination.

It is ironic that in this one personal and revealing view, Dempster, the man famed for being a rational and clear-headed lawyer, is profoundly irrational. Otherwise the narrative never offers his point of view: that startling shift to Casaubon's point of view at the beginning of chapter 29 of *Middlemarch* when the narrator, having told of Dorothea's uneasiness in her marriage, suddenly asks, "but why always Dorothea? Was her point of view the only possible one with regard to this marriage?" (228–29), never occurs in "Janet's Repentance." Although our view of Dempster is frequently colored by Janet's loving, yielding perspective, only this hallucination offers a clue to Dempster's own perception of Janet and of his married life. The broken, disconnected, and disjointed words of Dempster both demand and resist interpretation, forcing readers to bridge the gaps and fissures in narrative intelligibility.

There is at least one moment of coincidence between Dempster's hallucination and Janet's description of her relationship to Dempster, a moment that may suggest an explanation of the obscure seed of domestic violence. That coincidence is Janet's hair. In Dempster's hallucination, her hair is the hair of the Gorgon, odious and deadly; in Janet's memory, there is the treasured and vivid recollection of "the days when they sat on the grass together, and he laid scarlet poppies on her black hair, and called her his gypsy queen" (279). The scarlet poppies on the black hair catch the beauty of vivid contrast, and are a suggestive erotic metonymy, but at the same time the color red set against the black does hint at darkness, violence, and blood. She is hardly a Gorgon here, but her hair's dark beauty may intimate danger. Dempster's nickname for Janet, the "gypsy queen," may be a similarly shifting designation, referring both to her vibrant beauty and to something enigmatic, unpredictable, or unstable that she embodies. Gypsies were of course constructed as the exotic, fascinating, and dangerous Other of European culture, a paradox Eliot herself exploits in her depiction of gypsies in *The Mill on the Floss*. In chapter 11 of that novel, Maggie runs away to become the heroic and beautiful queen of the gypsies; when she encounters real gypsies, she finds them dirty, unappreciative, and frightening.[12] Being a "gypsy queen" in Dempster's imagination may be a similarly perilous designation; Janet's dark beauty and luxurious hair may themselves become a source of danger to her in her marriage.

The inevitable end of this interpretation—of both Dempster's hallucination and of Janet's memory—is the suggestion that in the past (the past to which Janet yearns to return) there is the seed of a very different memory for Dempster—an ambivalent memory of danger and fear. The "black hair" overlaid with "scarlet poppies," which arouses erotic longings in Janet, is the same black hair that arouses dread in Dempster. What is clear in this apposition is not only the incommensurability of an individual's psychic world with any objective reality, but the dreadful incommensurability of any one individual's psychic world with that of another.

Indeed when Žižek explicates Lacan's ideas on trauma as Cause, the gap between the real and psychical reality is highlighted. Žižek points out that, on the one hand, "the Cause is real, the presupposed reef which resists symbolization," so that "if we try to grasp the trauma directly, irrespective of its later effects, we are left with a meaningless *factum brutum*" of the event (*Metastases* 31, 32). On the other hand, "trauma has no existence of its own prior to symbolization"; "It is only through its echoes within the symbolic structure that the *factum brutum* . . . retroactively acquires its traumatic character and becomes the Cause" (31, 32). Thus, cause "not only exerted its efficiency after a certain time-lag, it literally *became* trauma—that is, Cause—through delay" (31). Žižek therefore claims that a powerful transformation takes place as the real event is, through time, incorporated into an individual's symbolization, an incorporation that may (but does not inevitably) take the form of trauma.

At the time when Dempster laid poppies in Janet's hair, then, the act was the cause of nothing. But as the powerful images of Janet's vibrant female body, her dark hair, and her exotic beauty echo "within [his] symbolic structure," one could argue that—in Dempster's psychical world—the event "retroactively acquires its traumatic character and becomes the Cause." The tragic irony for Janet in this model of interpretation is that her marital bliss is constituted and contaminated at the same moment. The seed of domestic violence is to be found retroactively in the "too short years of love" that Janet treasures, in a seemingly innocuous, loving act which later leads to loathing and violence: "[H]e could strike the soft neck he had once asked to kiss."

Thus, it is a symptom of Dempster's psychic destructiveness that he splits his beautiful and desirable wife into a Janus-faced creature whose obverse side is a loathsome monster that must be treated as if it were a recalcitrant horse or vermin, a split reminiscent of the separation of Jane Eyre and Bertha Mason into angel and monster. It is not, however, a seed in a scientific deterministic sense; the trauma becomes a seed only retroactively, so that it is, as Žižek argues, "the non-symbolizable kernel around which all later successive symbolizations whirled" (*Metastases* 31).

Two examples in the story concerning images of seeds support this view of cause as hermeneutic, rather than deterministic. Unlike the earlier image—"The seeds of things are very small"—where the narrator suggests a purely biological reading of how seeds grow to tragic effect, the seeds in these instances bring forth their fruit through a process that is not open to deterministic understanding. In the first, Janet's mother is despairing over Janet's difficult lot, and sees no escape for her. The narrator interjects, foreshadowing the hopeful influence of Tryan on Janet's life:

> She tried to have hope and trust, though it was hard to believe that the future would be anything else than the harvest of the seed that was being sown before her eyes. But always there is seed being sown silently and unseen, and everywhere there come sweet flowers without our foresight and labour. We reap what we sow, but Nature has love over and above that justice, and gives us shadow and blossom and fruit that spring from no planting of ours. (204)

In the second instance, Janet has received consolation from Mr. Tryan, and so the narrator rejoices:

> Blessed influence of one true loving human soul on another! Not calculable by algebra, not deducible by logic, but mysterious, effectual, mighty as the hidden process by which the tiny seed is quickened, and bursts forth into tall stem and broad leaf, and glowing tasselled flower. (263)

These seeds are of course not the seeds of trauma but the seeds of blessing; nevertheless their existence is exemplary. Everywhere there are seeds "being sown silently and unseen," which grow through a "hidden process" that cannot be explained by scientific determinism: "Not calculable by algebra, not deducible by logic." The logic of trauma and cause, similarly, cannot necessarily be read forward in time; seeds are sown "silently and unseen" and at the time are not recognizable as seeds at all. Likewise, trauma is only constituted after the fact, and the existence of a seed only conjectured as a result of apprehending the fully grown plant.

The seeds referred to in the passages above are best described as providential; the seeds of Janet's misery are quite different. To twist fearfully the happy words of the narrator about the seeds of happiness, one could say of Janet's misery: "We reap what we sow, but Evil has a hatred over and above that justice, and gives unhappy shadow and withered blossom and bitter fruit that spring from no planting of ours." Nothing "present or wanting in poor Janet . . . formed the motive of her husband's cruelty," the narrator has asserted; nevertheless, an unidentifiable hand planted a noxious seed in the midst of her early happiness. The seed of violence is thus at the moment of its planting early in the Dempster marriage an unrecognizable, non-symbolizable event; the seed only acquires its function as trauma, as cause, as it becomes symbolizable in Dempster's psychic realm—and is then cruelly acted upon.

THE MODEL OF CONFESSION

This chapter has argued that the deterministic, medical model of interpretation offers a solution to the problem of domestic violence that is really no answer at all: alcoholism causes domestic violence through a mysterious process. The hermeneutic model of interpretation identifies cause in the very earliest years of the Dempster marriage when a moment of loving play on the grass retroactively became a trauma suffered by Dempster, a trauma that led him unconsciously to view Janet as a creature who was both powerful and menacing. Yet this answer too must be radically inadequate. The narrative of trauma as cause offered by psychoanalysis may be an authentic account of the creation of Dempster's perverse and violent psyche; however this does not diminish or "explain" the monstrosity of Dempster's behavior. Having identified the seed or at least *a* seed only proves how unsatisfactory *any* answer will be to the question of the cause of domestic violence. Eliot's story thus leads us to question the sufficiency of any account of how past events lead to present conditions. The backbiting answers of Mamsey Dempster (Janet's poor housekeeping skills), the medical answer (Dempster's alcoholism), and the explanatory function of hermeneutics (Dempster's unnameable trauma) are all possible approaches to answering the question that must radically fail. To the dark riddle of Janet's life and to the identity of the seed of the contaminated marriage, they fail to provide ethically satisfactory explanations.

The story, however, offers a third model for understanding reality, a model not bound by temporal cause and effect or hermeneutic analysis, but by an atemporal divine understanding. As Tryan says to Janet when she is led to confess her sins: "He does not tell you, as your fellow-men do, that you must first merit His love; He neither condemns nor reproaches you for the past, He only bids you come to Him that you may have life" (260). The Christian model of confession and forgiveness makes the past a blank slate, where only the present moment of reliance on God matters. An inquiry into the *causes* of sin yields a simple and universal answer: human depravity. Human merit is impossible; only human weakness is real. The only sensible course is thus an entire reliance on God and God's commands:

> "There is nothing that becomes us but entire submission, perfect resignation. As long as we set up our own will and our own wisdom against God's, we make that wall between us and His love. . . . But as soon as we lay ourselves entirely at His feet, we have enough light given to guide our own steps; as the foot-soldier who hears nothing of the councils that determine the course of the great battle he is in, hears plainly enough the word of command which he must himself obey." (261)

In the Christian model, the human role is not to try to *understand* those factors that "determine the course of the great battle he is in"; the human role is simply to *obey* God's commands. Since human life is a battle, suffering—inexplicable suffering—will be an experience common to many.

In the story, the signal of such human obedience to God's will is confession, "repentance." When Janet confesses to Mr. Tryan in chapter 18 of the story, she is for the first time admitting her own despair and weakness. Her confession is followed by Tryan's own disclosure of weakness; he too is a sinner. Tryan confesses:

> "At college I had an attachment to a lovely girl of seventeen: she was very much below my own station in life, and I never contemplated marrying her; but I induced her to leave her father's house. I did not mean to forsake her when I left college, and I quieted all scruples of conscience by promising myself I would always take care of poor Lucy. But on my return from a vacation spent in travelling, I found that Lucy was gone—gone away with a gentleman, her neighbours said." (259)

Three years later he is walking in London and comes upon the scene of a woman who has poisoned herself: "[I]t was Lucy—dead—with paint on her cheeks" (259). This crisis determines the course of Tryan's future life. His mission thereafter is to try "to save others from the ruin I had brought on one" (259): "I asked for nothing through the rest of my life but that I might be devoted to God's work, without swerving in search of pleasure either to the right hand or to the left" (261).

The nature of Tryan's sin is not incidental. Although the tale of Tryan's seduction and abandonment of the young woman has been envisaged both in Eliot's own time and our own as "hackneyed" and "deliberately clichéd,"[13] it is worth reading the sordid tale in the light of J. W. Kaye's essay, "Outrages on Women," published in 1856, the year before "Janet's Repentance"; Kaye states that the *worst* "outrages" are seductions perpetrated by middle- and upper-class men on innocent and ill-educated women:

> There are various forms of man's cruelty to women of which wife-beating, we are afraid, is not the worst. To seduce, betray, and desert a young and beautiful woman, in the freshness and innocence of youth,—to leave her to die slowly of hunger, disease, or gin, or, suddenly, by a leap, on a cold winter's night, from the parapet of a bridge spanning the Thames, is to do what must be done amongst us on a much larger scale than wife-beating. (235)

Tryan's sin and Dempster's are thus both types of "outrages" against women, and the tale of Tryan's seduction is arguably a calculated choice by Eliot as she seeks to investigate the full spectrum of the bourgeois abuse of women.

If readers are led to consider the question of how Dempster's love for Janet became perverted into violence, they will thus also want to ask how Tryan's actions contributed to Lucy's death. What seems remarkable in Tryan's description of his relationship is the carelessness with which Lucy is lost. Although he promises himself that he will take care of her, he goes away on vacation and on his return is surprised to find that she is gone. One wants to know what provision he made in order that she be taken care of in his absence; one wants to know if she knew that he would return; one wants to know if he attempted to find her; one wants to know if she left voluntarily with the "gentleman," or through some kind of necessity. One wants to know, that is, the *cause* of Lucy's loss and eventual death. The confession does not allow us to know. Tryan's confession as *narration* has the irritating effect of a young child's explanation for losing some object in its charge: it was there and then it was gone. Read as a linear narration of cause and effect, the omissions in Tryan's confession of his sinfulness are remarkable.

In confession, however, questions of cause and effect are unimportant. As Tryan asserts: God "neither condemns nor reproaches you for the past, He only bids you to come to Him that you may have life" (260). The nature of his specific actions with regard to Lucy are almost irrelevant; indeed his own confessor tries to convince him that "[his] sin against God was greater than [his] sin against her" (261). Although Tryan still feels a "pang" when he thinks about Lucy, it is now only a spur which drives him to devote himself all the more fully to God's work (261). Confession permits one to turn away from determinations of cause into an atemporal and unquestioning present obedience. Thus, what confession allows, as is clear in both the case of Tryan and of Janet herself, is the ability to function in the world; Tryan, after the loss of Lucy, and Janet, after her repentance, both become effective agents in the world of good deeds and pious teachings. But what Tryan's example makes clear is that this ability to function is predicated on containing, but not incorporating into understanding, the traumas of the past. Confession may not exactly falsify one's past life, but it clearly offers an inadequate means of fully understanding it.

The ethical inadequacy of confession is underscored at the deathbed of Dempster, the character who, in conventional terms, is most in need of confession. The lack of any formal acknowledgement of guilt and repentance seems to be deliberately highlighted:[14]

> Suddenly a slight movement, like the passing away of a shadow, was visible in this face, and he opened his eyes full on Janet.
>
> It was almost like meeting him again on the resurrection morning, after the night of the grave.
>
> "Robert, do you know me?"
>
> He kept his eyes fixed on her, and there was a faintly perceptible motion of the lips, as if he wanted to speak.
>
> But the moment of speech was for ever gone—the moment for asking pardon of her, if he wanted to ask it. Could he read the full forgiveness that was written in her eyes? She never knew; for, as she was bending to kiss him, the thick veil of death fell between them, and her lips touched a corpse. (282)

The image of meeting Dempster again on the resurrection morning suggests a hopefulness that this last moment of consciousness will indeed prompt a death-bed confession, an explanation, a plea for forgiveness—all familiar scenes from early Victorian Evangelical fiction.[15] For Dempster, however, "the moment of speech is for ever gone." Janet's eager lips touch a corpse, not a human being capable of repentance; what he might have said remains unknown, and even his reading of the forgiveness in Janet's eyes remains conjectural.

Shoshana Felman suggests that scenes such as a death-bed confession are not only horribly clichéd, they are fundamentally false. To explain the causes of gratuitous cruelty—"I was cruel because . . ."—is to offer an excuse, a way out. As Felman says (pointedly quoting Paul de Man):

> The trouble with excuses (with confessions) is that they are all too *readable*: partaking of the continuity of conscious meaning and of the illusion of the restoration of coherence, what de Man calls "the readability of . . . apologetic discourse" (*Allegories of Reading*, 290), pretends to reduce historical scandals to mere sense and to eliminate the unassimilable shock of history, by leaving "the [very] assumption of intelligibility . . . unquestioned" (*Allegories of Reading*, 300). Confessions (or excuses) thus allow one, through the illusion of understanding they provide, to forgive and to forget. (Felman and Laub 151; parentheses and square brackets in the original)

A confession by Dempster would have functioned as an excuse, would have given an "illusion of understanding" to his auditors, providing the opportunity "to forgive and to forget." The narrative "offers" Dempster the opportunity for confession and then leaves the confession unspoken. That Eliot highlights the absence of Dempster's confession suggests that the absence of confession is a deliberate ethical choice on the part of the author; she wants the violence experienced by Janet to remain, not invisible, but "unreadable," morally incoherent.

One can ask, however, whether Felman's (and de Man's) objections to the very essence of confession obtain in the earlier confessions recorded in the text, those of Janet and Mr. Tryan. Do Janet's and Tryan's confessions also provide "an illusion of understanding" which "pretends to reduce historical scandals to mere sense and to eliminate the unassimilable shock of history"? We have already seen how Tryan's confession with regard to Lucy could be seen as evidence of an "illusion of understanding" that begs more questions than it answers, that contains the past without fully incorporating it into one's psyche. Janet's life viewed through the lens of repentance and confession has a coherence and stability that is illusory.

BODY AS MEMORY

Janet, like Dempster, is an alcoholic.[16] Her body is neither diseased nor in need of diagnosis, however, and her intake of alcohol is not related to either plethora or debility; instead, her body is repeatedly figured as mere blankness, vacancy. This figuration, related to alcohol but not solely determined by it, changes only after her confession to Tryan. For example, when she is beaten by her husband at the end of chapter 4, she has clearly been drinking: "Her wide open black eyes have a strangely fixed, sightless gaze" so that she stands "stupidly unmoved in her great beauty, while the heavy arm is lifted to strike her" (199). Later she looks "so blank and listless" (242) that Dempster believes she cannot hear him. Alcohol also fogs her memory, so that after one beating, "[t]he morning light" throws "its glare . . . on a hideous blank of something unremembered, something that must have made that dark bruise on her shoulder" (238). After Janet seeks refuge with her neighbour Mrs. Pettifer—who also sees blankness in her expression: "her eyes were fixed vacantly on the rushlight shade" (249)—she decides that she would rather endure the "misery" of violent abuse "than the blank that lay for her outside her married home" (240). In gazing at the "blank wall" that faces Mrs. Pettifer's window, she experiences a "sickening identity with her desolation of spirit and the headachy weariness of her body" (253). The world outside the marital home is not figured as safe, but rather as completely and deadeningly empty. There is a metaphoric blankness in a female existence that has no meaning or purpose outside of marriage: for "even [her husband's] absence—what was it? only a dreary vacant flat, where there was nothing to strive after, nothing to long for" (250). David Carroll calls the blankness when she is thrust from her home "the moment of non-meaning" (67) when all explanation and signification is drained from her life. Dempster's cruelty and violence open Janet to the unspeakable, to that place separated from the common world of meaning and explanation by an unbridgeable void.

Janet's body is also marked by blanks and gaps; it is, says the narrator, like a ruined temple:

> Janet had that enduring beauty which belongs to pure majestic outline and depth of tint. Sorrow and neglect leave their traces on such beauty, but it thrills us to the last, like a glorious Greek temple, which, for all the loss it has suffered from time and barbarous hands, has gained a solemn history, and fills our imagination the more because it is incomplete to the sense. (243)

Janet's body partakes of the purity and majesty of a Greek temple that, strangely, is all the more impressive—"it thrills us to the last"—because of the "loss" caused by "barbarous hands."[17] It "fills our imagination" because it is "incomplete to the sense." Like the story "Janet's Repentance" itself, the incompleteness of understanding with regard to Janet's life, and the violence at its source, makes the story all the more compelling to the reader.

When Janet confesses her sins, however, this blankness of her life appears to be dispelled. Tryan says to her: "Ah, dear Mrs. Dempster, you will never again say that life is blank and that there is nothing to live for, will you?" (262). At the end of the story, Janet's body is no longer figured as a damaged pagan temple but as a full Christian memorial to Tryan. Having noted the "meagre memorial" in the churchyard marking the place where Mr. Tryan's body is buried, the narrator remarks:

> But there is another memorial of Edgar Tryan, which bears a fuller record: it is Janet Dempster, rescued from self-despair, strengthened with divine hopes, and now looking back on years of purity and helpful labour. The man who has left such a memorial behind him, must have been one whose heart beat with true compassion, and whose lips were moved by fervent faith. (301)

Janet apparently now lives her life as a "memorial," as the "fuller record" of the achievements of Mr. Tryan. Janet's life, formerly a blank of alcoholic haze, a dark riddle which defied answer, seems to be no longer in question; rather, it is as though she has become a clear text of remembrance, of bearing witness to another's life. Her continuing life is now signified as a testimonial; she now carries out her good deeds—her "purity and helpful labour"—under the aegis of Tryan's doctrine of "fervent faith."

However, as Shoshana Felman and Dori Laub point out, the notions of memorial and testimonial are not simple. In their book on memory and recollection they argue that memorial or "remembrance" needs to be distinguished from testimony: remembrance is a complete statement, a totality of cause and effect, an understandable whole; testimony is always broken, partial, with the link between cause and effect incomplete or missing. Felman writes:

> As a relation to events, testimony seems to be composed of bits and pieces of a memory that has been overwhelmed by occurrences that have not settled into understanding or remembrance, acts that cannot be constructed as knowledge nor assimilated into full cognition, events in excess of our frames of reference.
>
> What the testimony does not offer is, however, a completed statement, a totalizable account of those events. In the testimony, language is in process and in trial, it does not possess itself as a conclusion, as the constatation of a verdict or the self-transparency of knowledge. Testimony is, in other words, a discursive *practice,* as opposed to a pure *theory.* (Felman and Laub 5)

Felman and Laub's book is about witnessing an actual historical event, the Holocaust; however, the book does include treatment of "literature and art as a precocious mode of witnessing":

> [O]ur ultimate concern has been with the preservation, in this book, both of the uniqueness of experience in the face of its theorization, and of the shock of the unintelligible in the face of the attempt at its interpretation; with the preservation, that is, of reality itself in the midst of our own efforts at interpreting it and through the necessary process of its textualization. (Felman and Laub xx)

In many ways, of course, "Janet's Repentance" is what Felman and Laub call a text of remembrance, that is, it constitutes itself as "conclusion" and establishes the "self-transparency of knowledge"; Janet's confession transforms her life into a complete and fixed "memorial." After all, the story is called "Janet's Repentance." However, the gaps and blanks that this chapter has pointed to—the gaps and blanks in Janet's own figuration, but also more importantly the gaps and blanks of explanation and cause surrounding the scenes of violence—suggest that this text also partakes of what Felman and Laub call testimony, that is, "language in process and trial," which retains "the shock of the unintelligible in the face of the attempt at its interpretation." Eliot's novels are all concerned with making intelligible the complex and fraught terrain of the human subject and human relations; this story's depiction of domestic violence also includes the unintelligible as it attempts to preserve what Eliot herself asserted was "essentially true" in the scenes witnessed by her in her childhood.[18]

The final image of Janet as "memorial" thus seems to partake of a doubleness. As a memorial that is as fixed and final as Tryan's grave marker, Janet's life appears to have a clarity of meaning that is complete but entirely reductive. As a memorial that is living and working, that bears the scars of suffering, Janet's body—and psyche—remain open, even resistant, to interpretation. This paradoxical resistance to and simultaneous insistence on explication and understanding arguably become characteristic of George Eliot's novels taken as a whole. While "Janet's Repentance" has not always been favorably compared with her later work, the power of the novella perhaps lies in its embryonic formulation of the questions that Eliot's later works address.[19] Carroll suggests that throughout her career Eliot's narratives "become increasingly enmeshed in interpretation as motives proliferate, contradict one another, and escape the constraints of any kind of maxim"; at the same time, he continues, there is a persistent "need to discover a world where motives are, however briefly, distinct and direct and acted upon" (140). The narrators of her fiction may thus *seem* to offer a totality of explication, a careful, patient, and sympathetic uncovering of the links in the chain of causation and understanding. However, as Dorothea Barrett argues, the "earnest, authoritative, and sometimes irritatingly arch persona" of the Eliot narrator is at times "out of control or absent" (29). Barrett asks:

> [I]s each of George Eliot's narrators possessed of "an intuition embracing the universe"? Is each narrative like a Rubik's cube, the confusion and complexity of which is ultimately resolvable into a tidy and symmetrical solution? Or is the pleasure of George Eliot's texts a Barthesian pleasure taken in the proliferation of complexity, a pleasure sustained and heightened by the constant and ultimate deferral of a solution? Do George Eliot's novels function as Proust believed that all novels must, by asking more and more questions, being able to answer none? (28–29)

Her answer is that the novels "are not static but dynamic. Their constant struggle, their lack of ultimate resolution, is itself a victory for the radical, passional, and unconscious" (32–33).

While the argument of this chapter does not contradict Barrett's overall conclusions, one must add that, in the case of "Janet's Repentance" at least, the lack of "ultimate resolution" also partakes of less attractive results. The "radical, passional, and unconscious," which remains resistant to interpretation, must include the violence that has so disturbingly marred Janet's existence. Janet's life as it is rendered in confession and as a memorial to Mr. Tryan gives it a clarity of purpose, a finality of closed interpretation; Janet's body as the collection of bruises and scars left by Dempster stands as a memorial to an evil that is as unassimilable as it is real. That so much of Janet's existence is figured as a blank points to the unreadableness of the text of her life, and to the "shock" of the history that was enacted there.

4

"The Sins of the Father" and "The Female Line"

Phantom Visitations and Cruelty in Elizabeth Gaskell's "The Poor Clare"

The previous chapter concerned the notion of causality in Eliot's fiction, and the sufficiency of cause and explanation that the narrative of "Janet's Repentance" could offer for the suffering of its protagonist. The various interpretative strategies offered by the narrative—deterministic, hermeneutic, confessional—render the cause of Janet's suffering and Dempster's brutality ultimately unreadable. While Eliot's realist mode thus preserves the "shock of history" suffered by Janet, the story's brief excursion into liminal awareness recorded in Dempster's hallucination indicates another avenue of investigation. This chapter will continue to investigate the notion of cause through an examination of Elizabeth Gaskell's ghost story, "The Poor Clare." By slipping the bonds of realist fiction, Gaskell's narrative is able to offer a portrayal of the female body (and the misery inflicted upon it) that stresses its intimate connection to an unknown family genealogy. Where Eliot exposes the power of the unconscious in human motivation within the mundane realities of married life, Gaskell employs a gothic ghost story. Gaskell's story taps into a powerful undercurrent of aggression and violence unconsciously directed at the woman's body. Most strikingly, the story demonstrates that both the "sins of the father" (Gaskell 309) and the affects attached to the "female line" (286) are so powerful that they threaten to overwhelm the protagonists of the story and even the logical progression of the narrative itself. The female body "inherits" a trauma and as the narrative veers away from expressing that trauma, the female body becomes its inexpressible symptom.

"The Poor Clare" was first published in *Household Words* in December 1856, and later reprinted as part of the story collection *Round the Sofa,* in 1859. It is curiously (and awkwardly) constructed as a set of discrete narratives that seemingly have no connection between them, told by a narrator who is "possessed" by forces beyond his control as he "researches" (293) what these connections might be. Gradually, the intergenerational saga that links the stories becomes clear; at their center is a phantom, invoked by a grandmother Bridget Fitzgerald, triggered by her son-in-law Gisborne, and unknowingly inflicted on her granddaughter, Lucy. Lucy is the pure innocent inexplicably afflicted by a ghostly and demonic double, a haunting that causes her father Gisborne to raise his arm to strike her, and then to drive her from her home just as Janet was. The presence of the phantom both points to repressed knowledge and indicates a route through which suffering, violence, and perversion are visited upon the female body. "Visited upon" is a particularly apt description of the haunting in Gaskell's text, and sets the work apart from the misery in "Janet's Repentance"; violence in "The Poor Clare" arises not only within the context of an intimate relation but within an intergenerational web that demonstrates, not only that "[t]he sins of the fathers are indeed visited upon the children" (309), but that the sins of the *mother* are. The work is fraught with intergenerational secrets in the "female line," with unspeakable and unspoken connections between people and between past and present events. The pressure of these secrets, of the unspeakable made incarnate in the female body, gives rise to a phantasmic presence within a triangulated familial relationship of dread and transgression.

Gaskell's deserved reputation as an important Victorian novelist rests upon her acute vision of societal and familial ills. From her ground-breaking portrayal of working-class life in *Mary Barton* to her compassionate depiction of unwed pregnancy in *Ruth* to the fine portrait of familial relations in *Wives and Daughters,* Gaskell's fame justly rests on what she calls, in a letter to her friend Mary Howitt "the beauty and poetry of many of the common things and daily events of life" (18 August 1838; *Letters* 12), or what Winifred Gérin in her biography terms Gaskell's "down-to-earth acceptance of the material world" (123). In this context, the ghost stories written by Gaskell are anomalous, out of place in an oeuvre of realist fiction. Thus, although Gérin notes that Gaskell "excelled at telling ghost stories round the fire at night," and "even claimed to have seen a ghost" (123, 122), Gérin gives short shrift to the ghost stories, simply mentioning that "The Poor Clare" was added to the collection *Round the Sofa* to assist Gaskell financially in a time of ill health and poor productivity (203–04). However, Gérin's sense that Gaskell is "haunted" (122) by the disappearance of her only surviving brother on a voyage to India when she was nineteen suggests the psychological energy that drives her stories of the macabre, an aspect of Gaskell's fiction taken up by Felicia Bonaparte in her treatment of Gaskell's "life and fiction as one continuous metaphoric text" (1). Bonaparte claims that Gaskell herself must be read "as though she were a poetic text" in order to "enter the private world that the inner woman inhabits" (1). This suggestive reading of Gaskell's fiction places a story like "The Poor Clare" at the center rather than at the margins of the author's work.[1]

Bonaparte argues that in her fictions Gaskell constructs an entity known as "Mrs. Gaskell," the woman who embodies all of the virtues of the angel in the house, a woman revered for her "femininity," her gentleness, and her "serene satisfaction" with domestic life (2). At the same time, Bonaparte contends, readers must be attuned to another Gaskell, a Gaskell whose "subtextual meaning" comes into "high relief" through an "imagistic vocabulary" and moments of "disproportion" and "disruption" (10). Bonaparte argues that "The Poor Clare" allows Gaskell to explore unconsciously the anger, bitterness, passion, and resentment of the child who was abandoned by her father after her mother's death (47).[2] In Bonaparte's allegorical reading, the three female characters in the story—Lucy, her demonic double, and her grandmother—are all aspects of Gaskell's own identity. She is the innocent child who loves her father; she is the child who must be demonic in order to have been rejected by her father; and she is the sinister grandmother, the "witch," who must learn "piety and prayer" to regain her father's love (53–54). The reading of the story in this chapter will build on Bonaparte's sense that Gaskell's ghost stories are not marginal but central to the project of mid-nineteenth-century social fiction. However, unlike Bonaparte, who states that she is "not as much concerned with the contents of the unconscious" but with

Gaskell's use of "metaphors and symbols to conceive her own identity" (11), this examination will probe the language of the textual unconscious, a language that produces a phantom in order to figure the inheritance of trauma visited upon Lucy.

"WHERE DOES THE MISERY COME FROM?"

In her essay, "Where Does the Misery Come From?: Psychoanalysis, Feminism, and the Event," Jacqueline Rose explores how a debate between Freud and Wilhelm Reich on the sources of misery—whether internal to the subject or "out there" in the world—also sheds light on ways of conceiving the problem of violence against women. Rose argues that nonpsychoanalytic feminists have been incorrect in their reading of misery and violence as emanating solely from the "outside" world, but that a purely "inside" answer has the effect of making female victims of domestic violence into "agents" of their own distress, ignoring the effects of, for example, law and cultural practices (32).[3] She concludes that "violence is not something that can be located on the inside or the outside, in the psychic or the social . . . but rather something that appears as the effect of the dichotomy itself" (28); in her view, a psychoanalytic feminism is uniquely positioned to undertake a deconstruction of this dichotomy.

Lucy's sufferings in "The Poor Clare" could be said to arise solely from the "outside," that is, from the familial and social world: after all, her father threatens to beat her and then drives her from her home, and those around her loathe the very sight of her. The demonic double could thus be read as a misogynist fantasy about the "true" nature of women. Indeed, critics of Gaskell's short story have tended to read Lucy's suffering as arising from "outside," from a Victorian society that denies bourgeois women a full expression of their sexuality. Maureen T. Reddy, for example, argues that the story is "a frightening depiction of the consequences of expressing female sexuality in a culture that insists that all good women are sexless angels, and that therefore requires women to repress their sexuality, under threat of ostracism or death" (261). Patsy Stoneman agrees: "In psychological terms . . . Lucy's double, which is seen, by everyone, makes visible the repressed sexuality of a whole society. . . . The Mary that Bridget wanted at home, the demure Lucy approved by her father, are only half human, the product of an ideology which denies female autonomy" (66). While not disagreeing with the precipitating effects of the societal and the paternal in Lucy's suffering, this chapter attempts to engage with the implications of the inside/outside dichotomy registered by Jacqueline Rose. In any purely "outside" reading, the relation of the phantom double to Lucy herself is an unexplained mystery; it *is* poised "outside" Lucy and yet it must be uncannily related to her "inside" psychical realm.

The figure of the "phantom," developed from Freud by Nicholas Abraham and Maria Torok, provides a striking model for understanding a misery that belongs neither simply to the "inside" nor to the "outside." Abraham and Torok argue that symbolizations in general, and the phantom in particular, are predicated on "the irrelevance of the world's reality without consciousness, which alone attributes sense or meaning" (Rand 5). The "world's reality," the subject's "outside," only matters insofar as it is incorporated, filtered, displaced or rejected by the "inside" of consciousness. The phantom is evidence of a disruption that exists neither simply *inside* nor *outside* the subject; it is of "a radically heterogenous nature with respect to the subject" since it "at no time has any direct reference" to the subject; nevertheless, it is the *subject* who is "haunted" (Abraham 174–75).[4]

What is particularly apposite in Torok and Abraham's conception of the phantom to the psychic phenomena studied in this chapter is that although the phantom fills a "gap" in an individual psyche, the *production* of that phantom is the result of an intersubjective and intergenerational process: "[W]hat haunts are not the dead, but the gaps left within us by the secrets of others" (171), the most important "other" being the mother herself. As Esther Rashkin says of Abraham and Torok's concept of maternal genealogy: "Every child's emergence as an individual is distinctive, constituted by repressions of uniquely charged pieces-of-the-mother, each bearing affects specifically related to the singular circumstances and psychic traumas of the mother's life. Moreover, since every mother is also the child of another mother, she must herself be understood as always already carrying the contents of another's unconscious" (18).

Abraham uses the metaphor of "ventriloquism" (173) to describe how the trauma of the other speaks through and possesses the subject. The phantom is thus one figuration of an uncanny inside/outside of the subject, of something that is experienced as self, as speaking through the self, and at the same time, as utterly estranged from the self and belonging to "someone else" (Abraham 188). The aim of analysis for these patients is to allow for a successful introjection of the unspoken mystery, a disinterring of the "crypt" of family secrets, which consists of gradually "appropriating" the traumatic event and bringing it into consciousness, giving it an identity. The struggle of the narrator of "The Poor Clare" to locate the complex and hidden strands of relationship between past and present, between parent and child, represents an attempt at such an appropriation.

MOTHER AND DAUGHTER

The narrator of "The Poor Clare" begins "that strange story connected with poor Lucy" by going back in time before, he says, he had any connection with "the principal actors in them, or, indeed, before I even knew of their existence" (271). Bridget Fitzgerald had married a man "above her in rank" (275) but when the story opens she is a poor widow who, with her daughter Mary, has become a servant and companion to the recusant Starkey family in order to survive. Bridget and her daughter are passionately fond of one another, but Mary "and her mother were too much alike to agree. There were wild quarrels between them, and wilder reconciliations" (276). These disturbed mother-daughter relations lead Mary to yearn for a life on the continent away from her demanding mother; she thus asks Madam Starkey to procure her a position abroad as a lady's maid. The parting from her mother is fraught with profound grief on her part and suppressed rage on her mother's. Bridget maliciously wishes that "her voyage might not turn out well" (291) and indeed after Mary goes, she is never heard from again. This is the first inkling of the power of Bridget Fitzgerald's desires; as she later laments: "my wishes are terrible—their power goes beyond my thought" (291). Her words in the story are destined to have a fatal and appalling power. Meanwhile, both of the Starkeys die, their son is taken away by his guardians, and Bridget Fitzgerald is left alone, with only her daughter's dog, Mignon—the precious and beloved one—to comfort her. Bridget and the dog go abroad in search of the lost Mary, and failing, come home. Bridget's subsequent wild and withdrawn ways lead her in later years to be regarded as a witch by the local villagers.

The precipitating act for the story's central events takes place when one of the boy's guardians comes to hunt on the boy's estate, and brings with him several companions, including one Squire Gisborne. Gisborne, frustrated after a day's fruitless hunting, comes upon the dog Mignon and, "partly for wantonness, partly to vent his spleen upon some living creature" (282), fires upon the dog and kills it. Bridget

Fitzgerald comes upon the scene just as Mignon dies; calling upon "the Saints in Heaven" to hear her prayers, she utters her curse upon Gisborne for killing "the only creature that loved me—the dumb beast that I loved" (282):

> "You shall live to see the creature you love best, and who alone loves you—aye, a human creature, but as innocent and fond as my poor, dead darling—you shall see this creature, for whom death would be too happy, become a terror and a loathing to all, for this blood's sake. Hear me, O holy Saints, who never fail them that have no other help!" (283)

Bridget's curse is specifically an intersubjective one: an "innocent and fond" person will become "a terror and loathing" *because* of Gisborne's love; the victim does not *deserve* this fate, and Gisborne himself will be unscathed.[5]

Gisborne tries to pass off his discomfort at hearing this curse by throwing a gold piece at the old woman. The money is rejected, and when he later hears that her name is Bridget Fitzgerald and that she had a daughter named Mary, his unease is palpable: "I could wish she had not cursed me. . . . She may have power—no one else could" (284). As the story progresses, the source of his unease becomes clear; he has married a woman named Mary Fitzgerald, and through "his wilful usage had caused her death" (303). The potency of Bridget's curse thus derives not from the death of the "beloved" Mignon, but from Mignon's metonymic displacement for Mary herself.

Having brought the account this far, the narrator interjects into the story of Bridget Fitzgerald and Squire Gisborne his own story; he explains that he must "make you understand how I became connected with them" (285). He is the nephew of and assistant to an eminent attorney whose "love of genealogy" (285) attracts cases of disputed inheritance and property law. A case has been brought to him concerning "the existence of any descendants of the younger branch of a family to whom some valuable estates had descended in the female line" (286). The "female line" is of course particularly difficult to trace since the surname changes with every generation. Since the uncle is "old and gouty" (286), the narrator takes up the investigation for him, and the narration of that investigation makes up the principal part of his tale.

The genealogical hunt that occupies the narrator foregrounds the central question this chapter examines: "Where does the misery come from?" In the story's terms, this question can be phrased as follows: can an inheritance, specifically an inheritance "in the female line,"[6] be traced back into the past to discover its origin, an origin that will resolve a current impasse? The trope of inheritance, like Abraham and Torok's trope of "ventriloquism," is a model for understanding how one generation "speaks through" or "bequeaths" to the next generation miseries and secrets that result in the production of a phantom. An inheritance comes from the outside but is incorporated into an inside, and becomes part of what constitutes the self.

The narrator, "following up a genealogical scent" (287), discovers that the nearest descendent to the estate in question is one Hugh Fitzgerald, the deceased husband of Bridget Fitzgerald. The narrator goes to interview Bridget, since, if she had a living child, that child would inherit the estate. Bridget informs him that to the best of her knowledge her daughter Mary is dead, and that if she is alive and married, the problem of female descent would still obtain: she would never recognize "the lost one under the appellation she then bore" (292).

The narrator loses all of his dry legal manner at this point and vows to take up the quest for Bridget Fitzgerald's sake. After his interview with Bridget, his reasons for pursuing the case—respect for his uncle, advancement of his own career—shift, and he finds that "some strange power . . . had taken possession of my will only that very morning, and which forced it in the direction it chose" (292). He is like "a child on a common blown along by a high wind, without power of standing still and resisting the tempestuous force" (293). This giddy feeling propels him on his whirlwind travels for information about Mary Fitzgerald or her children, but before long giddiness is succeeded by illness, illness that comes as a "positive relief" in comparison to the "visionary researches" which had previously possessed him. To recover from his illness, he makes for the "invigorating Yorkshire moors" (294), and there meets Lucy.

Then begins the third, and again seemingly disconnected narrative. The narrator, previously possessed by "some strange power," now finds himself possessed by another force: he is "irresistibly attracted" (294) to Lucy; he is "drawn towards [her] with a strange fascination" (295). Within ten days he is deeply in love with her, though curiously she does her best to avoid him. Again curiously, he is warned against Lucy both by her landlord, who says that "the young lady, for all as quiet as she seemed, played strange pranks at times" (295), and by her elderly servant who says that "Her father loved her well . . . yet he drove her out like some monstrous thing" (300). These warnings serve merely to confirm the narrator in his love, and he presses for a private interview with Lucy to declare his passion. In the interview, rather than listening to his protestations of love, Lucy insists that he hear her own story.

Thus begins the fourth narrative segment. Lucy tells the narrator that her mother died when she was very young, and that she formerly lived with her father, a soldier who was often abroad. Her childhood was happy, and she was confident that she was loved by her father, though that love was unstated. But one day, with his "tongue . . . loosened with wine" (302-303), he tells Lucy that he loves her more than anything in the world; then in a "strange, wild way" he turns and says that "there was many a thing he loved better—his horse—his dog—I know not what" (303). This statement of the father's love provokes disaster; the father's spoken word has loosed the unspeakable.

The very next morning he accuses Lucy of dancing on the young plants in the flower beds, later of "undue familiarity—all unbecoming a gentlewoman—with his grooms," and finally calls her names that "were such as shame any modest woman" (303). The break comes, she says, when:

> "he came in with a riding-whip in his hand; and, accusing me harshly of evil doings, of which I knew no more than you, sir, he was about to strike me, and I, all bewildering tears, was ready to take his stripes as great kindness compared to his harder words, when suddenly he stopped his arm mid-way, gasped and staggered, crying out, 'The curse—the curse!' I looked up in terror. In the great mirror opposite I saw myself, and right behind, another wicked, fearful self, so like me that my soul seemed to quiver within me, as though not knowing to which similitude of body it belonged." (303–04)

The father's violent action is checked by a disturbance in the field of vision, by a confusion between who can be struck and who in fact "deserves" the beating. Should he beat Lucy to chastise an interior evil, or is the evil already outside, free from his correction? Even Lucy herself does not know whether the *doppelgänger* is an inside or an outside; her soul does know "to which similitude of body it belonged."

The loving narrator, with commonsense notions of ghosts and apparitions, interjects into Lucy's story, and begins to reassure her and to rectify her fanciful notions by an appeal to positive knowledge: "'I fancy that some physician could have disabused your father of his belief in visions'——." Then, in a impressive narrative doubling that correlates with the presence of the *doppelgänger* itself, the narrator is himself struck dumb:

> Just at that instant, standing as I was opposite to her in the full and perfect morning light, I saw behind her another figure,—a ghastly resemblance, complete in likeness, so far as form and feature and minutest touch of dress could go, but with a loathsome demon soul looking out of the grey eyes, that were in turns mocking and voluptuous. My heart stood still within me; every hair rose up erect; my flesh crept with horror. I could not see the grave and tender Lucy—my eyes were fascinated by the creature beyond. (304–05)

The narrator's genealogical "visionary researches" have thus produced their "ghost." Although in love with Lucy, although "drawn towards [her] with a strange *fascination*" (295; our emphasis), he is forced to admit that "my eyes were *fascinated* by the creature beyond" (our emphasis). The word *fascination* is already ambiguous, implying both "to charm and enchant" and "to affect by witchcraft and magic" *(OED);* this double meaning is itself doubled when applied to Lucy and her *doppelgänger*. Lucy and her double are at once indistinguishable from each other—each is "fascinating"—, and completely dissimilar: where Lucy is "grave and tender," the phantom is "mocking and voluptuous"; where Lucy is decorous and marriageable, the phantom is sexually provocative and wanton.

Although the father's and the narrator's responses contrast radically with one another—the one a threat to strike, the other a reassurance of love—each motion is suspended by this double consciousness of her body. The phantom signals the difficulty of distinguishing the inside from the outside of Lucy's identity; Lucy's own body is fully present in itself and also fully present "outside" of herself, a discrete other. The father would strike her because she "deserves" punishment and discipline for her wanton ways, but the wanton body that he would strike is always beyond reach, and the available body is always an innocent one. The narrator, on the other hand, would love the innocent Lucy, speak words of reassurance and desire, but the available body, "mocking and voluptuous," leads the narrator to be not only fascinated by her but also disgusted. An object for punishment and an object for love, both roles for Lucy are disrupted by the uncanny double.

This characterization of Lucy and her double is conventional enough: woman as wanton, woman as virginal; woman as sinful, woman as pure. As Réné Girard says of monstrous doubles, the reader's initial interest in this uncanny and unsettling phenomena soon subsides into a mundane acknowledgment of the *fact* of the *doppelgänger;* having recognized antagonists as doubles, "there is really nothing very interesting to say about the hallucinatory aspects of an experience that for all practical purposes exists solely to divert attention from the essential fact, which is that [they] are truly doubles" (Girard 160). Having produced this double, the narrator, indeed the story itself, turns away from it, leaving Lucy's experience and the implications of doubleness largely unexplored. In spite of his proclaimed love for Lucy, the narrator cannot bear to stay near her after this experience. Just as her father drove Lucy from his home, so the narrator also deserts her since "the idea of her was becoming so inextricably blended with the shuddering thought of IT" (305). Clearly, for the narrator there is no possibility of a simple separation of inside from outside.

The narrator immediately returns to his rooms after this encounter and discovers a letter informing him that Gisborne is the surname of Mary Fitzgerald's husband. At first this piece of information means nothing to him, in spite of the earlier tempest that carried him in his genealogical researches, for now: "Nothing was real but the unreal presence, which had come like an evil blast across my bodily eyes, and burnt itself down upon my brain" (307–08). Nevertheless, he returns to speak with Lucy's servant, and discovers that Lucy's true surname is Gisborne. The mystery is solved: Lucy is the heir to the estate for whom he has so long been seeking, just as Lucy is also the heir to her grandmother's curse.

Readers are thus finally in a position to understand something of the phantom's genealogy. The phantom arises from the "crypt" of her family's repressed aggressions and desires; the intersection of Lucy with her past brings this unwanted and baleful inheritance. The proximate cause of the phantom's existence is the father's sudden and unwonted declaration of love for his daughter, a love that had been an unspoken "secret." Having been articulated, his love immediately turns to hatred, violence, and loathing. The declaration of love is itself not responsible for the phantom, but it announces the return of the repressed, triggering or bringing into effect the curse uttered by the grandmother—"to see the creature you love best, and who alone loves you . . . become a terror and a loathing to all." Moving back another step, the grandmother's curse was itself a response to male aggression—Gisborne's killing of Mignon, and more particularly his sinister but secret involvement with Mary, Bridget's daughter. Going back still farther in time, Mary's unhappy condition is also traceable to Bridget's own aggression, since she wished her beloved daughter ill as she set out on her voyage, and (as Bridget says) "my wishes are terrible" (291). Finally Bridget Fitzgerald's own history ("Her marriage—to one above her in rank—had been unhappy" [275]) suggests the misery of the "female line" goes back even farther in time than the story traces, indicating, as Esther Rashkin argues, that "[w]e are all the psychic products of our infinitely regressive family histories" (18). As we step back from the phenomenon of the phantom into the history which produced this phenomenon, we see that a mixture of repression, aggression, and desire motivates both male and female characters. Lucy bears the costs associated with this disturbed family history; the figure of the *doppelgänger* indicates that the violence and rejection she experiences in the story spring neither simply from who she *is* (from inside) nor from family and society (outside). The trope of inheritance explains how her body acquires and assumes that which is not self, but which becomes attached to or speaks through the self.

One might assume that the end of the story would now not be long in coming. The narrator should bring the grandmother and granddaughter together, the penitent but happy grandmother should remove the curse, and the now cheerful granddaughter should marry the narrator and live happily ever after. However, when the narrator *does* arrange for Bridget and Lucy to meet, it becomes clear that the curse, once spoken, cannot be simply retracted; the contents of the family "crypt" cannot be easily disinterred since they do not belong to an individual but adhere to a web of familial relations. The spoken curse cannot be unspoken; the repressions signified by the curse cannot be dissolved by the pure light of narrative clarity. Bridget is horrified by what her curse has accomplished, but seeing Lucy once, and discovering that she is powerless to eradicate the *doppelgänger*, also abhors the thought of seeing Lucy again; she thus flees to Antwerp in search of her confessor, Father Bernard. The narrator likewise abandons Lucy and resumes his travels, following Bridget (and as it transpires, Gisborne) to the continent.

The narrator learns from Father Bernard that Bridget Fitzgerald's attempts in Antwerp to confess her "deadly sin" (322) of witchcraft have been unavailing: "No words came. The evil powers had stricken her dumb, as I heard afterwards they had many a time before, when she approached confession" (323). That Bridget's confession is represented as literally unspeakable is a powerful metaphor for the entombment of the curse in the crypt of family genealogy; any representation Bridget could make of her own sins, fears, and aggression would never undo the curse, since the effects of it have already been dispersed throughout the family. As the curse itself was an intersubjective phenomenon, so relief from the curse must also be intersubjective; once spoken, Bridget's curse no longer belongs to her alone, but to the obscure and fraught familial history that produced Lucy and her double. For Lucy, the curse may be said to *be* the unspeakable family genealogy. Furthermore, Bridget's inability to confess may, like Dempster's inability in "Janet's Repentance," demonstrate again the radical insufficiency of confession as a means of forgiving and forgetting.

This dumbness in the face of culpability clearly relates to the larger trope of confession in the works that this book examines. George Eliot's story demonstrated that Tryan's and Janet's attempts to use confession to keep the past contained and suppressed were finally unavailing; past events, whether Tryan's abandonment of Lucy or the suffering of Janet, were foregrounded even as confession attempted to repress and silence the misery of the past. The relation of the unspeakable to confession, or the sense that confession does not possess the capacity to address the problem of the unspeakable, is also underscored in the final novel this book examines. In Wilke Collins's *Man and Wife,* Hester Dethridge cannot speak the history of her abuse; instead, she commits it to a paper she calls her "Confession," which is to be "buried" with her when she dies and "known to no other mortal creature" (581–82). Since confession requires an auditor with whom a narrative is shared, the notion that this confession is to be "known to no other mortal creature" foregrounds, in itself, the futility of Hester's attempts at reparation; her own clear knowledge of this hopelessness is manifested in the intended burial of the letter. Her confession cannot address the problem of her dumbness; indeed, under the circumstances, it merely functions as a metonymy for it, for the fact that she is already living out her life as one who is dead. All of this manifests itself dramatically at the level of narrative when the "Confession" is read by the violent Geoffrey Delamayn who, in using it to threaten and blackmail Hester, functions to extend the conditions of her earlier abuse at the hands of her husband. Hester's confession is a symptom of her suffering, not a "cure"; it is therefore not only grotesquely and ironically fitting that it should further the conditions of her agony and madness, but it is inevitable.

Indeed, in all three of these narratives, confession functions in precisely this way; not only does confession *not* resolve the problems it purports to address, it in fact exacerbates those problems, functioning in all instances as characteristics of them, rather than as remedies. These works seem to suggest, not only that the attempted entry into the language of trauma and transgression distorts and suppresses the past, but that "confession" is itself a form of subjection. Confession, by definition, belongs in the world of the conscious, the world of the speakable; it inevitably fails to address the unspoken and unspeakable miseries of the unconscious.

The notion that confession works as a form of subjection is elaborated by Michel Foucault: "Confession [names] . . . all those procedures by which the subject is incited to produce a discourse of truth about his sexuality which is capable of having effects on the subject himself" (*Power/Knowledge* 215–16).[7] This "discourse of truth" is of course not a neutral telling, but as Jon Simons explains, is "the main technique of power operating in the deployment of sexuality" (75). Thus, the dumbness of Bridget and Hester signifies a refusal of the technologies of self demanded by culture; in turn, the forcible extraction of Hester's "Confession" by Geoffrey Delamayn is a perfect demonstration of the work of power in enforcing these technologies.

Shoshana Felman also touches on the way in which confession actually perpetuates the predicaments or failings that it purports to address in her observation (cited in the previous chapter): "The trouble with excuses (with confessions) is that they are all too *readable*: partaking of the continuity of conscious meaning and of the illusion of the restoration of coherence" (Felman and Laub 151). This "restoration of coherence" is clearly illusory, if not actually damaging in these three narratives. In "Janet's Repentance," Janet and Tryan collude in their confessions to cast a pall of oblivion over past sufferings and culpability. In *Man and Wife,* Hester's "Confession" is precisely the instrument of her final ruin. In "The Poor Clare," Bridget has voiced what she can in speaking directly to her granddaughter, but these words have already been shown to be without power. What is unspeakable in the story *is* the enmeshment of the curse in the family genealogy, an unspeakability inscribed in the body of Lucy.

The failure of the confessional mode conceived of as a fully conscious procedure is repeated in the structure of "The Poor Clare" itself. If, as Felman claims, confession aims to establish the "continuity of conscious meaning and of the illusion of the restoration of coherence," the end of the story, which can only be termed bizarre and improbable, is an object lesson of a narrative where its ostensible "restoration of coherence" is simply a begging of the question. Gaskell has seemingly constructed a narrative for which no denouement could be achieved; the threads of narrative veer impossibly far from Lucy into the civic history of Antwerp. In the final pages of the story, Gisborne—now a soldier—and Bridget—now a nun, a Poor Clare—fortuitously meet in Antwerp, a city being consumed by war and famine. The latent familial aggression in the earlier part of the narrative has seemingly erupted into wholesale social violence. Yet the war is (miraculously?) ended by the self-sacrificing generosity of Bridget Fitzgerald; her silent starvation unites warring Antwerp in sorrow and repentance. When the people of the city come to hear of the Poor Clare's hunger, they lay down their arms and rush to the convent to feed the now noble starving nun. Bridget, meanwhile, has used the little food remaining to her to feed her enemy, Squire Gisborne, who has come to the convent a wounded and starving soldier. This generous and maternal act of feeding her enemy supposedly frees Bridget's tongue, so that she is suddenly able to confess her deadly sin, be shriven, and die. Her dying words are witnessed by the narrator, and they are also the ultimate words of the story: "She is freed from the curse!" (333).

However, while these words seem to indicate that the curse has finally been revoked, that confession has been adequate, the efficiency of these words is never meaningfully demonstrated for readers. The story ends with the narrator in Antwerp at the deathbed of Bridget Fitzgerald; readers are not shown Lucy's body as single and whole, nor is there any indication that the beloved Lucy will become the bride of the narrator.[8] Thus, although the plot trajectory of Gaskell's story seems to indicate that this confession is successful, any resolution to the curse takes place outside the story world, leaving the efficiency of confession to be taken on trust. More importantly, the narrative seems to remain haunted by the discourse of the curse even as the plot ostensibly resolves it.

"The Poor Clare" is thus a poorly focused narrative riven by uncertainty and divided aims: it is a ghost story, taken up with a complex raveling and unraveling of the genealogy of the curse and the creation of a phantom; it is a tale of violence, aggression, and rejection aimed against an innocent and yet abandoned daughter and lover; and it is a love story that receives no satisfactory or even acknowledged ending. The narrator's estrangement from Lucy—"for dread of the fearful Third" (319)—is never remedied within the context of the story; instead, he pours his energies into his genealogical researches and foreign travel. By the end of the narrator's tale, the afflicted Lucy has become irrelevant to his saga of intergenerational loves and hates. Thus, the narrative itself, like the father's blow and the grandmother's curse, is seemingly suspended or halted, sliding away from its original object and aim. The narration is "aimed" at the subject, but takes up a tangential course away from that subject. Although the narrator is at first "fascinated" by Lucy—her story, her beauty, his love for her—his narration gets caught in the fascination of the curse's own detour, traveling to the continent to complete the saga of Bridget Fitzgerald and never providing a satisfactory "happy ending." The violent hatred of Gisborne for his daughter is never resolved either. Lucy's body is thus the focal point at which the violence of the father, the ambiguous fascination of the narrator, and the curse of the grandmother all meet, but through which they pass; her doubled body is available for an interminable exploration of etiology, cause, and history, but is in itself only represented as the source of unease, disgust, and violent rejection. Her body *is* unspeakable. It is as though the text evades the implications of its own discourse; just as the narrator in "The Birthmark" colludes with Aylmer's world view or the narrator of "Janet's Repentance" employs ambiguous and sometimes tortuous indirections, so the narrator of "The Poor Clare" veers away from the consequences of his own narrative, dissolving the problematics of his investigations in the perfunctory ending.[9]

The resolution of the curse and the dispelling of Lucy's *doppelgänger* would involve, in Abraham and Torok's rendering of the phantom, a dispelling of the secrets of past generations, an opening of the crypt of family secrets. Bridget's feeding of Gisborne is clearly meant to indicate a level of intersubjective forgiveness and generosity that overcomes past aggression. But the secrets of the story remain at least partially untold; the father's suspended violence and the narrator's suspended desire suggest that the story's tangential course, veering away from the doubled body of Lucy, slides over the still-encrypted secrets of that body.

What is most clearly unresolved in the narrative of "The Poor Clare" is the story of Mary, Bridget's daughter and Lucy's mother.

This is also the point on which Margaret Homans focuses in her reading of the story. Homans, following Nancy Chodorow, reads Mary's story as an archetypal mother-daughter narrative; the relationship of Bridget to Mary, and by analogy, Mary to Lucy, is initially one of the daughter's pre-symbolic identification with the mother.[10] The tragic results for Lucy arise from the seductions of the symbolic order. Homans claims that "The Poor Clare" "exemplifies the literal power of the woman's word, a power beneficial when inherent in a mother's and daughter's presymbolic relation, but a power that is twisted to evil ends by the intervention of paternal authority between mother and daughter" (249). The daughter is seduced by the father to abandon the mother "and enter the father's law, the symbolic order" (249).

While suggestive, this reading seems to conflate the role of two daughters, Mary and Lucy, and to ignore the specifics of Mary's role, or perhaps more accurately the absence of Mary's role in the narrative. Mary is properly the heiress to the Fitzgerald estate, but her place and history remain largely unknown to daughter, mother, and narrator, although the latter two hunt for her eagerly. Mary is irrecoverable both *by* and *as* mother and daughter; that she is sought so avidly, however, suggests that the "female line" of descent, so much at question in the story, is marked by the trauma of her loss, by the unavailability of her story. Lacan's association of the maternal with the pre-symbolic suggests that the mother embodies a materiality that escapes representation. The materiality of the "female line" in Gaskell's story seems to make available an inheritance of wealth and rich estates, but the unrepresentable *trauma* of the female line, marked by the curse, is clearly at least a part of that inheritance. Mary's role in the line of female inheritance seems to remain untold in the story's ending.

The scandal at the center of "The Poor Clare," unnoted by the narrator with all his legal and genealogical expertise, is the status of Mary's marriage, and thus the ensuing legal status of Lucy, and therefore, of course, of her inheritance. In the briefly told story of Mary's marriage, the narrator learns from Lucy's servant only that Gisborne "practised some terrible deceit upon [Mary] and when she came to know it, she was neither to have nor to hold, but rushed off from his very arms, and threw herself into a rapid stream and was drowned" (308). What terrible "deceit" could cause this young wife and mother to kill herself? What are the "sins of the father" in this narrative? The most likely deceit is a sham marriage,[11] the same fate suffered by Anne's mother in *Man and Wife*. Throughout Gaskell's story, Gisborne's relations with women are entirely branded as projections; in Lacan's words, there is a complete "absence of sexual relation" (*Feminine Sexuality* 141). Gisborne's thoughtless killing of Mignon is an embodiment of all of his relations with women: his "love" for Mary takes the form of a "terrible deceit"; his "love" for Lucy is an unspoken secret, which, when spoken, leads to his violent loathing; his selfishness leads him to take food from the starving Bridget at the end of the story in order to save himself.

Gisborne's "thoughtlessness" is instrumental in creating what becomes the silencing effect of the "female line." For if Mary was deceived into a sham marriage, then the secret buried in Lucy's past is bastardy, and Lucy's claim to the estate in question is thus barred since only legitimate issue can receive an inheritance.[12] If Lucy is illegitimate, she cannot inherit anything through the "female line," or rather she cannot inherit anything through the "female line" *except* the curse. The only outside she can incorporate and bring inside is the taint of bastardy and of a shameful female sexuality. In Lacanian terms, it is the Name-of-the-Father that confers legitimacy and access to the symbolic order; denied legitimacy, cut off from the symbolic order and from representation, the daughter's body inherits only the pre-symbolic through the "female line." It is thus not surprising that the narrator ends his story with the death of Bridget Fitzgerald and gives no indication of Lucy's life after the curse is lifted, for what "after" is conceivable? In terms of plot, will he marry the woman he loves if she is tainted by sexual shame? Will he contravene the *law* and allow her to receive the inheritance, concealing—and therefore perpetuating the effects of—past secrets? Or will he reveal Lucy's illegitimacy, which will effectively disinherit her, such a disinheritance being perhaps both liberating and a profound loss? Rather than choose any of these options, the narrator does not reveal Lucy's fate, other than to make a passing retrospective reference at the opening of the narrative to "that strange story connected with poor Lucy" (271), leaving the sense of "poor" undefined. The final secrets are the narrator's.

The "female line" in "The Poor Clare" inherits or enunciates a misery that is not inherent in it—is outside in a social and paternal matrix—but which it comes to possess. The maternal relation, however loving and fond it may seem to be, necessarily makes this misery a part of its legacy. The "wild quarrels . . . and wilder reconciliations" (276) between Bridget and Mary Fitzgerald underscore the inescapable affliction of the maternal relation, an affliction that is revealed in both the physical body and in mental torment. This reading of the work leaves the social problem of familial violence explored but unresolved, which may be troubling for readers who expect from Gaskell, with her fine sense of social justice, a clearer etiology of this dysfunction and some remediation. Yet if the violence and rejection visited upon the female body are not problems resolved by the text, they nevertheless create and mark an instability, a disruption, which the text struggles to represent. The text's tortuous structure combined with its unstable inscription of the female body, its veering away from both Lucy's body and the mother's experience, indicates a failure of representation itself, and thus points to an eruption of the real. For Lacan the real, like the unconscious, is as much an "inside" as an "outside"; it is what he calls an "extimacy," an "intimate exteriority" (*Seminar VII* 139). The real in Gaskell's story is given body as the phantom and marks the intimate place of subjectivity that nevertheless is constituted by the Other in the form of intersubjective secrets, of unspeakable and unspoken connections between people and between past and present events. Analogously, as Jacqueline Rose claims, "violence is not something that can be located on the inside or outside, in the psychic or the social . . . but rather something that appears as the effect of the dichotomy itself." The distressed female body remains a persistent, irremediable, and real phantom.

"The Poor Clare" is thus a ghost story that demonstrates the persistence of the phantom's existence. That persistence is demonstrated both in the *excess* and *intractability* associated with aggression—the narrator's, the father's, the mother's, and the grandmother's—, and in the suggestion that there are further layers of secrets encrypted in Lucy's phantasmic body about which the narrator is silent. What is perhaps most remarkable about the persistence of the phantom is the accompanying aversion of narrator, father, and grandmother to Lucy. Her phantasmic body, driven out "like some monstrous thing," carries the weight of the narrative's secrets, anxieties, and aggressions, and produces fascination and cruelty, love and violence. The fascinated narrator turns from that real female body, necessarily leaving it unrepresented in the story's conclusion. The phantom as sign of misery is conjured but not dispelled in "The Poor Clare."

5

Rape, Transgression, and the Law

The Body of Marian Erle in Elizabeth Barrett Browning's Aurora Leigh

Elizabeth Barrett Browning's *Aurora Leigh,* published in 1856, the same year as "The Poor Clare," appears at first glance to situate itself, like "Janet's Repentance," firmly in the world of realism, far from the realm of occult haunting. While "The Poor Clare" moves beyond the bounds of realism and into the world of demonic possession and exorcism in order to investigate the violence in and misery of the lives of three generations of women, *Aurora Leigh* concerns itself with the growth and education of the eponymous heroine into artistry, womanhood, and marriage with the man she loves, appearing to follow what Helena Michie calls "the teleology of the conventional integrative plot of the Victorian novel" ("Pain" 200). However, although the text of *Aurora Leigh* ends with Aurora both artistically successful and happily married, and although most critics read the text as a triumph of psychological fulfillment and integration, representing as it does the coming into being of the female artist who manages both to be a successful writer and to find her heart's desire,[1] we read *Aurora Leigh* as a text that is haunted. And like "The Poor Clare," it is haunted once again by the body of a woman—that of the violated Marian Erle.

In contrast to most critics who perceive Marian Erle to be an important aspect of Aurora's political and psychological growth,[2] Marian's body appears to us as a site of fundamental disruption or crisis in the text; thus, not only is it not an aspect of Aurora's growth, it is a crucial interruption of it. Her body is a site of radical contradiction; appearing, disappearing, and remanifesting itself throughout the text, it disrupts the central autobiographical thrust of Aurora's narrative. She is a central aspect of the narrative yet the imagery with which she is most frequently associated functions to throw her very existence into question. She is described in terms of objects—she is Romney's "stool," his "cup" (6.908–09)—and in terms of animals—her love for Romney is "dog-like" (4.281) and in the final scene Aurora refers to her "spaniel head" (9.277). Most significantly, she is described in terms of the incorporeal—she is like mist, "not white nor brown, / But could look either, like a mist that changed" (3.810–11) or like water, so that her soul contains "cataracts" (4.184), her hair is a "sudden waterfall" (3.1046), and her heart "overflowed the world" (3.1086). At the end of the text, she appears as a phantom lacking substantiality, looking "[a]s if the floating moonshine interposed / Betwixt her foot and the earth, and raised her up / To float upon it" (9.189–91). The idea of Marian's incorporeality functions in conjunction with her own sense that she is not alive; she frequently, in the second half of the text, declares herself to be dead.

The phantasmagoric presence of Marian Erle is reminiscent of "The Poor Clare" and is, once again, helpfully illuminated by Abraham and Torok's notion of the phantom as a construct that emerges out of an intersubjective and intergenerational process, and which consists of the untold, unacknowledged secrets of families or of cultures. "The phantom is . . . a metapsychological fact," says Abraham, and goes on to explicate: "[W]hat haunts are not the dead, but the gaps left within us by the secrets of others" (171). The ghostly body of Marian Erle becomes the unresolved "gap" of *Aurora Leigh;* it is never entirely recuperated or integrated into the text, it carries unresolved secrets, and it remains as a trace, hovering unremembered and unaccounted for over its ending.[3]

The paradox of a text both realist and haunted might find its origins in Barrett Browning's statement of intention about *Aurora Leigh*. In a letter to Robert Browning, she writes:

> But my chief *intention* just now is the writing of a sort of novel-poem . . . running into the midst of our conventions, & rushing into drawing-rooms & the like "where angels fear to tread"; & so, meeting face to face & without mask the Humanity of the age,

> & speaking the truth as I conceive of it, out plainly. That is my intention. (1.10)

Barrett Browning's aim seems at least ironic, if not contradictory. Her stated determination to meet "without mask the Humanity of the age" is strangely juxtaposed with the idea of "rushing into drawing-rooms," a notion that conveys vividly the confinements and strictures of middle-class life. Thus, her realist intentions appear inadvertently, from the outset, to be compromised by being severely confined to a privileged, middle-class world of drawing rooms that, by definition, compromises the idea of an investigation into both "Humanity" and "the age."[4] Certainly, in spite of the fact that the text of *Aurora Leigh* concerns itself with pressing social issues of the time—poverty, rape, prostitution, illegitimacy, the constraints on women—the treatment of the working classes in the text often appears crude and dismissive.[5] Descriptions of the villagers entering the church for the ill-fated wedding of Romney and Marian evoke images of revulsion, of waste and debris, of that which ought to be expelled from a society:

> They clogged the streets, they oozed into the church
> In a dark slow stream, like blood. (4.553–54)

Later, when these guests become enraged by the non-appearance of Marian, they are described as vicious devouring animals of prey:

> the pack
> Who, falling on [the ration] headlong, dog on dog
> In heaps of fury, rend it, swallow it up
> With yelling hound-jaws. (4.851–54)

These descriptions, which convey contempt, even repulsion, contradict Barrett Browning's stated concern with social and political issues, with the "*Humanity* of the age" (emphasis ours). It is therefore perhaps not peculiar that what appears to haunt the text of *Aurora Leigh* is the body of a working-class woman, a body that does not inhabit drawing rooms, a body the story of which comprises, on the one hand, so large a part of Aurora's autobiography, and which is, on the other, so peculiarly dismissed at the end of the text. The body of Marian Erle thus haunts the text, not only compromising the growing subjectivity and psychological coherence of Aurora, but perhaps as a trace of Barrett Browning's own limitations or secrets, of that which remains personally or culturally unspeakable.

VIOLENCE AND THE MATERNAL RELATION

Aurora Leigh is a text imbued with violence and violent imagery: rape, prostitution, class violence, psychological violence. Domestic violence is thus only one aspect of the violence that is dispersed throughout the text of *Aurora Leigh,* but plays a central role in the narrative as a whole. It is most powerfully concentrated in the body of Marian Erle, which is, at various points of the narrative, hurt, persecuted, despised, beaten, raped, and left for dead. Marian Erle emerges from a situation of utter domestic horror; her body functions as the most specific site of violence in the text that winds itself through the central narrative as Marian Erle, a young working-class woman, comes to play a crucial role in the lives and narratives of the two protagonists, Aurora and Romney.

Beautiful, clever, and talented, Marian has run away from a life of domestic terror. The instability and constant threat of the life to which she is born manifests itself, from the outset, physically and spatially in the very dwelling in which her mother gives birth. This hut, made of mud and turf and hardly distinguishable from the ground out of which it is built, bespeaks the extreme marginality of Marian's existence. Her home barely exists or is only narrowly distinguishable from an animal's burrow. It has been built at night to avoid the knowledge of the landlord, and exists (just as the body of Marian comes to exist) in a state of imminent destruction; it is constantly liable to being "straight levelled, scattered by his foot, / Like any other anthill" (3.835–36). Where middle-class heroines find their homes denied to them by abusive fathers or husbands (expelled like Lucy or Janet, or moved, like Georgiana), Marian's actual house is threatened with literal physical disintegration.

When she is born, her body exists in the same marginal and dangerous space, in constant threat of total annihilation. Just as the physical structure that houses the infant Marian exists under constant threat, so is her mother unable to provide an emotional, containing framework in which the baby might be psychically housed. Her mother is constantly beaten by her father; it then seems inevitable that when the baby is born, there is "No place for her," her first cry is a "wrong against the social code" (3.841, 845). The beaten mother beats her baby:

> At which she turned
> (The worm), and beat her baby in revenge
> For her own broken heart. (3.868–70)

Marian's experience literalizes the fantasy of Gaskell's short story where the father's aggression is mediated through the maternal relation. Marian's only tolerable moments of childhood are spent out of her home and alone in the hills. Finally, Marian's mother, in response to a particularly savage beating from her husband, tries to sell Marian, quite deliberately offering up her daughter for rape; Marian escapes this time but her mother's action foreshadows the central act of violence that later is visited upon the body of Marian when she is actually raped. In this sense, her mother's gesture may be said to actually initiate this rape; the actual and later rape of Marian that occurs outside the home (and far away in both time and space) is begun inside Marian's home by her family relationships—that between mother and daughter and between mother and father. The rape is also initiated in the family's relationship with the landlord who might level their home with his foot and who has attempted to buy Marian. Both economically and psychologically, the body of Marian Erle seems born to be destroyed.

After her mother's attempt to sell her, Marian runs away, suffers a severe illness during which she almost dies, and finally finds herself in a hospital, the first safe place in which she has ever slept. It is here that her connection to the lives of Romney and Aurora begins. She meets Romney and he saves her life by providing her with a home and a livelihood when she is forced to leave the hospital. By the time her story is recounted to us by Aurora (who hears it from Marian), Romney has decided to marry Marian. Indeed, it is because of this decision that Aurora, prompted by Lady Waldemar, enters into Marian's life.

Marian's story is first narrated to us by Aurora because Marian has been so psychically destroyed that she has seemingly been rendered voiceless. Thus, while Marian is able to give some account of herself, it is so "meek" that it makes Aurora wonder at her being "so sad a creature." It is thus Aurora who grows "passionate" on Marian's behalf (3.847–50) and it is this "passionate" account that the reader receives. That Aurora speaks for Marian, the woman who cannot speak, is clearly manifested in the text. The corollary of this, however—that Marian also speaks through Aurora and that her narrative is made part of Aurora's—remains that which the text keeps obscured from itself. This imbricated relationship is not one that Aurora ever comes entirely to comprehend. Marian functions as an attribute of Aurora and by remaining metonymically linked to her throughout the text works as a constant disruption to her psychic integrity, a disruption that Aurora only dimly grasps. Abraham uses the metaphor of "ventriloquism" to describe how the trauma of the other speaks through and possesses the subject, functioning "like a stranger within the subject's own mental topography" (173). Marian is internally a "stranger" to Aurora (and remains so throughout the text); because she is never properly incorporated into Aurora's psychic world, she comes to signify the ways in which Aurora is strange to her very own self.

These problematics of subjectivity find their formal concomitant in the generic transgressions for which *Aurora Leigh* is well noted.[6] The presence of Marian's body and narrative serves not only to undermine the psychic coherence of the subject, but also to disrupt the formal coherence of the text as a whole by undermining the conventional generic expectations surrounding the constitution of the subject. Her body undermines the sense of the progress assumed by the plot of the Victorian *Bildungsroman,* opposing the teleological movement forward of Aurora's narrative. It disrupts the narrative's drive toward closure and the satisfaction of desire, serving to fragment and undermine this teleology, thereby interrupting the notion of a coherent subject, which the ideas of satiation and closure presuppose. Marian's body fills the text with contradictions, narrative confusions, peculiar psychological splits, fusings, and strange separations and reunions, with what Nicholas Rand calls a "configuration of incoherence, discontinuity, disruption and disintegration" (6). As in a palimpsest, fragments of Aurora's subjectivity are produced throughout the text, embodying themselves momentarily in other objects, then shifting, disappearing, and revealing themselves again. Although images and motifs of Aurora's subjectivity reoccur in unexpected places (in descriptions of Lady Waldemar, Romney, her dead mother and father) the most insistent and repetitive of these psychic appearances is that of Marian Erle. Structurally, then, the presence and significance of Marian's body is crucial. The violence figured most powerfully in her body becomes part of Aurora's story, and since her body is figured as the discarded female body, the other, the repudiated, it embodies the text's investigation into the notions of transgression, legitimacy, and the law.

Aurora's own life is not marked by physical violence, but the trauma of her early life is powerfully conveyed at the beginning of Book One. Because of the early loss of her mother, Aurora comes to consciousness possessed by an unidentifiable yearning:

> I felt a mother-want about the world,
> And still went seeking, like a bleating lamb
> Left out at night in shutting up the fold—. (1.40–42)

She is haunted by the sense of the lost object, "As restless as a nest-deserted bird / Grown chill through something being away, though what / It knows not" (1.43–45). The object is both lost and unrecognizable, an unknowable "something." Abraham, discussing the notion of loss and its subsequent manifestation as a phantom, describes loss as the memory of an "idyll, experienced with a valued object and yet for some reason unspeakable" (141). Such a memory, he says, is buried "*without legal burying place*":

> Between the idyllic moment and its subsequent forgetting (we have called the latter "preservative repression"), there was the metapsychological traumatism of a loss or, more precisely, the "loss" that resulted from a traumatism. (141)

Aurora's loss (resulting from trauma), symptomized by her indefinable yearning or craving for "something," manifests itself in her psyche in a repressed and distorted form—as guilt: she portrays herself as being responsible for her mother's death, indeed, as her mother's murderer. "She could not bear the joy of giving life, / The mother's rapture slew her" (1.34–35), she tells us, and a few lines later: "Aurora Leigh was born / To make my father sadder" (1.45–46). When she meets her cruel English aunt (after the death of her father), she describes her aunt searching her face in order to find "A wicked murderer in [her] innocent face" (1.330). Aurora's guilt, loss, and aggression are all figured in the terrifying portrait of her mother that is painted "after she is dead" (1.128) and which Aurora spends hours gazing at:

> Therefore very strange
> The effect was. I, a little child, would crouch
> For hours upon the floor with knees drawn up,
> And gaze across them, half in terror, half
> In adoration, at the picture there—
> That swan-like supernatural white life
> Just sailing upward from the red stiff silk
> Which seemed to have no part in it nor power
> To keep it quite from breaking out of bounds.
> For hours I sat and stared. Assunta's awe
> And my poor father's melancholy eyes

Still pointed that way. That way went my thoughts
When wandering beyond sight. And as I grew
In years, I mixed, confused, unconsciously,
Whatever I last read or heard or dreamed,
Abhorrent, admirable, beautiful,
Pathetical, or ghastly, or grotesque,
With still that face . . . which did not therefore change,
But kept the mystic level of all forms,
Hates, fears, and admirations, was by turns
Ghost, fiend, and angel, fairy, witch, and sprite. (1.134–54)

The portrait is evocative and multivalent; its "strangeness" for the child finds its origins in its peculiar blending of disparities. Crossing the boundary between life and death, the portrait, comprising the grotesque and the beautiful, the sacred and the damned, the clean and the unclean, engenders both hatred and adoration in the child Aurora. It is fascinating and terrifying; this split, fractured, broken image is the only mother that Aurora knows. Everything in her world, she narrates, becomes "confused, unconsciously" with "still that face"; the use of the word *still* is indicative of the lasting power this image holds over the growing Aurora. This is a central aspect of her inheritance; the dead maternal other, embodied in the portrait of Aurora's mother, is the first other that Aurora must assimilate.

Aurora leaves Italy, grows up, rejects Romney, and becomes a writer, but the dead face of her mother resurfaces in her life again—this time in relation to Marian, who becomes the other to whom Aurora is most crucially bound and from whom she never quite escapes. When Aurora first glimpses Marian in the streets of Paris, she describes the experience as being like that of a "meditative man" who, watching "gnats a-prick upon a pond," is abruptly horrified by the surfacing of "a dead face, known once alive . . . / So old, so new" out of the water (6.235–40). That the experience possesses the simultaneous quality of being both remembered and shockingly unexpected is conveyed by the notion that the face is both "old" and "new." The resurrection of Marian has the same uncanny, ghostly and ghastly effect of the portrait of her mother painted "after she was dead."

Indeed, Aurora's recognition of Marian in the crowd in Paris is a simultaneous recognition both of a "dead face" (6.239) and of the fact that Marian is a mother. The notions of death and motherhood occur simultaneously again for Aurora, echoing not only the death portrait of her mother but also the scene where Aurora's aunt, seeking "the murderer" in Aurora's face, searches Aurora's face with "two grey-steel naked-bladed eyes/ . . . —ay, stabbed it through and through" (1.327–28). Her aunt's stabbing eyes echo an image from her mother's death portrait—"Our Lady of the Passion, stabbed with swords"(1.160)—and are later fixed in her own death mask (2.942-43).

Aurora does not immediately inform the reader of her perception that Marian has a baby, and this narrative deferral is indicative of the complex, fragmented nature of their meeting. Each sees the other seeing; this recognition occurs not face to face, but as one that is, on both parts, splintered, fractured, evasive, deferred. Indeed, this scene of supposed recognition is most powerfully characterized by its misrecognitions, its confusions, its mistaken judgements, and its erroneous conclusions. Aurora's shocked question and its repetition—"God! what face is that?" she asks and, again, "What face is that?" (6.226, 231)—are indicative of the uncertainty and instability that suffuses this meeting. Aurora's belief that she reads the sign of Marian's damnation in the baby she sees Marian carrying is one of her most confused and alienated moments in a text otherwise characterized by the clarity and acuity of her perceptions. Believing herself to read the signs of Marian's transgressions correctly, her thoughts slip between wild imaginings of Marian as both dead and damned. Marian's supposed damnation is synecdochically signified by Aurora's characterization of Marian's face as a "dead face" (6.239):

> That face persists.
> It floats up, it turns over in my mind,
> As like to Marian, as one dead is like
> The same alive. (6.308–11)

In her subsequent imagined letter to Romney, Aurora, considering again Marian's illegitimate motherhood, reiterates this shift in Marian's imagined status from "dead" to "damned" with the implication that, at this moment, even Aurora thinks that Marian would be better off dead (6.365–66). These shifts are crucial. Death, damnation, somewhere between the two—Aurora, who loves Marian, can no longer find a place for her.

Both Virginia Steinmetz and Dolores Rosenblum connect Aurora's relationship with Marian to the ambiguities of her relationship with her dead mother. Virginia Steinmetz states that though "each has responded to loss differently, Marian . . . and Aurora are drawn to each other because they have experienced 'mother-want'" (352). Aurora manifests a "regressive identification with Marian as both mother and child in order that the poet may not only fulfill her mother-hunger, but also expel from her psyche the split mother image" (360). Rosenblum argues that the meeting with Marian allows her to "enact a symbolic resurrection of both the mother and the mothered child in herself" (333). For both Rosenblum and Steinmetz then, the connection with Marian allows Aurora to resolve her guilt and ambivalence about the maternal relation. But this scene of (mis)recognition arguably remains unresolved; each woman possesses the other in ways neither of them fully understands. The sense of psychic threat is conveyed when Marian, refusing to follow Aurora any farther, insists that Aurora follow her in order that she may return to her baby:

> Then she led
> The way, and I, as by a narrow plank
> Across devouring waters, followed her,
> Stepping by her footsteps, breathing by her breath. (6.500-03)

The precariousness, danger, and fear of Aurora's situation are powerfully conveyed as she follows Marian into a world Aurora is incapable of imagining (a world far removed from "drawing-rooms"); the sense that she may drown in "devouring waters" reminds us of the faces of the "drowned" Marian and her dead mother.[7]

Throughout the text, Aurora and Marian are the subjects and objects of each other's discourse and of their own. Indeed, the ongoing making and remaking, the dispersal, fragmentation, and fusings of their selves may be said to *be* the progression of the text. They are crucial aspects of each other; textually speaking, neither they nor their narratives can exist without the other. But as Aurora follows Marian across the streets of Paris, and as she confronts the fact of Marian's motherhood, she relegates Marian to the marginal, to a place that is no place because the subversion that Marian represents becomes too threatening to Aurora's own sense of integrity. In order, therefore, to retain her own subjectivity, Aurora must split off Marian.

VIOLENCE, TRANSGRESSION, AND THE LAW

The complexities surrounding Aurora's sighting of Marian and Aurora's subsequent bewilderment are caused not so much by her moral or spiritual difficulty in placing Marian (indeed, she believes herself to have a clear grasp of Marian's circumstances), but by the difficulty of *describing* what she thinks she has seen to Romney. She cannot *account* for Marian's behavior to Romney and finds herself repeatedly returning to the point where she imagines the letter she would to write to him:

> I ought to write to Romney, "Marian's here;
> Be comforted for Marian."
> My pen fell,
> My hands struck sharp together, as hands do
> Which hold at nothing. (6.333-36)
>
> I cannot write to Romney. (6.356)
>
> I will not write to Romney Leigh. (6.377)

Aurora has no difficulty in imagining Marian's predicament (however mistaken she might be); her difficulty lies in describing it. Aurora's difficulty in speaking of Marian's plight signifies the unspeakability of what has happened to Marian. Since Marian was raped when she was unconscious, the conception of her child occurs outside of consciousness and therefore outside of narrative:

> . . . when waking up at last . . .
> I told you that I waked up in the grave. (6.1217–18; ellipses in original)

The ellipses signify not only Marian's ignorance about what has befallen her, but also the fact that it cannot be recounted, that the event has no logical or narrative or social connectedness. Aurora's narrative difficulties are echoed by Marian herself who finds it impossible to place her experience within any system of signification to which she has access. On her first attempt to tell Aurora of her child, her lips move in a "spasm without a sound" (6.495). In a similar vein, she describes herself as being speechless after her rape, "[h]alf gibbering and half raving on the floor" (6.1232). She explains to Aurora:

> We wretches cannot tell out all our wrong
> Without offence to happy decent folk.
> I know that we must scrupulously hint
> With half words, delicate reserves, the thing
> Which no one scrupled we should feel in full. (6.1220–24)

Marian's description of her predicament becomes a statement about the cultural prohibitions to which her entire class is subjected. While she is made to suffer, to "feel in full" any indignity or violation, she is denied access to words, to a system of representation in which that violation might be defined, explicated, contained, or judged.

Marian's inability to describe her violation can be illuminated by Jean-François Lyotard's concept of the *differend*. The *differend* is precisely that which has been shut out of traditional legal discourse and out of social conventions of meaning. Lyotard explains:

> In the differend, something "asks" to be put into phrases, and suffers from the wrong of not being able to be put into phrases right away. This is when the human beings who thought they could use language as an instrument of communication learn through the feeling of pain which accompanies silence . . . that they are summoned by language, not to augment to their profit the quantity of information communicable through existing idioms, but to recognize that what remains to be phrased exceeds what they can presently phrase. (13)

Lyotard theorizes Marian's predicament precisely here. She recognizes that "what remains to be phrased exceeds what [she] can presently phrase"; her suffering either cannot be adequately signified or cannot be signified at all. The attacks on her body function to signify that which has been shut out of discourse.

Marian herself connects her rape back to her own early history, to her mother:

> —man's violence,
> Not man's seduction, made what I am, . . .
> When mothers fail us, can we help ourselves? (6.1226–27, 1229)

From birth, Marian's body is attacked and despised; her mother beats her as a baby, repeating the violence that she herself has suffered at the hands of her husband:

> One day, said Marian,—the sun shone that day—
> Her mother had been badly beat, and felt
> The bruises sore about her wretched soul. (3.1040–42)

It is in response to this particularly savage beating that Marian's mother tries to sell her to a man "with beast's eyes / That seemed as they would swallow her alive" (3.1050–51). The rape of Marian that occurs later in the text is, in one sense, an inevitable consequence of the physical violence to which her body has always been subjected. It is a repetition, an inevitable recurrence—the return of the repressed. Although Marian is unconscious when she is raped, she remains haunted by her mother's hatred and unconsciously fulfills her mother's earlier fantasy of selling her. The idea of being exchanged, thrown away, discarded, or violated has hovered around the body of Marian since she was born. From the time of her birth, we are told, she has had to "swindle a place" since "by man's law" there has been "no place for her" (3.840–42). But rape is also a very particular kind of violence. It serves, in this context, to make concrete the taboo or the prohibition that always hovered around the body of Marian.[8] It functions to shift her body structurally into the place of the unspeakable, the place that is no place, defined only by the violence, prohibition, and exclusion directed against it.

Many of the significations assigned to Marian are related to the notion of prohibition. Marian is other/outside/excluded/foreign because of her class, her sex, the violence to which she is subjected, and her illegitimate motherhood. Her markings and scarrings manifest the coming into being of a female body through pain, violence, and death. Aurora, the narrator, might be said to possess the capacity to transcend many of these exclusions, but even she assigns to Marian's body the notion of the unspeakable and (unconsciously) uses Marian's body to encapsulate unacknowledged and unrecognized aspects of her culture as well as of herself, things she "cannot name" (6.344–46).

This unspeakability becomes powerfully evident in the discussion between Marian and Aurora about Marian's rape; their discussion is figured in the language of the law. In a series of groundless reproaches, Aurora, functioning as judge, speaks of Marian's "vice," her "sin," of her having stolen her child (6.612–44), of her killing her child, and of her being "complaisant" to a wrong (6.736, 743). Aurora's moral and legal fluency exists in strong contrast to Marian's inarticulateness. Unable to "phrase" (Lyotard 13) an inexplicable set of relations, she helplessly sums up the horror of all that has happened to her by saying "I found the child" (6.670). The discussion reflects uncannily Lyotard's definition of a differend as a tribunal in which the accused has lost the means of proving that he or she has been wronged: "I would like to call a *differend [différend]* the case where the plaintiff is divested of the means to argue and becomes for that reason a victim" (9). He continues:

> [T]he "perfect crime" does not consist in killing the victim or the witnesses . . . but rather in obtaining the silence of the witnesses, the deafness of the judges, and the inconsistency (insanity) of the testimony. You neutralize the addressor, the addressee, and the sense of the testimony; then everything is as if there were no referent (no damages). (8)

Marian's body is this place of no "referent." Since "no presentation is possible of the wrong [she] says [she] has suffered" (Lyotard 8) her body is unspeakable, a place of psychic, semiotic, narrative, and cultural evasion. The world of law inside which Aurora safely resides is inaccessible to Marian and she describes her existence outside of the sphere of protection in terms that parody the safe assumptions of Aurora's world. Denying "perjury," she makes her "mother's oath" and claims her "right" within the "law" (6.661, 666, 754). But, paradoxically, the law on which Marian calls—a law of tradition and cultural assumption—is ironically one by which Marian can only be destroyed, "the law which now is paramount— / The common law, by which the poor and weak / Are trodden underfoot by vicious men, / And loathed for ever after by the good" (6.666–69). Aurora only ever attains a partial understanding of the excluded, prohibiting world that Marian inhabits.

Marian's liminal structural status is also constantly indicated by Marian herself who frequently claims that she is dead. She makes this claim three times; each time is a crucial moment involving the idea of reunion or integration for the three major characters—herself, Aurora, and Romney. In the first instance, she uses the notion of her death in life to undermine Aurora's insistence on a "reunion" between the two of them; since she does not believe she exists, the notion of a reunion, which presupposes two subjectivities or entities, is impossible:

> And she, I said, was murdered; Marian's dead.
> What can you do with people when they are dead. (6.813–14)

Her second claim to being dead is tied up with her refusal of Romney's second marriage proposal, another failed "reunion":

> Yet still it will not make her . . . if she's dead,
> And gone away where none can give or take
> In marriage—able to revive, return
> And wed you. (9.308–11)

And the third and most devastating instance is perhaps Marian's personal attempt at reunion with her own self, or a self she once had, or her past capacities. She says that she is no longer capable of love:

> But for me,
> Once killed, this ghost of Marian loves no more. (9.388–89)

All of these claims to being dead throw into question not only the very concept of reunion, but also the mutual subjectivities it presupposes. Marian's claim to be dead foregrounds the notion that the union of a subject with an impossible object (the object that both is and is not) renders the subject also unstable; in this way Marian's "death" becomes, at various points, a crucial aspect of the respective subjectivities of both Aurora and Romney, as well as of herself. Her death in life disturbs not only the psychic coherence of the subject, but, by disrupting the notion of reunion, disturbs the idea of simple closure with which the text supposedly ends. Her transgressive presence is there for most of the final scene between Aurora and Romney.

Marian's peculiar emotional liminality—her status of being both dead and alive—therefore becomes the most powerful place of disturbance in *Aurora Leigh*. She is constantly being written in and out of the narrative. As a signifier, she remains constantly volatile. Although she introduces, at various points, the role of pain, anger, violence, and victimization into the formation of female subjectivity, and therefore Aurora's subjectivity, her own liminality renders all of these constructs unstable. Lyotard states that "a case of differend between two parties takes place when the 'regulation' of the conflict that opposes them is done in the idiom of one of the parties while the wrong suffered by the other is not signified in that idiom" (9). Marian's dead and alive status, formed by her incapacity to function in the central idiom, forms a transgressive presence, which creates the space for new forms of subjectivity and legality, forms that appear, shift, change, and disappear through the progression of the text. Divested of the means to argue, her transgressive body suggests the possibility of being allowed, in Lyotard's terms, to "institute idioms which do not yet exist" (13).

THE MARKED BODY

The problematics of subjectivity that Marian manifests declare themselves in the various markings and transformations that occur on her body—her beatings, her rape, her pregnancy. Indeed, all of the crucial events in Marian's life occur through her body and, from the outset of her narrative, it is her body that is peculiarly foregrounded both for its extraordinary beauty (commented upon by every character in the text) and for the way in which it is victimized, attacked, or abused by almost everyone she encounters. Her parents, the squire who tries to buy her, the man who rapes her and fathers her child, Lady Waldemar, and Lady Waldemar's servant who sells her are a few examples. Throughout the text, Marian appears to function as a body on which stories are written, rather than as a subject in her own right; her body is the site for the inscriptions of others.

The most crucial event in Marian's troubled life—her rape and subsequent pregnancy—occurs when she is unconscious. In a discussion of Heinrich von Kleist's story "The Marquise of O—," where the protagonist is also raped and impregnated while unconscious, Mary Jacobus comments that "the rape takes place in the space of a narrative absence, not outside nature, but outside consciousness" (*First Things* 25). Jacobus continues:

> In Kleist's own discourse, it seems that feminine sexuality, however mediated, can never fully submit to textuality. The woman's body . . . remains the site of something at once undecidable and contradictory, in excess of narrative. (28)

In Kleist's story, the Marquise advertises for the perpetrator, finds him, and marries him, thus turning this tale of violation into one of sexual and emotional fulfilment with a happy ending. Jacobus concludes her discussion of the story by stating that it appears in Kleist's story that "feminine sexuality . . . can only be recuperated for narrative . . . by subordinating feminine sexuality to the Law of the Father" (28). The differences in the stories of these two women, Marian and the Marquise of O—, are as compelling as their similarities. The Marquise of O— is an aristocrat with a place, a home, a family, and a title; Marian has nothing. Indeed, Marian's surname—Erle—functions as an ironic commentary on the lack of any kind of place or position in the world which she inhabits. Much of the story of "The Marquise of O—" involves the Marquise's attempt to tell the story, to account for herself. The rape of Marian, on the other hand, and, for that matter, the identity of the father of her child remain a blank. She simply cannot tell her story and when Romney offers her his name for the child, she can only refuse, since this would constitute a false naming. Because her story remains in the realm of the unspeakable, "unrecuperated," occurring in excess of both narrative and the law, it returns as a symptom; it is written on her body. In this sense, if we return to Jacobus' comments about "The Marquise of O—," we might say that Marian's body refuses to submit to the Law of the Father and remains the site of contradiction and subversion.

The imagery surrounding the marking of Marian's body is echoed thematically in Aurora's exploration of her own writing. While conjuring Romney's imagined rejection of her work, she describes her writing in terms of a destroyed pregnancy:

> I ripped my verses up,
> And found no blood upon the rapier's point;
> The heart in them was just an embryo's heart
> Which never yet had beat, that it should die;
> Just gasps of make-believe galvanic life;
> Mere tones, inorganised to any tune. (3.245–50)

Later, the image is repeated in terms of childlessness: "I called the artist but a greatened man. / He may be childless also, like a man" (5.419–20). The connection between the markings on Marian's body and the markings of the text that constitute Aurora's work and narrative serves to emphasize not only the notions of instability, contradiction, and change that constitute the formation of the subject, but also the complexities that accrue around the writing of Marian into and out of the text and the exclusions that she suffers. The text is filled with metaphors of reading and writing, and also their antitheses—blindness and illiteracy. But where illiteracy in the case of either Romney or Aurora is metaphoric, it is a severe limitation in the case of Marian, who, because of her class exclusions, cannot (or does not) read as they do. Marian's body becomes the literal figuration of these prohibitions.

Throughout the ten long years in which Aurora and Romney are unable to come together, each is filled with the sense of the other's incapacity to read (correctly). After Aurora refuses Romney's proposal, he writes to her, paradoxically, to inform her that she is deliberately rendering herself illiterate:

> you read
> My meaning backward like your eastern books,
> While I am from the west, dear. Read me now
> A little plainer. (2.818–21)

Aurora responds by informing Romney that she, knowing more than any reading can inform her, considers herself to be too literate rather than not literate enough:

> I know your heart,
> And shut it like the holy book it is. (2.836–37)

In contrast with Aurora and Romney who are provided with texts they cannot and will not read, Marian's reading can only occur in fragments. Page halves cannot be matched, beginnings and endings of readings are never available to her; her reading is jumbled and jangled in accordance with her class deprivation, her personal fragmentedness, and her social and emotional exclusion. "'Twas somewhat hard to keep the things distinct," she tells us (3.983). In this sense, Marian's illiteracy is qualitatively different from Aurora's or Romney's. For Romney, textual coherence would be available if Aurora were only willing and able to read; for Aurora, the text is so plain that it is not worth reading. For Marian, however, the text is incomprehensible and unreadable because it is fundamentally unavailable. The belief held by both Aurora and Romney, at various points, that Marian can escape her chaotic, excluded, working-class world by marrying out of it, is undermined by Marian's own comments about her impending marriage to Romney, comments figured in terms of her longing, yet inability to read.

> While I shall set myself to read his eyes,
> Till such grow plainer to me than the French
> To wisest ladies. Do you think I'll miss
> A letter, in the spelling of his mind? (4.232–35)

Her language betrays not only her sense of foreignness, of talking a different language from Romney, but the hopelessness of ever translating from one world into the other. Romney's eyes, like French, will always remain incomprehensible to Marian.

When Romney and Aurora re-encounter each other at the end of the tale, their meeting is marked by misreadings and unexplained silences. He refers to himself as a "tedious book" (8.76), thereby missing the crucial fact that Aurora is unaware of his blindness, while she, in her blindness (about his blindness), reads a set of secret signs in the stars ("A secret writing from a sombre page" [8.91]) and invites the blind man to read these hieroglyphics. These almost farcical motifs are carried out until the end of the scene. Aurora tells him her heart is "writ in Sanskrit" (8.476–78), while he, insisting on the notion of his "legible life-signature" (8.1234) tells Aurora, who does not understand what he is saying, that his secret (that he loves Aurora best) is "writ/ Too plainly in the book of [his] misdeeds" (8.1217–18). The notions of reading and writing here are inextricably mingled with the idea of blindness, a concept that has also threaded its way through the entire text.

Marian's "blinded face" (3.1049) at the moment that her mother is attempting to sell her strangely foreshadows her response to Romney when he asks her to marry him and she "look[s] blindly in his face" (4.118). Aurora says of herself that she "shuts her eyes" (4.465) in order to avoid grasping the complexities of the marriage and compares herself to a "blind man" (5.1028) when Lady Waldemar tells her that she is going to marry Romney, taunting Aurora at the same time with a letter she may not read. Aurora's metaphorical blindness is a crucial aspect of the final encounter with Romney, where she remains bizarrely blind to his blindness. Romney's literal blindness then is passed between all three of the main characters. Since his blindness is a partial figuration for Marian's "blinded face," it serves to retain the trace of Marian even after she leaves the final scene, insistently reminding us of that which may not be absorbed into a completed and readable world. The violated, raped, unspeakable body of Marian remains an inextricable part of Aurora and Romney's final union. Both dead and alive, inscribed with horror, she reminds us of what cannot be translated, what cannot exist in a legible, comprehensible world.[9]

Throughout the text, Marian's body continues to know and speak what her society will not; it therefore exists as a space and a trace in the text refusing to be written out. Aurora's final description of Marian's physical appearance evokes that of a ghost. Marian's body is insubstantial, incorporeal, just as it is in Aurora's opening description of her:

> As if the floating moonshine interposed
> Betwixt her foot and the earth, and raised her up
> To float upon it. (9.189–91)

Her ghostliness is even more powerfully conveyed in her final conversation with Aurora, which echoes the legal terminology of their earlier discussion of Marian's transgression. Marian places her "case" (9.239) before Aurora and asks her to "judge" her (9.379). The language in which she makes her request, however, reminds us that she cannot be judged because her life is over:

> Have I not the right
> To take so mere an aftermath from life,
> Else found so wholly bare? (9.223–25)

The juxtaposition of "right" (with all its overtones of fairness, legal or moral claim, entitlement, privilege, and even immunity) with "aftermath" reminds us that Marian is outside of the legal (and emerging domestic) framework that the text presupposes.

Marian is tangential to the tale and part of its subplot yet in disturbing the central notions of psychological growth, of contented domesticity, and of happy unions, she is a crucial figure of transgression. The tale of Aurora Leigh's development remains filled with blanks, illegibilities, and contradictions which are largely figured in the body of Marian. Marian's body, connected to the dead body of Aurora's mother, hovers over the final union of Aurora and Romney as a phantom of whose existence Aurora is only partially aware. As the embodiment of Barrett Browning's interrogations of issues of class and violence when they are visited upon the female body, she remains a phantasmagoric presence which both reveals and conceals the unspeakable aspects of her culture.

6

"Will She End Like Me?"

Violence and the Uncanny in Wilkie Collins's Man and Wife

Marital cruelty is the central subject of Wilkie Collins's novel *Man and Wife*. The novel, published just before the passage of the Married Women's Property Act in 1870, concerns itself fundamentally with the institution of marriage, its social and political presuppositions, its legal and economic implications, and its psychological and spiritual dimensions. The very title of the novel announces its focus; the phrase *Man and Wife* reverberates through the text with varying degrees of irony. This text, in its investigation into pressing social, political, and contemporary questions of its time, is, with "Janet's Repentance," the most realist of those investigated in this book. However, as this chapter will argue, by the novel's end, the narrative paradoxically appears to undermine its own enterprise. As the novel inexorably explores and exposes the failure of both society and the law to protect its members, the realist enterprise appears to give way under the weight of its own investigation and reframes itself in other terms, thereby formally imitating that which it investigates—the collapse of possible restitution in the real world itself. Although this collapse is signaled in several parts of the narrative, it is the body of the haunted and haunting character of Hester that finally interrupts or breaks the realist surface of the text; it is her damaged and battered body that causes the novel to succumb to phantasmagoria, to the uncanny.

Reframed in formal terms, the body of Hester posits the question: at which point is realism no longer a useful means of investigation? Although Collins keeps attention focused on the political and social world that structures and comprises the conditions of an individual character's personal choices and under which a specific marriage occurs,[1] this text, like "The Poor Clare" and *Aurora Leigh,* also appears to be haunted, presenting gaps and irresolutions that are once again figured in the battered and, in this case, crazed body of the woman. And like those two texts, the haunting is, once again, located through the agency of a maternal inheritance.

THE MATERNAL INHERITANCE

The opening section of *Man and Wife* concerns itself with the failed life and somber death of Anne Silvester, the mother of Anne Silvester, the main character in the novel. The mother's life has been destroyed by the (thoroughly legal) abuses to which her husband has subjected her; her dying words manifest her terror that her daughter may be subject to her own fate:

> "She is Anne Silvester as I was? *Will she end like Me*?"
>
> The question was put with the labouring breath, with the heavy accents which tell that death is near. It chilled the living woman who heard it to the marrow of her bones.
>
> "Don't think that!" she cried, horror-struck. "For God's sake, don't think that!" . . . Lady Lundie put her ear close to [Anne's lips], and heard the dreadful question reiterated in the same dreadful words:—"She is Anne Silvester—as I was. *Will she end like Me*?" (42–43)

This scene of the mother's death manifests itself almost as a kind of haunting; the representation of the realistic concerns of a dying mother for her child is shifted and intensified here to the point where Anne Silvester appears spellbound, possessed. Collins creates this atmosphere through his use of italics, of repetition, of heightened language: "chilled," "wildness," "horror-struck," "dreadful." He also moves beyond the bounds of realism by conveying the sense that the dying woman may see something that her listener cannot.

The brief appearance of Anne Silvester (the mother) in the opening chapters in the novel appears almost inexplicable in narrative terms; its function is precisely to anticipate the impossible hauntings that occur later in the novel by foregrounding the very question that she asks: will the daughter who bears the same name as the mother be cursed as the mother was cursed? Will the daughter be an uncanny double of the mother and the mother's experience?

The terror inherent in Anne's mother's repeated question hovers in one form or another over almost all of the texts that this book examines. The question of whether the child's maternal inheritance is determining and inescapable is thus not only of great psychological and emotional significance in these texts, but is powerfully linked to these texts' representation of violence. In almost all of the texts in our study, the bond between mothers and daughters is one of misery, grief, and even complicity in the scene of violence: in "Janet's Repentance," Janet's mother is the passive and silent, if suffering, onlooker at the brutal abuse Janet suffers; in "The Poor Clare," Mary Fitzgerald decides to abandon her harsh and demanding mother Bridget and then Bridget herself abandons her afflicted granddaughter Lucy; in *Aurora Leigh*, Aurora's connection to Marian Erle is powerfully bound up with Aurora's unresolved relationship with her dead mother while Marian's own mother (herself a beaten woman) attempts to sell Marian in order to be raped.

While silent, absent, or complicit mothers haunt all of the texts we discuss in this book, the maternal relationship is particularly intensified and foregrounded in the last three texts under examination. In all these texts, domestic violence is figured as an inherited curse or affect passed down through the maternal line. This concept is obviously crucial to "The Poor Clare," the plot of which actually revolves around an inherited curse, but it is also central in both *Aurora Leigh* and *Man and Wife*. The rape of Marian Erle, as noted in chapter 5, is inextricably connected to her mother's earlier actions and unconscious fantasies about her; while in Collins's novel, Anne Silvester appears destined, in ways that are never fully explicated by the text, to be haunted by the pattern of her mother's life. Lucy and Aurora Leigh are also haunted by their mothers' secrets (most of them untold and unconscious) and even Hester Dethridge, "born of pious parents" (582), makes the decision to marry Joel Dethridge—a drunkard and a brute—in order to escape her jealous, sick, and increasingly bad-tempered mother. In all three of the texts, the protagonists are haunted by an intersubjective and intergenerational process that consists of the untold and unacknowledged secrets of their families and culture, secrets that are powerfully related to the maternal inheritance.

These secrets are complex and multilayered. They may be indicative of ways in which mothers, both consciously and unconsciously, participate in the horrors suffered by their daughters, in which case, although the violence suffered by the women in these works is directly caused by the men with whom they are intimate, the maternal is also powerfully implicated in their representation of the unspeakable aspects of the scene of violence. But these intergenerational and cultural secrets may also be indicative of the social and political complexities and impossiblities surrounding the bonds between mothers and daughters, of a matrix from which escape is essentially impossible. Joan Manheimer analyzes the proliferation of "Terrible Mothers" in nineteenth-century literature in precisely these terms, seeing it as a function of an impossible social institution. She states: "In their creation of Terrible Mothers, nineteenth-century novelists leave an indictment, like an open wound, pulsing against a society which is unable, without prohibitive cost, to secure a meaningful continuity for itself" (545). Her metaphor of the maternal "pulsing open wound" seems uncannily connected to the pattern of violence in these texts; this pattern seems to exist suggestively and subliminally in *Man and Wife* but is never fully explicated.[2]

VIOLENCE

The story of *Man and Wife,* which progresses through two generations, revolves around a number of interconnected marriages, focusing particularly on the position of women in marriage. Indeed, by examining the psychological, spiritual, legal, and economic complexities of marriage, the novel inevitably highlights the position of the wife, who, as the most legally unprotected of the parties, is most subject to these complexities. As the novel proceeds with its investigation of women's circumstances inside the marriage laws, it explores various types of marriages in all their manifestations—illegal marriages, forced marriages, private marriages, and, in one case in the novel, a marriage that is both publicly sanctioned and happy. Most particularly, in its investigation of the potential imbalances and abuses of power inside the institution of marriage, it examines the possibility of violence and the related physical, legal, and psychological vulnerability of women who are subject to it. Indeed, since physical violence, by its very essence, depends on inequities of power, Collins utilizes violence as an image and analogue of all possible inequities. Cruelty and violence within individual marriages become a mode of investigating large social, cultural, and legal problems.

One of the most pivotal and hidden aspects of violence inside a marriage is sexual violence. Besides the inevitably private nature of this particular form of "marital cruelty," the law also allows it to continue. James A. Hammerton states that "marital rape *per se* was not an offence in criminal or divorce law; only violence associated with it might be successfully pleaded to sustain a charge of cruelty" (*Cruelty* 108). In *Man and Wife,* the legal and cultural "acceptability" of marital rape is textually manifested through narrative indirections or omissions. One example of this is the experience of Hester, the worst victim of marital cruelty in the novel. Although she refers in her "Confession" to her husband's sexual abuse of her, she evades a detailed account of what occurs. She states that on the night in which she killed her husband, she "suffered the last and worst of many indignities at [her] husband's hands" (599), but refuses intimate explanation. Even here, in her Confession which is "known to no other mortal creature" and which is to be "buried" with her (581–82), her terrible sense of shame is evident. "No mortal eyes but mine will ever see these lines. Still, there are things a woman can't write of even to herself," she states (599). The unspeakability of her experience is a function not only of her own shame, but also of a culture in which she has no voice. Indeed, it is in part because she has no voice in the culture that she takes the shame for her own in the first place. The gaps—"no mortal eyes," "can't write of," "known to no other"—all work to create the sense of the extremity of her experience and her terrible isolation. The words that she does use—"the last and worst of many indignities"—convey powerfully to the reader the duration and intensity of the abuse.

Her textual omissions indicate a peculiarly disconnected acceptance of the physical violence to which she is subjected, an acceptance which is indicative of an intractable legal and cultural norm. This is clearly evidenced in the interaction between Hester and the magistrate to whom she appeals:

> "I must take the law as I find it; and so must you.—I see a mark there on the side of your face. Has your husband been beating you? If he has, summon him here. I can punish him for *that*."
>
> "How can you punish him, sir?" says I.
>
> "I can fine him," says he. "Or I can send him to prison."

> "As to the fine," says I, "he can pay that, out of the money he gets by selling my furniture. As to the prison—while he's in it, what's to become of me, with my money spent by him, and my possessions gone—and when he's *out* of it, what's to become of me again, with a husband whom I have been the means of punishing, and who comes home to his wife, knowing it? It's bad enough as it is, sir," says I. "There's more that's bruised in me than what shows in my face. I wish you good morning." (587)

Thus, the unspeakability of Hester's experience is inextricably related to the fact that it is rendered normative by the culture she inhabits. The magistrate can punish her husband because he can see the bruise but her real injury remains unresponded to and uninscribed. "Magistrates and lawyers; relations and friends . . . I had tried all these, and tried them vainly," Hester states (593).

If violence in the marriage between the Dethridges is only partially inscribed, its inscription is almost entirely avoided in the middle-class marriage between Anne and Geoffrey. The possibility of violence is conveyed in overtones and indirections, in innuendoes and incompleted exchanges between them. The horrors of the sexual situation in this marriage are implied (rather than played out) when Geoffrey informs Anne "loudly and brutally" that she will enter their marital home "on any terms [he] please[s]" (541). Since Geoffrey's physical size and strength are his most noteworthy and remarked upon characteristics, and since Collins utilizes this huge and powerful physique as a motif by which to convey the savagery of the man, Anne's response—"nothing will induce me . . . to live with you as your wife"—seems frighteningly puny (541). Courageous though her response is in the circumstances, it also functions to foreground her helplessness.

Animals are also used to convey Geoffrey's capacity for violence, as they are with Dempster in "Janet's Repentance": "The grand secret in dealing with a woman, is to take her as you take a cat, by the scruff of the neck—" (104), he comments. This sentiment is picked up slightly later in the novel when Geoffrey stops a dog from barking by breaking its ribs with a kick (171). The similarities between domesticated animals and women in the domestic sphere has, ironically enough, already been conveyed by Geoffrey's own observation, but the notion of defenselessness conveyed in the idea of a "dumb beast" is also paralleled in Hester's "dumbness," which is a result of her husband's attacks upon her. Geoffrey's own animality is also conveyed in the "hideous, tigerish glare" he gives Anne when he realizes he is *irrevocably* married to her and comments that he knows what he "owe[s] her" (517), another statement that possesses extremely sinister sexual overtones. The situations in both of the marriages described above ultimately point to the same source, the law that upholds the institution of marriage and protects women no better than it protects cats and dogs.[3]

The problematics of marriage and the law are explored through a number of marriages in this novel, but most particularly through the two marriages described above—the one middle-class and the other working-class. The two marriages work in structural relationship with each other, displaying hidden aspects of each other and reflecting each one to the other. The degraded violent marriage of Hester and Joel functions throughout the novel as an echo and reminder of that which is inchoate in the middle-class marriage. Before the two plots actually wind in on each other, the parallels are drawn in Hester's early "recognitions" of Geoffrey and in her warnings to Anne (543). The overt coming together of the two plots takes place in chapter 49, entitled "The Letter and the Law," which occurs toward the beginning of the third and final volume of the novel.[4]

The chapter opens in Drury Lane where Anne Silvester and Sir Patrick Lundie are meeting in order to solve the complicated legal web that has left Anne in the situation of being potentially legally married to either Arnold or Geoffrey or to neither of them, or to both. The law in this case turns on a letter which has appeared and disappeared through the complex twistings and turnings of the plot and which is currently in Anne's possession. Although this chapter concerns itself with the crucial discovery contained in the letter—that Geoffrey Delamayn has declared himself to be Anne's husband previous to her private meeting with Arnold—the main body of the narrative in the chapter consists of Anne's account of her visit that morning to Fulham where Hester Dethridge now owns a cottage.

The account of this visit is crucial in a variety of ways. When Hester opens the door to Anne, Anne is "startled" by Hester's knowledge of Anne's intimate affairs (not only that she has swooned in the library at Windygates but also that she has been "brought to it by a man") and by the "dead-cold look" in Hester's eyes (473). Anne is again "startled" when Hester asks her if her man has "knock[ed her] down" although Hester's question occurs only a few minutes before Geoffrey does, indeed, attempt to hit Anne (474). If anything appears strange in this interaction, it is Anne's surprise. She was, in fact, "brought" to her swoon at Windygates "by a man" and the likelihood of Geoffrey beating Anne is not new to the reader. Thus, what is surprising is that Anne be taken aback by Hester's comments, that she appear so peculiarly ignorant about her own misery. Hester's insights highlight information that Anne (and even to some extent Sir Patrick, who is listening to Anne's narrative) refuses to know and attempts to repress. Hester possesses knowledge and empathy that both Sir Patrick and Anne are currently incapable of apprehending but do come to recognize before the almost fatal denouement of the novel. Hester's empathy exists in spite of, or perhaps because of her own capacity for violence. Certainly the violence in this chapter manifests itself almost as much in Hester (between Hester and Anne), as it does in Geoffrey (between Geoffrey and Anne). Hester is delighted and fascinated at the possibility of Anne being beaten (474, 475, 476) and, by making the "motion of striking a blow with her clenched fist," twice plays out for Anne, in graphic detail, the action of being beaten. The immediate threat of violence that her little mime brings home to Anne causes Hester to "smile" for the only time in Anne's experience of her (477–78). Mr. Speedwell comments that they are "well matched in that house. . . . The woman is as complete a savage as the men" (478). There are, however, aspects to their meeting that are indicative of less savage characteristics in Hester. She allows Anne into the house, overlooking her own instructions to her servant, and offers her tea. Her fascination with Anne is a sign not only of her sadism, but also of her recognition of the similarities between the two of them, a connection that she perceives and that both Anne and Sir Patrick deny.

The narrative focus of this chapter finally moves from Hester back to the letter and Anne's marital status. But the narrative indirections here have been suggestive. Even at the moment that the law is supposedly (through Sir Patrick's discovery of the letter) resolving the confusion, fraud, and betrayal that have thus far occurred, the dramatic action of the chapter announces the futility and uselessness of the law in relation to the emotional and spiritual disaster that has been Hester's life and that will comprise a large part of Anne's. Anne's account of her morning functions representationally as an account of that which the law has failed to solve and will continue to fail to solve. This failure also announces itself in the final workings out of the plot; the only possible escape from the trap in which Anne finds herself lies in the death of Geoffrey and the incarceration of Hester, both of which occur in the most sensational of ways. The very extremity of Geoffrey's death and Hester's madness are indicative of the impossibility of a reasonable social or legal solution to Anne's crisis, or Hester's (or even Geoffrey's).

Indeed, the novel's excursions into the realm of the sensational and the bizarre become a formal concomitant to the notion of the impossibility of a rational or realistic resolution to its thematic crises. In breaking the bounds of its own realism, the text declares the failure of society; in realistic terms, the law cannot and will not offer its protection. This notion is most clearly figured in the character of Hester. Hester is a person who has been utterly destroyed by the pressures that society has forced her to bear and is the greatest victim of the law in the novel. As the novel progresses, she shifts from one world into another, from being a sane married woman of property who exists inside society to being a person who lives in the excluded world of the marginal, the strange, and finally the utterly mad. As this psychological progression occurs, she is also shifted from one narrative mode into another, from the realm of realism into the realm of the uncanny. By the end of the novel she hardly belongs in the world of the living. Indeed, the narrator comments after the reader's first introduction to Hester that the "woman was alive in the world, and working in the world; and yet (so far as all human interests were concerned) she was as completely out of the world, as if she had been screwed down in her coffin, and laid in her grave" (116–17).[5]

THE UNCANNY: HESTER

Hester enters the realist narrative as the quiet, slightly strange cook with a sad past:

> Elderly and quiet; scrupulously clean; eminently respectable; her grey hair neat and smooth under her modest white cap; her eyes, set deep in their orbits, looking straight at any person who spoke to her—here, at a first view, was a steady, trustworthy woman. Here also, on closer inspection, was a woman with the seal of some terrible past suffering set on her for the rest of her life. You felt it, rather than saw it, in the look of immovable endurance which underlaid her expression—in the deathlike tranquillity which never disappeared from her manner. (113)

The slightly overstated conventionality of the early part of the opening description of Hester exists in stark disparity with what follows: "Elderly," "quiet," "clean," "respectable," "modest," and "neat" all contrast sharply with "terrible," "suffering," "immoveable endurance," "deathlike tranquillity." Indeed, the very incongruities in this description function as early portents of the psychological splits inside Hester, so that even though she is for the first two-thirds of the novel a fairly plausible and realistic figure, she is also, even from the outset, a peculiar and ambiguous presence in the story.

Although hardly the literal *doppelgänger* of "The Poor Clare," she functions throughout the novel in structural and thematic parallel with Anne and Geoffrey. She is called upon to leave Windygates at virtually the same time that Anne leaves; significantly, the chapter entitled "Gone" refers to both Anne and Hester. The terrible isolation of both women is described in virtually identical terms. Hester is described as being as "completely out of the world, as if she had been screwed down in her coffin, and laid in her grave" (117). Of Anne's imprisonment at Fulham, we are told that she is "as absolutely isolated from all contact with the humanity around her as if she lay in her grave" (556). The sense that they are both irretrievably connected to the grave is also picked up by Hester who, when Anne faints in the library, writes: "Shivered when I touched her. That means, I have been walking over her grave" (254). As Geoffrey stumbles upon a solution to his dilemma about how to ensnare his best friend and his fiancée, he associates his solution with having seen Hester. The delivery of his final blow of betrayal to Anne is directly preceded by, and juxtaposed with, his first encounter with Hester:

> How came he to have seen it now?
>
> The dumb old woman reappeared in his thoughts—as if the answer to the question lay in something connected with *her*. (242)

The parallels are not only structurally and thematically maintained, but also insisted upon by Hester herself. Her grasp of this is evident in chapters 53 and 54 in her warnings to Anne, her moments of compassion toward Anne, and even in her peculiar exultation in Anne's sufferings, which seem to function momentarily to release her from her own. This occurs before Anne herself is able to acknowledge the similarities between Hester's situation and her own. Anne is initially skeptical of, even insulted by, Hester's warnings to her (474), "startled" when Hester asks her if Geoffrey has ever hit her (474), and repulsed by Hester's peculiar involvement with her. It takes a long time for Hester's recognitions to be matched by Anne's. In the same vein, her early explanations of Hester's behavior are peculiarly limited: "I believe she felt a certain hard-hearted interest in seeing a woman whom she supposed to be as unfortunate as she had once been herself," she tells Sir Patrick (475). The mixture of sadistic delight, identification, and compassion that Hester directs toward Anne is far more comprehensive, honest, and insightful than Anne allows for or is capable of confronting at this time.

In this sense, Hester functions as a repressed aspect of Anne and Geoffrey's relationship. Her rage, her deformity, her own capacity for violence figures that which is inchoate in the relationship of Anne and Geoffrey, and which takes a long time to surface. In terms of Hester herself, her silence is indicative of her withdrawal from the world of communication and community and also of the unspeakability of her suffering. However, her dumb suffering also figures the suffering of Anne and of her mother before her. Thus, Hester functions as the return of the repressed—the unspeakable and unspeaking return of all the unacknowledged secrets in the novel.

Repetition and recurrence are carefully orchestrated in *Man and Wife*. Indeed, the recurrences and connections in this novel enter increasingly into the world of the preternatural, the uncanny. Motifs and concepts develop and disappear without rational explanation; extraordinary and inexplicable connections form between different characters. For example, the narrator points out the potential patterns of generational repetition between Anne and her mother:

> Who could imagine a contrast more complete than the contrast between her early life and her mother's? Who could see anything but a death-bed delusion, in the terrible question which had tortured the mother's last moments:—"Will she end like Me?" (48)

When Anne receives her message of betrayal from Geoffrey, she drops "senseless at his feet: as her mother had dropped at his father's feet, in the bygone time" (252). As Blanche's mother has attempted to revive Anne's mother, so Blanche attempts to revive Anne. But Anne is only able to be revived by Hester, who has herself been physically knocked senseless many times (594) and who herself suffers repeatedly from fits in which she passes out and loses count of time: "The instant Hester Dethridge touched her, the swooning woman gave signs of life" (254).

Other connections between Anne, her mother, and Hester emerge in these two latter scenes. When Anne's mother finds out in the presence of Lady Jane that she is not married, Lady Jane feels terrified of her response:

> After a moment's hesitation, Lady Jane looked around at Mrs. Vanborough, standing silent by her side—looked, and started back in terror. "Take me away!" she cried, shrinking from the ghastly face that confronted her, with the fixed stare of agony in the great glittering eyes. "Take me away! That woman will murder me!" (37)

The description of Anne's mother's face here is very similar to the descriptions of Hester's face each time she sees her apparition. In her first encounter with Geoffrey, we are told: "Her dull eyes slowly dilated; looked away, sideways . . . started, rigid and glittering" (241). Her look is very similar the night she actually murders Geoffrey:

> Her lips were parted in horror; her eyes, opening wider and wider, stared rigid and glittering at the empty wall. (636)

Hester doubles not only for repressed aspects of Anne and of her mother, but also for Geoffrey. Hester's "glittering eyes" and her silence are matched by the "evil light" in Geoffrey's eyes when he betrays Anne and his silence, which "was the brute silence that threatens dumbly" (251). When Geoffrey and Hester first see each other, their response one to the other is almost identical. Of Geoffrey, we are told:

> [T]he eyes of the dumb cook slowly penetrated him with a stealthy inner chill. Something crept at the marrow of his back, and shuddered under the roots of his hair. He felt a sudden impulse to get away from her. (240–41)

Hester's response to him is very similar:

> Her dull eyes slowly dilated; looked away, sideways, from *his* eyes; stopped again; and started, rigid and glittering . . . stared as if they saw a sight of horror behind him. . . .
>
> The woman had left him, under the influence of some sudden panic. (241)

Each of these two is terrified by the sight of the other. This is indicative not only of the peculiar connection between them but also of the fact that each appears to possess uncanny knowledge of the other, that knowledge being that each will be the source of the other's destruction.

Their mutual "recognition" of each other is reminiscent of Hester's first recognition or vision of "herself," which is heralded by the same icy coldness and creeping feeling that Geoffrey experiences when he first lays eyes on her. In her Confession, Hester describes the experience of herself as being absolutely divided. She states:

> I felt, for the first time, what I have often and often felt since—a creeping chill come slowly over my flesh, and then a suspicion of something hidden near me, which would steal out and show itself if I looked that way. . . .
>
> The Thing stole out, dark and shadowy in the pleasant sunlight. At first, I saw only the dim figure of a woman. After a little, it began to get plainer, brightening from within outwards—brightening, brightening, till it set before me the vision of MY OWN SELF—repeated as if I was standing before a glass: the double of myself, looking at me with my own eyes. (605)

This doubling is the ultimate consequence of Hester's terrible suffering; she, like Lucy in "The Poor Clare" finally doubles as herself. In functioning as the return of the repressed for Anne, she also comes to embody even the repressed aspects of herself. The dangerous divisions inside her become a symptom of her madness; in response to the unbearable pressure that has comprised her life, she breaks in two. Her second self exhorts her to murder; by the end of the narrative, she has, indeed, become both victim and perpetrator.

Hester's split (victim and killer), ironically, becomes another aspect of her connection to Geoffrey who also ends as both killer and victim. The peculiar bond between them is manifested in and sealed by Geoffrey's reading of Hester's Confession. Hester has written her manuscript for her eyes alone; it is to be "buried" with her when she dies and "known to no other mortal creature" (581–82). "No mortal eyes but mine will ever see these lines," she states (599). She is to be her own and only reader. This splitting is another aspect of the divisions within her; she is both actor and watcher, teller and told. It is a terrible irony that the reader would finally come to read this manuscript through Geoffrey's eyes; it is as though Geoffrey has come to stand in for Hester's other self. This is a bizarre twist on the horror in which Hester is trapped since his reading of her manuscript enhances, indeed seals, the "relationship" between the two of them. Each of these two functions for the other as gazer and gazed upon, subject and object, victim and killer. They come to be the object and sign for each other. The encounters described above hint at the bizarre, the preternatural. The terror between all of these characters is created by that which cannot be realistically seen or heard; through them, we enter the world of the uncanny—the "thing" that terrifies, that hints of connections to the supernatural, and that defies rational explanation.

Hester is the most powerful figuration of the uncanny in the novel and this accounts not only for the strange distortions in her own behavior but also for the peculiarities that accrue around her relationships with almost every character in the novel. In his essay "The 'Uncanny,'" Freud comments on the part played by doublings, repetitions, and recurrences in the manifestation of the uncanny. The notion of repetition is not only a phenomenon of subjectivity, but something that occurs *between* people, something that can occur over generations, that can occur even between the living and the dead. Freud states:

> [T]he subject identifies himself with someone else, so that he is in doubt as to which his self is, or substitutes the extraneous self for his own. In other words, there is a doubling, dividing and interchanging of the self. And finally there is the constant recurrence of the same thing—the repetition of the same features or character-traits or vicissitudes, of the same crimes, or even the same names through several consecutive generations. (356)

Hester's relationship with Anne, with Geoffrey, with Anne's dead mother, and with herself are all manifestations of the uncanny, of "something repressed which *recurs*" (Freud 363) not only in these characters, but over generations. "[T]his uncanny," states Freud, "is in reality nothing new or alien, but something which is familiar and old-established in the mind and which has become alienated from it only through the process of repression" (363–64). Hester's ambivalent responses to Anne, her terrified collaborations with Geoffrey, and her dread of the spectral manifestations of her own self point not only in the directions of her madness and terror (and the madness and terror that is dispersed through all the characters), but also at earlier origins of familiarity and belonging. This uncanny duality would explain not only the apparently inexplicable familiarity she appears to experience with Anne, but also her collusion with Geoffrey, the greatest object of her terror and dread. There was a time, writes Freud, when the double "wore a more friendly aspect" (358); Hester embodies the perversion of that friendliness into shame, dread, and violence.

The uncanny connections between Hester and the main protagonists are also borne out by the use of coincidence in the novel. Coincidence always interrogates the boundaries of the realistic and the probable, since it tends to foreground a deliberate patterning or orchestration of events. In this sense, it appears unrealistic, or at least utterly improbable, that Hester should unexpectedly and without explanation open the door of the cottage at Fulham. But the use of coincidence here fulfills another function. The appearance of Hester at Fulham bears its own kind of psychic realism, manifesting aspects of Anne (and of Geoffrey) that will have to be confronted at Fulham. Thus, her presence functions to confirm a deep psychic reality. From this point on in the novel, Hester's role changes. As that which she embodies becomes momentous and overwhelming, she, who has been a minor character through the first two-thirds of the book, becomes a major actor in the development of events.

As the figure of Hester becomes increasingly sensational, she disrupts the realism of the narrative. In *Fictional Consensus and Female Casualties,* Elizabeth Ermarth argues that realism is "fundamentally a form of consensus"; for representational or realist fiction "consensus *creates* continuous time, the medium of growth and development" (2). Although it is possible at the level of story for individual characters to challenge the social consensus, "at the formal level . . . the consensus of realism cannot be challenged successfully without disturbing the effect of verisimilitude" (2). Thus, the maintenance of the illusion of verisimilitude presupposes social and political consensus, the maintenance of a common world. It follows that the breaking of the (realist) illusion implies disagreement, nonconsensus, subversion. "When the common medium is not sustained the represented world develops fissures, cracks in its identity," Ermarth states (5).

Hester functions as an ambiguous structure of indirection in the novel. On the one hand, as a figure of melodrama and of the sensational, she might be said (in Ermarth's terms) to intensify protest against convention and the law; she becomes a figure of hidden revolt figuring what Anne's veneer of middle-class respectability prevents her from confronting. On the other hand, the very use of melodrama might be said to detract from the realism of the text, implying that Hester's sufferings are somehow less than real (or so outside the realm of reality), that the very figure of extremity that Hester cuts renders her sufferings implausible.

Certainly, Hester's sufferings are extreme and so is her response to her suffering. In terms of the realistic narrative the figure that she finally becomes does emerge as extraordinary, unfamiliar, implausible. She exists on the margins of realism, questioning the boundaries of the probable. But Hester's shift into the world of the incredible is indicative of the fact that she has been *made* extreme; she is a symptom of the ills of a society that will not confront its own brutality. Thus, as the narrative progresses, Hester inhabits increasingly the world of the sensational and the bizarre. Jenny Bourne Taylor states that "Hester Dethridge, becomes an uncanny figure by both functioning as the extended analogue of Anne's position, and as the literal manifestation of a psychic response to violence and repression" (216).[6] Hester straddles two (at times contradictory) modes in the novel. Her shift in mode becomes the formal concomitant to her psychological story, namely, the tale of someone who has been forced over the edge. Thus, as the narrative progresses, the figure of Hester becomes increasingly bizarre, peculiar, strange; it speaks not so much of Hester's individual psychological response to her suffering but, much more significantly, of a world that can no longer contain her.

TEXTUALITY AND IDENTITY

Hester is one of the crucial structures of indirection in the novel. There are, however, other disruptions to the consensus engendered and demanded by realism. The text is filled with letters, telegrams, and notes, which create a formal fracturing and engender a sense of the text's fictionality by drawing attention to the writerliness of the text. Just as Hester functions as a disruption of the text, so does the writerliness of the novel undermine its own supposed truths by implying other texts (or many possible texts), other narratives, other lives that may have been lived. The text is formally fissured by its own repressions and the ambiguous mixture that this text comprises—of both announcing these repressions and also colluding with them—comes to function as a peculiar kind of subversion. These texts then speak indirectly to the unspeakability of the violence that Hester has suffered; they too become signifiers of the unrepresentability of real suffering.

Indeed, the most compelling, and most numerous, alternative texts in this novel are Hester's, which exist in the form of her manuscript—her letter written to herself—and the letters she constantly writes on her slate. Her letters function as arcane texts from another world, as prophecies, intimations, and warnings that underwrite her peculiar appearances and sightings. They provide a series of powerful questions and warnings that wind themselves through the dominant text; they are uncanny chantings from the underworld that exist beneath the supposedly rational world of propriety and the law. The single sentences and fragments that she writes on her slate, which appear as strange or even incomprehensible when read in isolation, join together to form an extremely coherent text which, surrounded by her customary silence, becomes quite powerful:

> "I keep nobody's secrets but my own." (116)
>
> "Who has done it?" (254)
>
> "Brought to it, by a man." (254)
>
> "I said, at the time, brought to it by a man. Did I say true?" (473)
>
> "Who is the man?" (474)
>
> "Tell me how he served you; did he knock you down?" (474)
>
> "We are loth to own it when they up with their fists and beat us—ain't we?" (474)
>
> "Frightened of *him*?" (567)

Her utterances frighten, embarrass, even enrage people. She infuriates Lady Lundie (and loses her job), devastates Blanche, frightens Anne, and terrifies Geoffrey. But her refusal to apologize, shift, or dilute her commentary becomes its own form of protest—a mute revolt based on immobility and silence. Hester's slate is one form of protesting the life and living death that has been hers.

Hester's second text—her Confession—is her other form of protest. The Confession is deeply poignant in itself because it is here that the dumb woman "speaks," and most eloquently, of her suffering. The Confession also functions as an interpolated narrative; it is an important disruption in the text which emerges as the "voice" of the silenced, the voice of the woman. It disrupts not only the current narrative voice and time, but since it is a voice from the past that was, in fact, designed to be buried with Hester, it also manifests itself as the voice from beyond the grave. Hester's muteness is, of course, the consequence of the violence that she has suffered since the blow she receives does, quite literally, silence her. But her muteness is a symptom not only of the fact that she has been personally beaten into silence but also of a legal and emotional world that has rendered it futile for her to speak. The magistrate, himself, comments:

> "Poor people in this condition of life don't even know what a marriage settlement means. And, if they did, how many of them could afford to pay the lawyer's charges?" Upon that, he turned to me. "Yours is a common case," he said. "In the present state of the law, I can do nothing for you." (586)

Hester finds no one who can do anything for her. "My story," she says "is always the same thing, over and over again. Best get to the end" (590). Since it is not possible for Hester's story to be heard, it is never possible for it to be different; she becomes that which Drucilla Cornell names as "the 'dumbness' before what cannot be 'heard' or 'read' because it cannot be articulated" (3). Since she cannot be articulated (culturally), she ceases to exist, as it were; we are reminded again of the narrator's comment that "(so far as all human interests were concerned) she was as completely out of the world, as if she had been screwed down in her coffin, and laid in her grave" (117). Collins utilizes the figure of Hester in order to convey the ways in which women can be psychically written and erased. All that remains of Hester are traces and tracings upon a slate and a Confession—and even that is stolen from her. Having begun her adult life with "a spirit of my own," as she terms it (586), her writings are the only ways left in which she can construct herself. They are all she is; one may indeed say that the loss of her Confession is the very death of her.

Thus, through the figure of Hester, Collins investigates the problematic questions of identity and subjectivity. He investigates the ways in which they are constructed and also the ways in which they are shattered. In this text, it is violence that functions as an image of the way in which a culture or a society can join in destroying its members. This shattering is conveyed in various ways.

One motif that is used in order to manifest the ways in which personalities can be torn apart is that of doubling. Hester functions as an image through which Anne both defines herself and fails to recognize herself. As Anne progresses through her nightmarish journey, she becomes like Hester, a writer of letters. She also becomes a blank text, that is, a text without letters that must be rewritten. She loses her name and becomes the generic Mrs. Graham, a name that obscures both her true identity and her true marital status. When she becomes delirious, her loss of identity is described in terms of texts, of lost markings and lost lettering. Her linen is unmarked, her handkerchief is unmarked, she carries no letters and no cards: "In every case the marks had been cut out" (327). For a long time following her illness and loss of identity, Anne has no home; existence is defined only by the letters between her and other people. These texts are for a time her only manifestation of existence in the story. Like Hester she becomes identified with modes of signification; like Hester she becomes a text without a context (she has lost her place in the world); and like Hester, her letters are read as communications from another world. Finally, like Hester, this move into textuality is a result of the violence that Anne suffers.

The loss of Anne's identity is inextricably bound up with the loss of her place. Like her mother, she is deprived of a socially sanctioned moral base, a surname (belonging to a man), and hence of a home. This also parallels Hester whose loss of self also begins with the loss of place. She describes the first traumatic incident in her marriage as the illegitimate selling of her furniture. There is an intimate connection between place and property, on the one hand, and identity, on the other. Since, as Bourne Taylor points out, "feminine identity is constituted through marriage as a property relationship" (213), it is logical that Anne ceases to exist when she flees; she becomes a text without a context and therefore one that cannot be read. Without this context, she becomes blank: "[T]he animating spirit was gone—the mere shell of the woman lived and moved, a mockery of her former self" (248).[7]

Anne's journey is marked by the series of locations, from which she is either locked out or locked in. Each of these functions as a not-home in which she does not belong and must not stay. The story opens with her panic-stricken expectation that expulsion from Windygates may be "a question of a few hours" (82). Indeed, her desperate desire for a private marriage with Geoffrey is to attain legitimacy in order that she be allowed *back* to Windygates, that she may be allowed to have a home with Blanche. The respectability that she would attain by her marriage to Geoffrey is a prerequisite for that home. Once she leaves Windygates, she is locked out; she has sealed her fate and may never return. Her next place is the Inn at Craig Fernie, which is as closed to Anne as if she had been a "stray dog" (121)—again, one is reminded of Geoffrey's treatment of animals. As with Windygates, once she leaves the Inn, she is locked out and has no option of returning.

The notion of being locked in or locked out is a crucial indication of the impasse that marriage creates for women. As Anne becomes a woman without a place, the focus on entries and exits, doors, windows, locks, and walls grows in the text. The motifs of boundaries and confinement wind their way through the novel, emphasizing Anne's position as a transgressor.[8] Anne develops a morbid suspicion about her place of abode becoming publicly known. When she finally goes home in response to Geoffrey's sinister "Mrs. Geoffrey Delamayn come home," it is to the "lonely house, isolated amid its high walls" (526). The narrative description here is carefully focused on the house and the way in which space is articulated. This detailed attention to the layout of the house becomes particularly significant at the end of the novel when Anne's confinement becomes literal, absolute, and potentially deathly.[9] Like Georgiana in "The Birth-Mark," she has been placed inside a space in which she can be killed. Anne's personal and sexual safety comes to rest on the architectural layout of the house:

> To a woman, escape from the place was simply impossible. Setting out of the question the height of the walls, they were armed at the top with a thick setting of jagged broken glass. A small back door, in the end wall (intended probably for the gardener's use) was secured by a lock—the key having been taken out. There was not a house near. The lands of the local growers of vegetables surrounded the garden on all sides. In the nineteenth century, and in the immediate neighbourhood of a great metropolis, Anne was as absolutely isolated from all contact with the humanity around her as if she lay in her grave. (556)

Fulham is, of course, Anne's second last home and it is here that her story reconnects with that of Hester. By the end of Anne's stay at Fulham, the walls must literally be taken apart to penetrate the space and to reveal its secrets. It is also here that Hester becomes overtly mad and is taken to her final home—the asylum.[10] At this point, the two women split irrevocably. Anne finds a home and a position once again, this time as Sir Patrick's wife. Marriage to Sir Patrick is the only way in which she can escape the prison of Fulham. Aspects of her psyche and of her former suffering appear to be simply buried at the end of the novel. (The death of her baby is one more version of this.) But these aspects of Anne remain alive in the form of Hester who figures as a symptom of both of their stories and is permanently incarcerated.[11]

The ambiguities and contradictions in the ending allow the novel to both announce and pull back from acknowledging the crises that it has investigated. The very neatness of the ending paradoxically highlights the lack of resolution and reminds us of Anne's suffering and of what is omitted. The arbitrariness, the extreme convenience of the death of Geoffrey, and most importantly, the removal of Hester serve to remind us of that which has not been resolved, but simply dispensed with, occluded, or denied. We are denied a final glimpse of Anne's psyche; aspects of her self and her suffering remain silent. The smoothly polished surface of the ending becomes indicative of disruptions the narrative voice prefers to avoid.[12]

But these very agitations, ambiguities, and contradictions are wound into the central concerns of *Man and Wife*. The story of Anne and Hester cannot be satisfactorily concluded because the society that has allowed violence to destroy them has not been rectified. Since women are not able to determine their future, they always hover potentially at the edge of social and sexual disaster. The labyrinth of individual psychological relations that occur in this novel is indicative of larger repressions and problems in the culture. If Hester is a repressed aspect of the relationship between Geoffrey and Anne, she also figures that which is repressed in the culture itself. The complex of misery in which Anne and Hester find themselves are not manifestations of their individual psyches, but of a society that destroys them.

THE LAW

The very title of the novel—*Man and Wife*—draws attention to the legalities of marriage and announces the *institution* of marriage to be its true subject. The phrase resonates through the text as it investigates the multiple marriages that occur in the novel, and is picked up in one of the most powerful passages in the text, in reference to the wedding ceremony of Blanche and Arnold:

> Then, the service began—rightly-considered, the most terrible surely of all mortal ceremonies—the service which binds two human beings, who know next to nothing of each other's natures, to risk the tremendous experiment of living together till death parts them—the service which says, in effect if not in words, Take your leap in the dark: we sanctify but we don't insure it! (374)

The passage is filled with its own ironies—"next to nothing," "risk," "leap in the dark" (even "mortal" carries overtones of death)—but its context renders it even more ironic. At the very moment that the narrator comments drily that "[t]he sun shone on Blanche's marriage," the reader is aware of Arnold's potentially bigamous status. Besides, this moment of ecstatic happiness—the sun, the "strewed flowers," the "joy-bells" (372–73)—exists in juxtaposition with the ominous narrative voice that has been warning of impending doom since the time that this wedding date has been set (292, 311, 314, 317). This voice rises to apocalyptic overtones on the night before the wedding:

> The first hour of the wedding-day was at hand, as the Truth made its final effort to struggle into light. The dark phantoms of Trouble and Terror to come, were waiting near them both at that moment. Arnold hesitated again—hesitated painfully. Sir Patrick paused for his answer. The clock in the hall struck the quarter to twelve.
>
> "I can't tell you!" said Arnold.
>
> "Is it a secret?"
>
> "Yes." (370)

The striking clock, the personifications of "Trouble" and "Terror," and the notion of a struggling Truth making its "final effort," all convey the sense that this marriage must and will be doomed. As events unfold, the marriage of Blanche and Arnold does, in fact, escape disaster, but almost every other marriage in the novel is blighted. The laws surrounding marriage wind their peculiar web of psychological and social constraints around people's lives; each case is different yet each case provides a ruinous example of what the law can do. The marriages of Hester, of Anne, of her mother before her, of Mr. and Mrs. Karnegie of the Sheep's Head Hotel are all examples of dreadful unions. Sir Thomas and Lady Lundie's marriage is also a bad one but its consequences tend to be comic rather than tragic. Society's laws for these arrangements appear to be largely economically motivated and it is the economic impact of these arrangements that appears most crucial.

The novel opens with an investigation into the economic prospects of the mothers of Anne and Blanche:

> Both were the children of poor parents; both had been pupil-teachers at the school; and both were destined to earn their own bread. (15)

From the outset what is emphasized is the relationship between marriage, property, and the law—the ways in which power is distributed through a society. When Vanborough becomes dissatisfied with his marriage, he carefully analyzes these constructions (indeed, it is these constructions that render him dissatisfied with his marriage in the first place) and with the help of his clever, inhumane lawyer, utilizes them to his own advantage and to his wife's destruction. The story of Anne's mother, and therefore of Anne's own childhood, is the story of legally constructed iniquities, iniquities that are passed on and replayed in the second generation.

This second generation's story—the story proper—opens with a description of the owls at Windygates who have lived "by the oldest of all existing rights—the right of taking" (53). This comic investigation of the owls who have come "with the creepers, into possession of the summer-house," who have lived comfortably with the "sense of superiority which the large bird feels everywhere over the small," and who have "slept their happy sleep by day, and found their comfortable meal when darkness fell" (54) becomes an analogue for "some human owls" whose predatoriness is investigated throughout the novel. Indeed, the economics of social relations dominate the plot of the novel. Sir Patrick's power and position in society, as well as "head of the household," makes it possible for him to protect Anne eventually, although even this protection is dependent upon the death of her husband who has absolute power over her:

> What can a married woman do for herself? . . . There were outrages which her husband was privileged to commit, under the sanction of marriage, at the bare thought of which her blood ran cold. . . . Law and Society armed her husband with his conjugal rights. Law and Society had but one answer to give, if she appealed to them:—You are his wife. (550)

Much of Hester's anguish is played out through property and the law. Unlike Anne who has Sir Patrick, Hester has no protection from a husband who destroys her. His physical attacks on her signify his economic power over her, and indeed it is for *economic* reasons, rather than for personal sadistic reasons that he remains with her. This is clarified repeatedly in Hester's Confession:

> "My good creature," says [the magistrate], "you are a married woman. The law doesn't allow a married woman to call anything her own—unless she has previously (with a lawyer's help) made a bargain to that effect with her husband, before marrying him. You have made no bargain. Your husband has a right to sell your furniture if he likes." (586)

> As long as I could make a farthing, he stuck to his wife. Being married to him, I had no right to have left him; I was bound to go with my husband; there was no escape for me. (589)

> All he had to do, was to put his hand into my pocket, and take what he wanted. (590)
>
> For the second time, he had robbed me of my own property, and had turned it into money to be spent in drink. (593)

In both the working-class and the middle-class marriages, the abuse suffered by the women is motivated by economic rather than psychological concerns. The violence, cruelty, and sadism manifested by both Joel and Geoffrey are presented as unfortunate byproducts, or consequences of, economic considerations which are actually sanctified by the law.

These economic negotiations are linked by the narrative voice to the violence in the novel. When Geoffrey takes Anne out of the room as his wife, he says to Sir Patrick:

> "The law tells her to go with her husband," he said. "The law forbids you to part Man and Wife."
>
> True. Absolutely, undeniably true. The law sanctioned the sacrifice of her, as unanswerably as it had sanctioned the sacrifice of her mother before her. In the name of Morality, let him take her! In the interests of Virtue, let her get out of it if she can! (526)

The narrator's use of the word "take" with its overtones of both sex and death hangs ominously over the scene and the threat of Geoffrey literally raping or killing Anne is horribly present. But the narrator also connects this scene back to Anne's mother who, although also destroyed by her husband, is never actually physically harmed by him. His act of destruction is an economic act, an act of fraud that is legally upheld; significantly enough, however, the narrative imagery used is the same as that which is used for the more literally violent marriages in the novel. The legal fraudulence of economic, sexual, and social relations is directly connected by the narrative voice to the violence in the novel. The narrator states that Vanborough is determined to "bury" Anne's mother (a word frequently associated with both Anne and Hester) and we are told that his abandonment of her is her "death blow" (22, 41). Vanborough's and Delamayn's abuse of power, which is not physical but is economically and gender based, becomes linked with actual crime. Economic social deception and murderous violence come to function together and mirror each other; they are both analogues for a whole system of corrupt power relations. Thus, Delamayn, the fraudulent lawyer of the first generation, is the father of Geoffrey, the murderous husband, in the second generation. Geoffrey begins by planning an escape from Anne that is reminiscent of the legal one that his father plans for Vanborough. But he ends up as a murderer—just like Joel Dethridge. Richard Barickman, Susan MacDonald, and Myra Stark point out that in "the sensational novels of Dickens and Collins . . . elaborate criminal intrigue is the truest analogue to respectable social relations" (26).

Étienne Balibar states that for Marx "legal forms" are "necessary and yet 'irrational,' *expressing and codifying* the 'economic' reality which each mode of production defines in its own way, and yet simultaneously *masking* it" (229). The law possesses a dual function; it expresses the values of a society (and maintains its order) and conceals and obscures some of the primitive structures on which the laws themselves may be based, namely, the maintenance of economic dominance. This is similar to the point made by Foucault (quoted in the Introduction) when he points out that "a legal decision . . . bears within it an assessment of normality and a technical prescription for a possible normalization" (20–21). The law upholds the state of affairs—indeed, it *is* the state of affairs. In *Man and Wife* the laws of marriage become a central focus through which the novel explores the "ambivalence" and "irrationality" built into the maintenance of the law.

Morality, virtue, and the law are all used to mask the social horror beneath. The novel is permeated with secrets that cause confusion and bewilderment and become an intricate aspect of the plot of the novel as it becomes increasingly unclear who knows what. The narrative is filled with indirections and ambiguities; there are "private" marriages that become indistinguishable from secret marriages that run into a series of escalating deceptions. Even the one happy marriage in the novel (that of Arnold and Blanche) is almost destroyed because of a secret between them, a subterfuge that enters their life the very day they become engaged. Hester Dethridge's marriage against the wishes of her family is semiprivate in the beginning (in that it lacks public endorsement) but by the end is hideously private in the isolated horror in which she comes to live. Her secret that is buried in the walls mirrors the larger deceptions of society. Although one of her first statements in the novel is "I keep nobody's secrets but my own" (116), her life and death embody the secrets of an entire culture.

Ultimately, the sense of secrecy inside the novel mirrors its own peculiar ambiguities. The novel both expresses and represses the terrible secrets of the culture it investigates.[13] On the one hand, the very neatness of the ending announces the lack of resolution and highlights that which has been occluded. On the other hand, the writerliness of the novel, its use of the uncanny, its complex investigation into violence and the law all function as subversive elements in the prevailing order. Collins's focus is not on the one happy marriage in the novel but on the outcast Anne, the victim Hester, on marriages and families as an implied center of crisis in a culture which deserves serious investigation. His use of arbitrary plot resolutions, which function to release his victims from truly impossible circumstances, is one way of conveying this crisis. Two of the central marriages in the novel are ended by the deaths of the husbands; that both of these deaths are excessively violent speaks to the violence and horror of the domestic situations in which Collins's victims are trapped. The only escape for the brutalized wives that the novels can conceive is, as in the case of "Janet's Repentance," the death of the husband. The home, in many instances in the novel, becomes not so much a sanctuary as a prison; it is a physical structure that upholds laws and institutions from which women have little chance of escape. The suffering of women, translated into the prevailing norms of a system, is only escaped in extraordinary and insane circumstances. In this instance the mutilations, madness, self-destruction, and death of Hester Dethridge function as signifiers for the unacknowledged and unresolved violence of the culture.

Conclusion

In "Janet's Repentance," Janet who has been, repeatedly and for years, beaten by her husband, finds herself unable to recall what has happened to her the night before. The morning light "throws its glare" onto a "hideous blank of something unremembered, something that must have made that dark bruise on her shoulder, which aches as she dresses herself" (238). Janet's dissociated confusion in regard to the bruise highlights the bruise's presence as a site of utter contradiction; it is both aching and unremembered, a "hideous blank" and darkly visible. Just as the "glare" of revealing light falls not on the "bruise," but on the "hideous blank of something unremembered," so the discursive illumination of this passage falls on a "blank" that is yet "something." The visible bruise acts as a marker for an invisible, denied, unremembered, and unrecorded act of violence, and at the same time is a synecdoche for her whole wounded body.

The repetition—"something . . . something"—emphasizes that the scene of violence is marked by an indefinable, unknowable quality; it is "something" which is both present and forgotten. Janet's bruise that is a "blank" thus constitutes a secret, one that she keeps from herself, one that she does not even know that she possesses. Distinguishing unknown and unknowable secrets from the ordinary secrets designed to preserve privacy or keep peace, Esther Rashkin defines the former as "a situation or drama that is transmitted without being stated and without the sender's or receiver's awareness of its transmission. . . . [It] is an interpersonal drama, experienced as too shameful to be articulated, which must be kept silent" (4). Janet's secret of unconscious shame and dread, however, is not only a manifestation of an "interpersonal drama"; it is also a secret that Janet's entire social and familial world insistently maintains. It is, in this sense, not only a secret kept *from* someone, but also a secret kept *for* someone. Janet herself might thus be said to be unconscious of this function in herself; her resistance to knowing is mirrored in the culture of denial which surrounds her.

This secret world evades articulation or explication; all attempts at speaking the secret are destined to fail. It is for this reason that confession, which belongs in the world of articulated speech, fails all of the characters in our texts. In contrast to the world of the confessional, psychoanalysis stresses what the subject (or the culture) does *not* know (or only partially knows), that is, what is unconscious; it positions itself uniquely between the inarticulable, which constantly attempts to speak, and that which must be spoken. In a debate with Foucault on the subject of confession and psychoanalysis, Jacques-Alain Miller foregrounds precisely this point as he exposes the essential limitations of confession: "In confessional procedures it is assumed that the subject *knows* the truth" (*Power/Knowledge* 216), he states. Our psychoanalytic study has attempted to penetrate the *unknown* and *unknowable* truths of nineteenth-century culture.

Psychoanalysis then, unlike confession, bridges the world of the unknown and the known, that which is inarticulable and that which attempts to speak. In the texts under consideration here, one manifestation of this unlikely place, this undefinable bridge between two worlds, is the uncanny, that "class of the frightening," as Freud says, "which leads back to what is known of old and long familiar" (340). The uncanny emerges in various forms in the texts we have considered here, but the proliferation of doublings, coincidences, repetitions, recurrences, and spectral presences is suggestive, always gesturing in the direction of that which cannot quite be spoken. The strange and estranged sense of something known, yet forgotten and lost suffuses the texts: Aurora Leigh's strangely haunted and haunting recognition of Marian Erle in Italy ("that face persists"); Hester Dethridge's bizarre connections to most of the main characters in *Man and Wife,* including her own double and Anne's dead mother; Lucy's spectral self; the mysterious atmosphere of "The Birth-Mark," are all manifestations of unknown and unknowable secrets, secrets that are attached to the marked, reviled body of the woman.

But psychoanalysis possesses its own secrets. At the end of his essay "The 'Uncanny'" (1919), Freud remarks that psychoanalysis, which is "concerned with laying bare . . . hidden forces, has itself become uncanny to many people" (366). As a corollary to this, we may say that the frequent occurrences of the uncanny in the texts under consideration here may stand in not only for the unspeakable aspects of culture and family that we have investigated, but also for psychoanalysis itself. Psychoanalysis, like the uncanny, is both profoundly estranging and intensely familiar. While it is, on the one hand, intensely bound up with the intimacies of desire, self, family, and sexuality and is in this sense deeply known, it is, on the other hand, concerned with the unconscious manifestations of these phenomena and is therefore also utterly strange and estranging. Like its subject matter, psychoanalysis is itself uncanny, destined always to conceal as it reveals. Lacan states:

> Until further notice, we can say that *the elements do not answer in the place where they are interrogated.* Or more exactly, as soon as they are interrogated somewhere, it is impossible to grasp them in their totality. (*Séminaire II.* 281; qtd. in and trans. by Felman, *Lacan* 78)

Psychoanalysis finds the objects of its analysis to be perpetually elsewhere, "impossible to grasp." It is uncanny; in turn, the uncanny comes to function as a figure of psychoanalysis' own (inevitable) resistance to itself.

The mutually implicated relationship that is revealed here (between psychoanalysis and the uncanny) also uncovers the singular connections between psychoanalysis and the domestic worlds that we investigate. While these fictional worlds reveal thoroughly familiar forces of society and family to be at work, the secrets of these worlds are half-revealed and half-concealed by uncanny ghostly presences, presences that point in the direction of a meaning that is in excess of itself. These uncanny presences are manifestations not only of the unconscious shame and dread associated with the domestic realm, but function in turn as figurations of psychoanalysis, the very process that is used to investigate these worlds, these secrets, and indeed these ghostly presences themselves. The intricate family relationships in these texts uncover psychoanalysis as surely as it uncovers them. Each reveals and exposes the other, attempting to render visible that which is otherwise obscure. Out of the same culture that produced these texts comes psychoanalysis; both disciplines produce their culture and expose it; both reveal its secrets and keep them.

Two key secrets haunt the edge of each text we investigate, and hover over its ending, defying closure or resolution: the secret of male violence, and the secret of the reviled, abjected body of the beaten woman. Since these secrets are unspeakable and unrepresentable, they manifest themselves in what Steven Marcus terms the "deformed language of symptoms, the untranslated speech of the body" (196); through this opaque enunciation, we might apprehend the bruised body of Janet, the spectral body of Lucy, the deformed body of Hester. These figurations render the body both present and absent; they evade signification; they gesture in the direction of meaning and simultaneously deny its existence; they are an injunction to silence, to evasion, to dread.

Indeed, the extent of the representational complexities that accrue around the marked body of the woman speaks to the extent of evasion or deferral on which culture insists. There is an inextricable relationship between the representation of the marked bodies, which emerges as a site of contradiction and of phantasmagoria, and the hegemonic discourse that ostensibly denies the existence of that site. Foucault discusses this phenomenon in *The History of Sexuality*, where he explains how dominant discourses *produce* the very discourses they repress or obscure:

> We must make allowance for the complex and unstable process whereby discourse can be both an instrument and an effect of power, but also a hindrance, a stumbling-block, a point of resistance and a starting point for an opposing strategy. Discourse transmits and produces power; it reinforces it, but also undermines and exposes it, renders it fragile and makes it possible to thwart it. (101)

This powerful dialectical relationship (between the hegemonic discourse and its opposition) manifests itself in each of the texts in our study. Inextricably related to the detailed explorations of middle-class domestic life are the spectral manifestations of what may not be mentioned, ghostly presences that hover at the interstices of the texts. Each text first gives rise to such disclosures and then, as though unable to tolerate the force of its own disclosure, returns the reader to a comfortable, customary domestic middle-class environment. "The Birth-Mark" might provide the best example of this, not least because it is the only text in our study in which the consequences of domestic violence are followed through to their horrific conclusion: the death of the protagonist. After Georgiana's death, we are returned to the real world by the bland, normative comments of the narrator. He comments on the tale's outcome twice: at the beginning of the story, he tells us that the marriage "was attended with truly remarkable consequences" (37); at the end he tells us regretfully that Aylmer "need not thus have flung away . . . happiness" (56). Although he finds the "consequences" of the marriage to be truly "remarkable," he fails to "remark" that the young, beautiful bride has ended up dead.

This pattern is followed variously by the texts in this study. Both Janet Dempster and Anne Silvester are saved by the timely deaths of their brutal husbands; Marian Erle, who has died psychically, conveniently no longer wishes to be married to Romney; Lucy is putatively but unconvincingly "restored" to her own self. These spectral, subversive presences appear to dissolve as the female body is returned to the normative domestic realm and succumbs to it. (Women in nineteenth-century fiction who do *not* return to this realm end up dead: Georgiana, Bertha Mason, Lady Dedlock, Emma Bovary, Tess). In the texts we examine, these bodies step back from the liminal into the consensual world of community; yet in each case the destroyed body haunts an ending that attempts to ignore its very existence. The reader is thus insistently returned to an environment that is haunted by the very discourse it has both created and then suppressed.

The imbricated relationship between the hegemonic discourse and that which it attempts to repress accounts for the occluded, distorted representation of the bodies of the women who haunt these texts, and for the deformed, secretive forms of evasion to which these repressions have given rise. Janet's "blank" is echoed repeatedly; Marian Erle is unconscious when raped; Lucy is literally haunted by a phantom of which she has no knowledge or understanding. In "The Birth-Mark," Georgiana wakes from a charmed sleep to find herself in a scene that "looked like enchantment" (44), the very scene in which her husband will kill her; "For aught Georgiana knew, it might be a pavilion among the clouds" (44), states the narrator, utilizing an image that highlights not only the unreality of her prison, but also ironically foreshadows her death. Even in the case of *Barchester Towers,* where we are not taken out of the realist world, middle-class violence occurs in a foreign country, which is figured as "another world" from the perspective of the English middle class. In every text we have explored in this book the moments of violence, the marking, the beating, and (in the case of "The Birth-Mark") the killing are represented as moments out of the real world or real time, moments of liminality. In each case the reader is thrust into a phantasmagoric, haunted, alien environment, which functions to signify the supposed unreality (impossibility) of bourgeois domestic violence.

The relationship between the represented realistic bourgeois world and that which is occluded or rendered invisible by that world is not, as Foucault's comments cited above indicate, one of simple opposition. Indeed, throughout the century, as nineteenth-century realist texts concern themselves increasingly with human consciousness and with psychical reality, it might be said that it is the very *intensification* of realism that gives rise to these hauntings. The mid-nineteenth century embarked upon intense scrutiny of divorce law and marital cruelty; that the realist texts of this era simultaneously awaken themselves to these issues and deny them, seems to arise from the pressure of a knowledge that is in excess of realism's capacity to represent it. This excess is in part formally represented by the infiltration of other generic modes into realism. Thus, realism might be said to give way to romance in chapter 1, to sensationalism in chapter 6, or to function in the strangely hybrid way that it does in *Aurora Leigh* (a prose poem) in chapter 5. But even in the texts that might be defined as fully realist, there are moments when realism appears to overleap itself, when, through a paradoxical trope that encapsulates simultaneously both intensification and denial, it topples over into phantasmagoria, liminality, the spectral. The concept of an intensified realism, of a realism that almost sickens on itself is touched upon by Erich Auerbach in his accomplished study of the representation of the "real" in European literature. Discussing Balzac's representation of contemporary life, he demonstrates how Balzac creates a sense of reality by appealing to the mimetic imagination of the reader and then uses that very reality to create a "sort of second significance which, though, different from that which reason can comprehend, is far more essential—a significance which can best be defined by the adjective demonic" (472). Auerbach's use of the word *demonic* encapsulates precisely how realism, in its very efforts to represent the "real," can in itself become spectral. Out of the interstices and gaps of its own symbolic order, realism creates the other, which announces its presence through a subliminal absence and haunting of the text.

Naomi Schor identifies the haunting and haunted "other" produced by realism quite precisely as the figure of the woman. "Realism," she states "is that paradoxical moment in Western literature when representation can neither accommodate the Otherness of Woman nor exist without it" (xi). This is echoed by Shoshana Felman who also utilizes the language of the supernatural in her analysis of the status of women in critical readings of Balzac's realism. She states in *What does a Woman Want?* that in critical readings of "Balzac's 'realism' . . . the woman is relegated to non-existence, since she is said to partake of the 'unreal' ":

> A subtle boundary line, which gives itself as a "natural frontier," is thus traced, in the critical vocabulary, between the realm of the "real," and that of the "unreal," between the category of "realism" and that of the so-called supernatural. (29–30)[1]

"Unreal," "supernatural," or "demonic," these female presences that haunt the edges of the realist text are the silenced, abjected others who express that which cannot be contained or articulated inside the realms of realism. They speak a misery that may not necessarily have been inherent in their own beings, which might be outside in a social, cultural, and paternal matrix—but which they come to possess. This misery is revealed in both the physical body and in mental torment, in both daughters and mothers, in afflictions that are passed on through the generations. The abused female body is one such haunted other.

Notes

INTRODUCTION

1. Although this book does not undertake an analysis of male victims of domestic violence, there are, of course, instances of female aggressors represented in Victorian literature. When Mr. Bumble in *Oliver Twist* asserts to his new wife, the workhouse matron, that within marriage, "[t]he prerogative of a man is to command" (227), Mr. Bumble finds his hat knocked off, and his head exposed:

> [T]he expert lady, clasping him tight round the throat with one hand, inflicted a shower of blows (dealt with singular vigour and dexterity) upon it with the other. This done, she created a little variety by scratching his face, and tearing his hair off; and having, by this time, inflicted as much punishment as she deemed necessary for the offence, she pushed him over a chair, which was luckily well situated for the purpose: and defied him to talk about his prerogative again. (228)

Similarly, Mrs. Joe throwing Pip at Joe Gargery as a "connubial missile" in chapter 2 of *Great Expectations* and the story of the "churning" of Jack Dollop in chapter 21 of *Tess of the d'Urbervilles* are also comically rendered but clear instances of violence. Thackeray's drawing of Becky "in the character of Clytemnestra" in chapter 67 of *Vanity Fair* suggests an even more sinister propensity for female violence. Yet all of these instances, at least, contain a comic germ unlike most of the representations of male violence which this book examines. Even the comic novel, *Barchester Towers,* does not treat male domestic violence itself as a comic event.

2. The *Oxford English Dictionary* first cites the colloquial "wife-beating" from Mary Russell Mitford's *Our Village: Sketches of Rural Character and Scenery* (1830), when she makes reference to the "wife-beating tyrant." Frances Power Cobbe's graphic enumeration of the spectrum of "wife-beating, wife-torture, and wife-murder" (132) appears in 1878.

3. Woolf's other solution to female invisibility is to call for a "supplement to history" (*Room* 58), which would provide factual rather than imaginative evidence of women's lives. Such "supplements" documenting marriage laws and domestic violence have now been written by social historians such as Maeve Doggett, James A. Hammerton, Lee Holcombe, Joan Perkin, and Mary Lyndon Shanley.

4. Critics of the Gothic such as Kate Ferguson Ellis in *The Contested Castle,* Michelle A. Massé in *In the Name of Love*, and Anne Williams in *Art of Darkness* comment on the bourgeois realism that inhabits such tropes as the "haunted castle."

5. In justice to Cobbe, one should note that she is caught in something of a dilemma; her political project requires assistance from the very "gentleman" whose actions she might in some instances condemn: "I entreat my readers not to turn away and forget this wretched subject. I entreat the gentlemen of England,—the bravest, humanest, and most generous in the world,—not to leave these helpless women to be trampled to death under their very eyes" (Cobbe 164). The most that Cobbe is willing to admit is that "[w]ife-beating exists in the upper and middle classes rather more, I fear, than is generally recognized; but it rarely extends to anything beyond an occasional blow or two of a not dangerous kind. . . . The dangerous wife-beater belongs almost exclusively to the artisan and labouring classes" (Cobbe 134).

6. The notion that poor and working-class women form a "victim type" is indebted to Marie-Christine Leps's analysis of the medical and anthropological discourse of the "criminal type" in the nineteenth century. Leps analyzes how this discursive construction "indicates both the limits and the origins of the power exercised by a knowledgeable white male bourgeois elite" (Leps 64).

7. The great exception in Dickens's work is the honest blacksmith Joe Gargery; he submits to Mrs. Joe's tyranny because he thoroughly appreciates the results of male violence against women. Explaining to Pip why he does not "rise" in rebellion against her persecution, Joe recounts his own history:

> "And last of all, Pip—and this I want to say very serous to you, old chap—I see so much in my poor mother, of a woman drudging and slaving and breaking her honest hart and never getting no peace in her mortal days, that I'm dead afeerd of going wrong in the way of not doing what's right by a woman, and I'd fur rather of the two go wrong the t'other way, and be a little ill-conwenienced myself. I wish it was only me that got put out, Pip; I wish there warn't no Tickler for you, old chap; I wish I could take it all on myself; but this is the up-and-down-and-straight on

> it, Pip, and I hope you'll overlook shortcomings." (*Great Expectations* 79–80)

Having seen his own mother being beaten by his father, Joe takes the moral path in marriage, as in all else. Never a "gentleman," never comfortable with the clothes, conduct, or codes of that class, he is nevertheless the novel's only true man, transcending what Pip discovers to be the pettiness of "middle-class morality." Still, Joe's exemplary treatment of Mrs. Joe does not save her from a beating; Orlick's aggression, mirroring Pip's, renders Mrs. Joe a permanent invalid. There is no marital cruelty in *Great Expectations,* but there is "a woman being beaten."

8. Nord (8–11) also discusses the extension of this literal contagion into images of, for example, the streetwalker as "an agent of far-reaching contamination" (11). Similarly, typhus and cholera passed from poor to bourgeois neighbourhoods.

9. Before 1857, divorce was only available to those few whose wealth allowed them to pursue a divorce *(a vinculo matrimonii)* through a private act of Parliament. Poor women faced with persistent "cruelty" could apply to the ecclesiastical courts for a legal separation—divorce *a mensa et thoro*—which allowed women to live separately from their husbands, but it did not allow them to remarry, or control their property or their wages. They could also "pray the peace" against their husbands before a magistrate; the husband who failed to keep the peace would be fined or forfeit a security (Doggett 100, 5).

The Divorce and Matrimonial Causes Act of 1857 took marital matters out of the ecclesiastical courts and into the new civil Divorce Court. The Divorce Act imposed a double standard, however, in that a man could obtain a divorce for his wife's adultery but a woman could only obtain a divorce if her husband combined adultery with another offense—cruelty, bigamy, bestiality, incest, rape, sodomy, or desertion (Doggett 100). The wife would thus not be granted a divorce if her husband were cruel but not adulterous, though she could apply for what in 1857 was called a judicial separation.

Refinement of what constituted marital cruelty occurred in the 1878 Matrimonial Causes Act, which specified that a judicial separation would be granted to the wife of a cruel but nonadulterous husband only if that husband had been convicted of aggravated assault against her, and only if the magistrate was "satisfied that the future safety of the wife [was] in peril" (qtd. in Doggett 131). By the end of the century the grounds for separation were broadened; the Summary Jurisdiction (Married Woman) Act (1895) allowed a woman to separate from her husband if he "deserted her, forced her by wilful neglect or persistent cruelty to leave him, or was sentenced on indictment to pay a fine of more than £5 or to a term of imprisonment exceeding two months for assaulting her" (Doggett 144). Both before and after 1857, then, the definition of cruelty was a crucial one.

10. James Hammerton claims that it is only after 1869 that physical violence ceases to be a requirement for a finding of cruelty ("Victorian Marriage" 282). For instance, in 1854 Lushington ruled in *Chestnutt v. Chestnutt* that there was no legal cruelty:

> Here is no charge either of bodily violence inflicted, or of threats of personal ill treatment. However disgusting the language charged, if proved, may be—however degrading habits of intoxication—however annoying to a wife, especially the wife of a gentleman and a clergyman—these facts standing alone, do not constitute legal cruelty. If it be said that the consequences to the wife are mental suffering and bodily ill-health, I do not think that the case would be carried further. The same might be said of other vices . . . [which] might occasion great mental suffering, and consequent thereon, bodily ill-health to the wife; but they do not constitute legal cruelty. (1854: 164 *English Reports* 115, qtd. in Hammerton, "Victorian Marriage" 282–83).

The 1869 case of *Kelly v. Kelly* saw a significant extension in the definition of cruelty from physical violence to mental suffering. The couple argued about many things, including the disposition of a sum of money bequeathed to Frances Kelly and the treatment of their son. James Kelly claimed that his wife was plotting against her, forbade visitors from coming to see Frances, and told the servants to take no orders from her, which, Hammerton argues, is a striking and humiliating displacement from the sphere of authority supposedly granted to middle-class Victorian women. Under the strain of his demands, Frances's health broke down. In her petition to the court in 1869, Frances Kelly was indeed granted her request for separation; the judge Wilde was struck by her unfair removal from her proper position—"she was entirely deposed from her natural position as mistress of her husband's house"—and concludes that "without disparaging the just and paramount authority of a husband, it may be safely asserted that a wife is not a domestic slave, to be driven at all costs, short of personal violence, into compliance with her husband's demands" (qtd. in Hammerton, "Victorian Marriage" 287, 288). The case thus ended in a finding of cruelty, for even though James Kelly's actions were not violent, the consequences of his actions on his wife—the loss of her health—still constituted cruelty (Hammerton, *Cruelty* 129).

For a more detailed analysis of *Evans v. Evans* see Andrew Dowling's essay on the Divorce Court in Eliot's fiction.

11. Even when violent physical cruelty had been proven, separation did not automatically follow. As Caroline Norton says in her *Review of the Divorce Bill of 1856,* even "a long course of misconduct" by the husband, which the wife "*condoned,*—as the law calls amiable, Christian-like forbearance," stripped the wife of the right to use that cruelty as legal evidence against her husband (12). For example, Frances Curtis petitioned the Divorce Court for a judicial separation from her husband in 1858 on the grounds of cruelty; the judge Cresswell agreed that there had been cruelty, but found that the "continued cohabitation for years afterwards constituted condonation of the offence, which could only be revived by further violence or threats of violence" (Hammerton, "Victorian Marriage" 284–85).

12. Andrew Dowling argues that the new court "fuelled an interest and created an audience for tales of matrimonial breakdown" (328).

13. Joan Copjec argues in *Read My Desire* that psychoanalysis is uniquely positioned to account for a desire that reveals both that which "*must be articulated*" and that which "*is inarticulable,*" that which will "register itself *negatively* in speech" (14).

14. Bronfen is speaking here specifically about representations of the "beautiful feminine corpse"; however, her larger argument about seeing beyond "what is not in fact visibly there" (xi) also obtains in our study.

CHAPTER 1. "A FRIGHTFUL OBJECT"

1. In *Body Work,* Peter Brooks discusses the ways in which the literary notion of the token or identifying mark comes to look "suspiciously like a linguistic signifier. The sign imprints the body," he says, "making it part of the signifying process. Signing or marking the body signifies its passage into writing, its becoming a literary body, and generally also a narrative body, in that the inscription of the sign depends on and produces a story" (3).

2. The narrative ambiguities of this tale may, to some extent, mirror the authorial ambiguities present in Hawthorne's two entries in *The Notebooks* in his preparatory notes for "The Birth-Mark." The first reads: "A person to be in the possession of something as perfect as mortal man has a right to demand; he tries to make it better, and ruins it entirely:—For instance, a noble mansion, and in his attempts to improve it, he causes it to fall to the ground" (*Lost* 56). In the second, he writes: "A person to be the death of his beloved in trying to raise her to more than mortal perfection; yet this should be a comfort to him for having aimed so highly and holily" (*American Notebooks* 8:184). The differences between these two entries are extremely instructive.

In the first, the subject "ruins" the object of his attentions, which is specified as a magnificent possession—a noble mansion. In the second, the object of attention is a human being and the situation has been gendered; the subject is male, the object is female, and the "nobility" of the object in the first entry has been reassigned to the subject who has aimed "highly and holily." In short, the potential censure implicit in the first entry ("ruin") has given way to a kind of admiration in the second ("highly and holily"). In turn, however, the echo of *Macbeth* rings the changes on further ambiguities; Lady Macbeth's words—"What thou wouldst highly,/ That wouldst thou holily" (1.5.17–18)—are spoken in the context of her murderous determination to shift these noble qualities. The allusion then enhances the ambiguities that haunt the entries in Hawthorne's notebooks as well as the text of "The Birth-Mark" itself.

3. It is possible to divide the critical response into two large camps. Critics who read the mark with the assumption that it is a "blemish" tend to see Aylmer, in one form or another, as an idealist, albeit failed, whose "fault" then lies in having longed for perfection on earth. Concomitantly, Georgiana's collusion with him is a sign of her spiritual perfection. See, for example, Cleanth Brooks and Austin Warren: "What the story emphasises is not Aylmer's self conceit but rather his possession of the questing spirit which will not resign itself to the limitations and imperfections of nature" (104); Arlin Turner: "Two concluding sentences detract nothing from the loftiness of Aylmer's purpose or from his wife's understanding and heroism. . . . In 'The Birthmark' an obsession with a noble purpose produces tragic results" (163–64); and Richard Fogle who states that Aylmer "is punished . . . because of his genuine idealism" (187).

Critics who read the mark as a signifier for Georgiana's femininity and sexuality see Aylmer as sexually perverse, sadistic, and a murderer. See Allan Gardner Lloyd Smith who discusses Aylmer's perversion (97–98), or Frederick Crews who discusses his sadism (20). For other readings along these lines, see also James Quinn and Ross Baldessarini 92; Simon Lesser 88; Jules Zanger 368; Richard Millington 27; and Judith Fetterley 25.

4. Compare Steven Youra who also highlights the absoluteness of Aylmer's vision when he points out that Aylmer invests his reading of the mark with "transcendental significance" (44).

5. Jules Zanger highlights the narrative collusion in the way the story is read pointing out that the interpretation of the story that regards the mark on Georgiana's cheek as "the external sign of her human, imperfect condition and understands Aylmer's attempt to remove it as the expression of either scientific, rational, reformist presumption, or of too aspiring an idealism . . . is suggested by the narrator's comments" (364).

6. Judith Fetterley attributes this desire for concealment to Hawthorne, stating that he seems as "eager to be misread and to conceal as he is to be read

and to reveal" (31). It seems more useful to focus on the narrative ambiguities, noticeable throughout, but most particularly at the end of the tale.

7. For other discussions of the Pygmalion motif in the tale, see Robert Arner 168–71; Robert Heilman 577; Youra 46, 47; and Crews 156.

8. When Aylmer the artist attempts to take Georgiana's portrait, he fails:

> Georgiana assented—but, on looking at the result, was affrighted to find the features of the portrait blurred and indefinable; while the minute finger of a hand appeared where the cheek should have been. (45)

His portrait of her results in the further reduction and fragmentation of his object from hand to finger. Indeed, as Youra points out, he actually produces "a true picture of how he sees her—a blurred image whose only distinct feature is the minute hand imprinted on her cheek" (47).

CHAPTER 2. DOMESTIC VIOLENCE, ABJECTION, AND THE COMIC NOVEL

1. "But, in general, he has a wholesome mistrust of morbid analysis, an aversion to inflicting pain. . . . There was nothing in his theory of the story-teller's art that tended to convert the reader's or the writer's mind into a vessel for polluting things. He recognised the right of the vessel to protest, and would have regarded such a protest as conclusive" (James, "Trollope" 1883: 57).

2. See Nicola Thompson for an analysis of how Trollope's interest in domestic realism and in the psychology of his female characters resulted in his fiction being considered "feminine" by his contemporaries.

3. On the representation of the crippled body, compare Lennard J. Davis, who remarks that critical accounts of the broken body in the realm of sculpture, of the Venus de Milo, for instance, "[look] away from incompleteness . . . [in a manner] that allows the art historian still to see the statue as an object of desire" (57).

4. The specific context of Michie's remarks is the figuration of Lily Dale's body in Trollope's *The Small House at Allington,* and the way in which William Dean Howells, in his *Heroines of Fiction* (1901), provides a fantasized "full" description of Lily's body.

5. Cindy LaCom claims that while it may appear that "Trollope . . . challenge[s] cultural norms by making Neroni sexual [rather than asexual], he also condemns female sexuality by implying that it is inherently deformed" (194). Noting the Signora's powerfully satiric critique of marriage

and sentimentality, Richard Barickman, Susan MacDonald, and Myra Stark argue that Neroni's crippled status "is evidence of Trollope's ambivalent attitudes toward such an open challenge by a woman to the respectable system of sexual relations and toward even such a subdued expression of female sexual desire" (55). Christopher Herbert, in his reading of the novel, argues that Signora Neroni's "compulsive seduction of men clearly is a pathological compensation for the absence of all hope of erotic pleasure" (170).

6. Compare U. C. Knoepflmacher who asserts that the novel "relies on the juxtaposition of the ostensible and the implied . . . between facade and motive, between . . . the 'outer' and the 'inner' man" (*Laughter and Despair* 27).

7. The sight of a "physical defect" (102), a blemished body, is included in Kristeva's list of experiences that lead to abjection.

8. LaCom argues that Signora Neroni finally articulates bourgeois cultural values; she wants at the end of the novel a "union with a good man and a body/object that can nurture such a union and produce the children so important to her role in the domestic sphere" (196). Thus, her expulsion from Barchester is almost tragic. Compare Sheila Burgar, who claims that "Trollope ends Madeline's connection with Barchester on a generous and humane note" (44) by allowing her a crucial role in the successful romance of Eleanor and Arabin.

9. An almost identical scene occurs in Trollope's *He Knew He Was Right;* Nora Rowley reflects that Hugh Stanbury "had behaved very badly to her, certainly, taking her by the hand and putting his arm around her waist. And then had he not even attempted to kiss her?" (301) However, Nora's anger at the "violence of her lover"(300) soon shifts since his romantic attentions are, in fact, not unwelcome:

> She had never thought that he had been such a one as that, to ill-use her, to lay a hand on her in violence, to refuse to take an answer. She threw herself on the bed and sobbed, and then hid her face,—and was conscious that in spite of this acting before herself she was the happiest girl alive. (301)

Slope's behavior, then, is ungentlemanly only in its particularity, not as an absolute.

CHAPTER 3. VIOLENCE, CAUSALITY, AND THE "SHOCK OF HISTORY"

1. Andrew Dowling examines marital conflict in Eliot's fiction as a response to the Divorce Act, and suggests that "Janet's Repentance" is Eliot's first attempt at representing matrimonial cruelty. The physical violence of this

story, he argues, yields to more subtle explorations of psychological cruelty in later works such as *Middlemarch* and *Daniel Deronda*.

2. George Eliot's editors agree that the story of "Janet's Repentance" is based on events that occurred in Nuneaton during her stay at Mrs. Wallington's school from 1828–1832. Mr. Jones, the original of the Evangelical clergyman Mr. Tryan, died when the young Mary Anne Evans was twelve years of age; the details of his story were impressed on her by Maria Lewis, the principal teacher at Mrs. Wallington's school and an ardent supporter of Jones. In his biography of George Eliot, Gordon S. Haight writes: "Mr Tryan, her hero, is an idealized portrait of Mr Jones, the Evangelical curate at Nuneaton. Her version of his persecution at the hands of Janet's husband, the brutal Lawyer Dempster, was derived from Jones's staunchest disciples, Maria Lewis and Mrs Buchanan, and heavily slanted towards the Evangelical side" (Haight, *Biography* 227). Facts about the originals for the Dempsters—the lawyer J. W. Buchanan and his wife Nancy Wallington (a friend of Maria Lewis)—are less clear: "The Buchanans appear as the Dempsters in all the 'keys' to the originals of 'Janet's Repentance' circulated in Warwickshire after its publication in 1857" (Haight, *Biography* 9–10). For the most detailed account of the lives of Mr. Jones and the Buchanans see Haight (*Originals*) 5–7.

George Eliot herself testifies to the essential truthfulness of the story. In a letter to John Blackwood on June 11, 1857, Eliot replies to some of the concerns her publisher had expressed after he read the manuscript of the early chapters of "Janet's Repentance." He has requested that she "*soften*" the harshness of her story, and in response she claims to have already allowed as much softening as the story will permit:

> Everything is softened from the fact, so far as art is permitted to soften and yet to remain essentially true. The real town was more vicious than my Milby; the real Dempster was far more disgusting than mine; the real Janet alas! had a far sadder end than mine, who will melt away from the reader's sight in purity, happiness, and beauty. . . . There is nothing to be done with the story, but either to let Dempster and Janet and the rest be as I *see* them, or to renounce it as too painful. (*Letters* II: 347)

3. U. C. Knoepflemacher complains that the novella is "sentimental and schematic," and at times "smacks of . . . cheap melodrama" (*George Eliot* 79, 83); Thomas A. Noble claims that the domestic plot has "serious defects," including a "crude sentimentality" (176) but commends the social portrait of Milby and Evangelicalism, a point taken up by Suzanne Graver in her study of Eliot and community.

4. Gilbert and Gubar claim that Eliot's depiction of domestic violence is not done directly, but rather "very tactfully, from her description of Janet's

'wounded' consciousness of 'the riddle of her life' (chap. 13) to a factual explanation that her husband" controlled the family property (488).

5. The extreme realism of the story has prompted twentieth-century "diagnoses" of Dempster and Janet. Stephanie Demetrakopoulos claims that "Janet's recovery rests on the principles set forth later in the twelve steps of Alcoholics Anonymous" (96). J. W. Bennett assigns Janet and Dempster to "Type 1" and "Type 2" classifications of alcoholism according to their drinking patterns. Dempster as a Type 2 alcoholic is "tough-minded, confident, uninhibited, impulsive, excitable. Onset is early; fighting, accidents, and arrests are common; and guilt about alcohol dependence is infrequent" (60). Janet on the other hand is a Type 1 alcoholic: "eager to help others, sentimental, shy, and loyal. Age of onset is usually after twenty-five, fighting and arrests while drinking are rare, and guilt feelings about drinking are common" (60). Sheila Shaw reads the incident of Janet's discovery of the brandy bottle as an example of what Alcoholics Anonymous members call "budding," that is "Building Up to a Drink" (176).

Peter Fenves is an example of a critic who strongly resists this medical/sociological pattern of reading, and suggests instead, for instance, that given the text's own construction of the term "alcoholic," "Janet does not fit the species 'alcoholic' at all" (428).

6. See Matthew 13:31–32.

7. Critics such as David Carroll and Andrew B. Lynn have addressed epistemological questions in Eliot's work in general and in *Scenes of Clerical Life* in particular. Sally Shuttleworth claims that by late in her career—in *Daniel Deronda*—Eliot's narrative methodology resembles that of "the creative, experimental scientist" (xii). Our chapter suggests that Shuttleworth's claim also holds true for Eliot's earlier work, that is, that in "Janet's Repentance" Eliot offers various paradigms for understanding the cause of domestic violence, and then tests the efficacy of these paradigms.

8. The stimulant "bark" refers to the bark of the Cinchona tree, which is powdered and administered to reduce fever. Quinine is derived from this bark (*Oxford English Dictionary*).

9. Medical practitioners in "Janet's Repentance" provide a curious match for their patient's illnesses. Although Mr. Pratt originally attends Dempster, when Pratt becomes a Tryanite, Dempster switches his allegiance to Pilgrim. Dempster would seem to be the ideal patient for Pilgrim; he is naturally plethoric, his face "purple and swollen" in illness, his "eyes dilated" (276), and his symptoms heightened by the unwise taking of stimulants. Tryan, not surprisingly, is attended by Pratt and would seem to suffer from debility; his is a "sensitive failing body" (229), a "pale wasted form" (299), in need of the

strengthening stimulants a practitioner such as Pratt would prescribe. Although neither system of diagnostic technique is endorsed by the narrator, it would seem that patients seek out doctors whose methods best correspond to their particular ailment.

10. J. W. Bennett seems to favor a purely physiological model of interpretation of the story; he asserts that Eliot presents the symptoms and behavior of the alcoholic with the accuracy of an experienced medical practitioner. Yet when he turns directly to the question of violence, Bennett's answer is as limited as Pratt's and Pilgrim's:

> [Dempster] is a brilliant lawyer with a successful practice. He has a loving mother, and a beautiful and once loving wife. Yet now he drinks prodigiously, bullies everyone around him, whips his horse and his driver, and torments Janet. Why? It remains one of the mysteries of alcoholism. (60)

At the end of his essay, however, Bennett himself notes the paradox in his explication of the medical model of alcoholism: "[T]he modern medical community [has] worked hard to get alcoholism defined as a disease and hence something to be treated sympathetically by doctors"; nevertheless "the disease concept may hinder progress in treatment" since alcoholism, he concludes, is "a disease that afflicts the soul" (66).

11. One can compare here, J. S. Mill's remarks on the case of William Burn. Burn was convicted of savage brutality against his horse, but was let off lightly due to the judge's consideration of the man's wife and children. Mill writes scathingly in the *Morning Chronicle* of 17 November 1846:

> Real consideration for the wife and children would have spoken a very different language to the magistrate. It would have said something like this—A man capable of the act of which this man is found guilty, must be one of two things. He is either a wretch who wantonly ill-treats a helpless being, for the pleasure of tyranny, . . . or an irritable, violent creature, who on the smallest provocation . . . flies into an uncontrollable rage, and cannot restrain himself from wreaking a savage vengeance. One of these two characters the man must be; and on either supposition we may infer what sort of a taskmaster he is to the unfortunate woman and the unfortunate children, who are as much in his power, and much more liable to rouse his ferocious passions than the animal over whom he tyrannised. (24: 954)

For a further discussion of the relation of violence against women to cruelty to animals see chapter 6; see also Surridge, "Dogs' /Bodies, Women's Bodies."

12. For a discussion of the sources for and implications of Eliot's treatment of Gypsies, see Bernard Semmel. He notes the Gypsies' paradoxical figuration in nineteenth-century England: on the one hand, they embody "Bohemian exoticism" and a delightful "freedom from the restraints of middle-class Victorianism" (108); on the other hand, "their enemies charged, they cheated and stole, and . . . consequently, they were feared and reviled" (104).

13. A unsigned review in the *Saturday Review* (29 May 1858) calls the story "hackneyed" (*Critical Heritage* 69); Kristin Brady describes it as "deliberately clichéd" (84).

14. Gilbert and Gubar argue that Dempster's delirium indicates that he "is simply mad with guilt over his mistreatment of her" (489); if this is true it is madness and guilt that have not led to repentance and confession.

15. See Eliot's essays "Silly Novels by Lady Novelists" and "Evangelical Teaching: Dr Cumming" for a scathing view of trite Evangelical novels and teachings.

16. For a discussion of Eliot's representation of the bourgeois woman as alcoholic see Shaw.

17. See Dorothea Barrett for a further analysis of Eliot's representation of Janet's body; Barrett describes her as the first of Eliot's "monumental women" (24–25).

18. See endnote 2 for information about Eliot's adaptation of local history into the plot of her story.

19. For example, Noble claims that "[t]he distance between 'Janet's Repentance' and *Middlemarch* is immeasurable" (151). More approvingly, Kerry McSweeney notes that aspects of Janet's characterization make her "an early sketch of Romola" since "[i]n both characters there is a certain strain of visionary possibility that is discontinuous with realistic presentation" (61); Dowling argues that the unspeakable nature of domestic violence in "Janet's Repentance" anticipates *Daniel Deronda* in which Grandcourt's "silence operates as a sign of some truth beyond itself; of an unspeakable, and specifically sexual, horror" (323).

CHAPTER 4. "THE SINS OF THE FATHER" AND "THE FEMALE LINE"

1. Carol Martin's reading of the story, although very different from Felicia Bonaparte's, agrees that "The Poor Clare" vitally relates to the central body of Gaskell's fiction; she argues that Bridget Fitzgerald is in fact

a character in the same mould as Margaret Hale of *North and South* or Cynthia Kirkpatrick of *Wives and Daughters*. What sets the ghost story apart is that "in the remote time and place and the supernatural context of the ghost story, a special wildness, an uncontrolled power, can be allowed to the women characters without their forfeiting the reader's sympathy" (Martin 38).

2. Gaskell's mother died when she was thirteen months old; she then went to live with her maternal relatives. According to Winifred Gérin, Gaskell did not see her father again until she was twelve years of age, her father having remarried. Her annual visits to her father after age twelve (until his death seven years later) are not happy ones. See Gérin, chapter 2 for more details.

The role of the absent or dead mother in Gaskell's fiction has been commented on frequently. Barbara Thaden's chapter on "The Dead Mother" provides a useful overview of the daughter's relation to the dead mother in nineteenth-century fiction in general and Gaskell's work in particular. Like many critics, Thaden comments specifically on the phantasmic return of the dead mother in *Mary Barton*, where "Mary's mother returns to her in the symbolic form of a 'guardian angel' at the time of her deepest distress" (29). Hilary Schor (28–37) examines the same scene in *Mary Barton* in terms of the maternal function of the onlooker, as a semiotic eruption in the symbolic order, and as an indication of Gaskell's political interest in women's social roles. In *Bearing the Word*, Margaret Homans provides an extensive analysis of mothers and daughters in Gaskell's fiction in general and in "The Poor Clare" in particular.

3. Wilhelm Reich asks the question: "*Where does that misery come from?*" because he is dissatisfied with what he takes to be Freud's answer: "The misery comes from inside" (Reich 42–43). Deciding where misery or violence comes from is naturally of central importance in discovering how that misery or violence is to end. For Reich, since misery is "out where the people [are]" (Reich 43) and not "a privatized, internalized angst" (Rose, "Misery" 25), the seeming psychoanalytic focus only on the *internal* workings of the unconscious, and of id, ego, and superego, is mistaken. In order to relieve misery, says Reich, we must recognize its origin in repressive social, political, and cultural forces.

Jacqueline Rose points out that Reich does not always portray Freud's views accurately since Freud's ideas are often not capable of an either/or formulation. For instance, Rose quotes Reich's puzzlement over Freud's reaction to a question about masochism: "When I asked [Freud] whether masochism was primary or secondary, whether it is turned-back sadism or aggression or a disturbance of aggression outward, or whether it's a primary death instinct thing, Freud, peculiarly, maintained both" (Reich 89; Rose, "Misery" 29).

Different as they are from Reich, nonpsychoanalytic feminists, says Rose, have tended to see violence against women as originating in the outside, as they pit "politics . . . against psychoanalysis," and demands for social and cultural change against "the vicissitudes of psychic life" (Rose, "Misery" 26). Many contemporary feminists tend to view violence against women as an "outside" problem; Andrea Dworkin's *Pornography: Men Possessing Women* (1981) and Catherine MacKinnon's *Only Words* (1993), for example, both see pornography as an origin— "out there" in the world—of violence perpetrated by men against women. Freud's abandonment of a literal for a fantasized seduction theory is also cited as an example of Freud's inherent rejection of "outside" forces.

According to Rose, this type of argument makes woman a "pure victim" ("Misery" 32) who is helpless against the outside forces that threaten her. Only a massive state apparatus of laws especially designed to protect woman from what is "out there" can thus save her. As Wendy Brown argues in *States of Injury*, "Legally codifying and thereby ontologizing a cultural construction of male sexual rapaciousness and female powerlessness, such appeals for protection both desexualize and subordinate women in assigning responsibility to the state for women's fate as objects of sexist sexual construction" (170).

4. When the subject suffers a trauma, it may symbolize that trauma in a phantom, a symbolization that on the one hand allows the subject to continue to function, but on the other creates within that functioning a "configuration of incoherence, discontinuity, disruption, and disintegration" (Rand 6). Abraham argues that the phantom, whether the ghost of Hamlet's father or the phantasmic possession of delirium such as Dempster's in "Janet's Repentance," is "nothing but an invention of the living," an invention that is "meant to objectify, even if under the guise of individual or collective hallucinations, the gap produced in us by the concealment of some part of a love object's life" (171). The haunted ones

> are caught between two inclinations. They must at all costs maintain their ignorance of a loved one's secret; hence the semblance of unawareness (nescience) concerning it. At the same time they must eliminate the state of secrecy; hence the reconstruction of the secret in the form of unconscious knowledge. This twofold movement is manifest in symptoms and gives rise to "gratuitous" or uncalled for acts and words, creating eerie effects: hallucinations and delirium, showing and hiding that which, in the depths of the unconscious, dwells as the living-dead knowledge of *someone else's secret*. (188)

5. Gaskell clearly has a deep interest in the intersubjective phenomenon of the curse; both "The Doom of the Griffiths" and "The Accursed Race"

(Cousin Phillis and Other Tales) trace the effects of curses in innocent succeeding generations. A third tale, "The Old Nurse's Story," resembles "The Poor Clare" in that familial disruption leads to the production of a child double. Alan Shelston argues that the "idea of the family curse," in Gaskell in particular and in cultural life in general, "is readily associated on the moral level with the theme of nemesis, on the economic with property rights, and on the anthropological with evolutionary and genetic theory" (144). Shelston concludes that, for Gaskell, curses sow "seeds of destruction that foredoom the future" (144–45). Compare to the seeds of violence discussed in chapter 3.

6. Shelston discusses the "matriarchal line of succession" in the story (145). Bonaparte also argues that "the demon Lucy repudiates is the demon she inherited ancestrally through the female line"; thus the demon represents both the "hate" that is "in Bridget's heart," and the sexual freedom of her mother Mary (53). However, Bonaparte's treatment of the three women as all aspects of Gaskell's own personality makes her treatment of the "female line" a simultaneity rather than historically determined.

7. Where our study diverges with Foucault is that Foucault sees a direct continuity between the confession and psychoanalysis, the "talking cure." We, however, regard the methods of psychoanalysis as precisely different from the methods of the confessional as the former concerns itself with what the subject does *not* know or have access to, is *unable* to confess. Foucault makes these claims about the continuity of the confessional and the psychoanalytic method in several of his books, including *The Order of Things*, *Power/Knowledge*, and *The History of Sexuality*. Although the aims of confession remain the same, he claims, the methods have changed through time:

> [I]t's true that these procedures were often profoundly altered at certain moments, under conditions which are often difficult to explain. In the eighteenth century one finds a very sharp falling away, not in pressure and injunctions to confess, but in the refinement of techniques of confession. During this period, where the direction of conscience and the confessional have lost the essential force of their role, one finds brutal medical techniques emerging, which consist in simply demanding that the subject tell his or her story, or narrate it in writing. (*Power/Knowledge* 215)

8. Of the ending Shelston writes, "Her release from the curse would have left them free to marry, but there is no indication that this has ever happened: the horrors of the past may therefore have been compounded by domestic unhappiness in the life of the narrator himself" (144).

9. This reading disagrees with Patsy Stoneman's, which argues that the ending of the story "is not open-ended but offers an ideological resolution of

the 'terrors' it has disclosed" (66). Stoneman argues that Bridget's life as a nun "represents a breach of her claustrophobic obsession with her daughter's chastity and a move towards an adult involvement in the community" (66–67).

10. Margaret Homans claims that although "the daughter does enter the symbolic order, she does not do so exclusively. Because she does not perceive the mother as lost or renounced . . . she has the positive experience of never having given up entirely the presymbolic communication that carries over, with the bond to the mother, beyond the preoedipal period" (13). She thus retains "the literal or presymbolic language" as well as "symbolic language" (13).

11. This is the assumption that Maureen Reddy makes also (see Reddy 262).

12. We have been told by the narrator that there are legitimate claimants in another branch of the family, though in a later generation. If Lucy is illegitimate, she would be disinherited unless she were named specifically in her ancestor's will. That she would be so named is highly unlikely as the claim seems to go back four generations, that is, to before Lucy was born. If the ancestor in question died intestate, only legitimate issue could inherit the estate.

CHAPTER 5. RAPE, TRANSGRESSION, AND THE LAW

1. Almost all of the critical discussion surrounding *Aurora Leigh* does presuppose a coherent subject who progresses along a path of reintegration: Margaret Reynolds, discussing the split between Aurora Leigh the poet and Aurora Leigh the woman, states that it is "ironically . . . the mediation of the conventional (albeit invented) poetic stereotype of the male/female relation between poet and Muse that precipitates the restoration of Aurora's sexual identity" (6); Joyce Zonona claims that at the conclusion of *Aurora Leigh*, Barrett Browning "offers a striking image of a woman artist who is simultaneously poet and muse" (241); Dolores Rosenblum discusses the incorporation of Marian into Aurora's self and states that "looking into the mirror of a mother-sister marks Aurora's discovery of an integrated self and a poetics" (335); Marjorie Stone discusses the ways in which Barrett Browning uses gender reversals to undermine conventional expectations, allowing Aurora ultimately to emerge as both an artist and a woman (103); Gail Turley Houston, discussing the powers of women's bodies and the body of writing they produce, demonstrates how "Barrett Browning's *Kunstlerroman* replaces the phallic gesture of the male-authored *Kunstlerroman*'s assumption of manhood with the abundant, erect, tangible female breast, which, instead of reiterating the

old flaccid dead mythologies, engenders a new metaphor for woman as writer" (233); Helen Cooper claims that "through her close contact with the procreative role of woman enacted by Marian Erle in the second half of her story, Aurora finally claims her female identity" (169).

Alison Case is exceptional in that she does not plot a path of reconciliation and reunion. She discusses the coexistence of two reemerging, incompatible plots: "a female *Kunstlerroman* and a feminine love story, for both of which Aurora serves as heroine/narrator" (17) while maintaining an "uneasy coexistence" (18) between "dual narrative possibilities" (19) that results in the coexistence of "two kinds of stories" (21).

2. Cooper perceives her to be the "instrument of [Aurora's] transformation" (172); Rosenblum discusses the incorporation of Marian into Aurora's self and states that "looking into the mirror of a mother-sister marks Aurora's discovery of an integrated self and a poetics" (335). However, Linda Lewis gestures in the direction of Marian's disruptive function when she states that "only the case of Marian Erle troubles our sense of how things ought to be . . . and Marian's insistence upon her unresurrected state seems to deny closure in a work where all other loose ends are neatly tied" (59–60).

3. Other critics have commented on Marian's peculiar state of nonexistence. Houston points out that "Aurora, Romney and Lady Waldemar all relate to Marian as though she were an item of exchange between them" (227–28). Patricia Murphy states that she "seemingly takes on the qualities of all women" (23). Our concept of the phantom, however, functions not so much as a signifier of how characters in the text might use or relate to Marian Erle, but as a signifier of the fact that she ultimately cannot be "used," incorporated, or integrated fully into Barrett Browning's text. She appears to us to remain outside of the realm of integration.

4. What Barrett Browning *intends* in her reference to "drawing-rooms" is, to some extent, clarified in Book Five of *Aurora Leigh* by Aurora's theory of poetry:

> Nay, if there's room for poets in this world
> . . . .
> Their sole work is to represent the age,
> Their age, not Charlemagne's—this live, throbbing age (201–03);
>
> this is living art,
> Which thus presents and thus records true life. (221–22)

The "true life" that is referred to here might be compared with Barrett Browning's stated wish in her letter to Robert Browning to "[speak] the truth as [she] conceive[s] of it, out plainly" (1.10). The "drawing-rooms" into which Barrett Browning wishes to "rush" are therefore signifiers for "this live throbbing age . . . which . . . presents . . . true life" and Aurora's conceptualization of the subject for poetry is intended to signify everyday life (true life in drawing rooms) which is contrasted with a mythologized, idealized, and distanced past (the world of Charlemagne). Our point is that the idea of "true life" that occurs primarily in drawing rooms does seem a contradiction in terms.

5. Several critics have commented on the limitations and prejudices evident in Barrett Browning's treatment of the working classes in *Aurora Leigh* and the way in which they appear to contradict the feminist concerns of the text. Cora Kaplan, for example, referring to the "conflict and contradiction in [Barrett Browning's] position on female sexuality and class" (25), states that *Aurora Leigh* emerges with "a theory of art and politics unconnected with material reality and deeply elitist" (12); she concludes: "nowhere in the literature of the mid-century is the bourgeois rejection of working-class consciousness more glaring than in *Aurora Leigh*" (35). Cooper states that "Aurora's middle-class fiction allows her, like Romney, to feel charity toward a poor sufferer while scorning her class" (165). Louise Hudd points to the text's "problematic depiction of class politics and social reform" (63) and states that "the poem's critique of social conditions for the urban masses [is] uneasily subordinated to its feminist message" (66). See Hudd (64–66) for a further discussion of the poem's attitude to social reform in relation to the critics of the time. Hudd also discusses the way in which Barrett Browning's class prejudice or social conservatism may interrupt the realism of her text, stating that "the one thing that *Aurora Leigh* isn't, is realist in the sense in which George Eliot conceives the term" (65–66). Gilbert and Gubar do not read this text as a triumph of feminist assertion at all. In contrast to most readings of *Aurora Leigh* (see note 1 above), they read the end of the text as a statement of Aurora's compromise with the docility demanded of her by Victorian marriage. Aurora, they claim, will labor for her "glorious blind master . . . in . . . [an] 'unwearied' trance of self-abnegation"; she will fulfill "the role of dutiful handmaiden to a blind but powerful master" (578).

6. A number of critics have explored the implications of the generic complexities of *Aurora Leigh.* Stone discusses the ways in which "women write between existing genres" (101); Susanna Egan analyses how the "genres seem to work against each other" (284) in *Aurora Leigh* since the success of the woman poet seems to work against the novelist who chooses a socially acceptable climax; Houston, discussing the notion of the *Kunstlerroman* as a genre that "constructs and is constructed by gender," explores the problematics for a woman of the construction of the self as artist within the constraints of the "market system" (213); Case comments that Barrett Browning's violations

of novelistic genre are a response to "restrictions which generic conventions imposed on the expression of female artistic self-determination. The narrative confusions result from the coexistence of two seemingly incompatible plots" (17); Susan Stanford Friedman remarks that genre anxiety for women poets originates in the "interface between genre norms and gender codes" (203). Aurora, herself, also questions generic conventions (5.230).

7. Stacey Gottlieb points out that "Barrett Browning's clear intent to deny Marian any personal responsibility for her misfortunes has been taken by critics as evidence for both the poet's political progressiveness and political conservatism" (58); however, what is significant here is precisely the issue of unconsciousness. Marian's "act" only becomes tolerable to Aurora when she discovers that she was "absent" when it occurs and this seems to reveal as much about Aurora's own "absences" as it does about Barrett Browning's political convictions.

8. In her discussion of rape and resurrection in *Aurora Leigh,* Lewis points out that all of the major characters in *Aurora Leigh* "die" but that Marian is the only one who "remains dead" (56) and that this is because Barrett Browning, in her exploration of rape, "illustrates the death from which there is no resurrection" (56).

9. Zonona reads Marian's disappearance from the narrative as an endorsement of the mutual subjectivities of Marian and Aurora saying that Barrett Browning "refuses to place her in any position in relation to Aurora. Aurora must speak her own truth, affirming—and naming—a muse (the dawn) who is nothing less than her very self" (243).

CHAPTER 6. "WILL SHE END LIKE ME?"

1. A number of critics have commented on the fact that Collins is more concerned with the political, economic, and cultural system than with individual psyches. Richard Barickman, Susan MacDonald, and Myra Stark comment that Collins's "focus on courtship, marriage, and the family . . . is a means of locating the primary source of social disorder" (7); D. A. Miller says of *The Woman in White* that the end of the novel "has merely discovered its beginning, in the family matrix where such violence has acquired its specific structure" (212); Jenny Bourne Taylor comments that "*Man and Wife* in particular is an extraordinary exploration of male violence and the position of women in marriage" (213).

2. The question of absent, dead, destructive, and silenced mothers and their relationship both to subjectivity and authorship in nineteenth-century literature has been exhaustively discussed in the critical literature. Sandra M. Gilbert and Susan Gubar see motherlessness as a signifier for powerlessness in

nineteenth-century society, stating that the recovery or memory of the "lost foremother" would enable the female subject to "find [her] distinctive female power" (59). Adrienne Rich, in her essay on *Jane Eyre,* believes that it is Jane's motherlessness that provides her with the freedom to find a "nurturing, or principled or spirited woman" on every step of her journey which allows her to create her own subjectivity (91). Marian Hirsch sees "maternal repression . . . at the very basis of the structure of the plot" of the nineteenth-century novel (50), and Margaret Homans claims that women writers "articulate thematically a daughter's bond to and identification with a vulnerable or vanished mother" (16).

3. For a further discussion of the relationship between women and animals, see Lisa Surridge, "Dogs'/Bodies, Women's Bodies."

4. Barickman, MacDonald, and Stark comment on the way in which the very linking of "respectable characters to the 'lowest' in their society" functions as a questioning of "the very basis of Victorian social and moral hierarchies" (27).

5. Stana Nenadic points out that the essence of the sensation genre is that it "overturns and subverts domestic reality and domesticity. It takes everyday and commonplace family situations or relationships, with which the mainly middle-class and female readership would readily identify, and presents their threatening, sinister, and nightmarish possibilities" (143); Miller comments that the "sensation novel [might be allowed] to 'say' certain things for which our culture—at least at its popular levels—has yet to develop another language" (188) and that when the norm of the Victorian household is "recontextualized in a 'sensational' account of its genesis, such a norm risks appearing *monstrous*: as aberrant as any of the abnormal conditions that determine its realization" (198–99).

6. In contrast to Bourne Taylor who argues that Hester functions within the "overall naturalistic narrative by remaining embedded within its implied terms of reference as pathological" (217), we are arguing that Hester is figured as being outside the human cultural norm and thus functions as a critique of culture.

7. Others have also commented on the inextricable relationship between place and a sense of self, particularly for women. Nenadic states that the "identity and status of the middle-class woman came through reference to husband and family" (140); Melynda Huskey points out that "women exist only in context, and context can change at any time, in any direction" (5); Jonathan Loesburg discusses the relationship between identity and its legal and class manifestations in sensation literature, pointing out that the "loss of legal identity entails loss of class identity" (119).

8. The only alternative for Anne to being locked out is being locked in, which is what happens at Fulham. It is also interesting to note that the motif of confinement is expressed not only through the series of locked rooms in the novel, but also through the idea of the secret pregnancy Anne undergoes, since it is this pregnancy that functions as the original signifier of her locked out status.

9. Gilbert and Gubar point out that dramatizations of imprisonment and escape are "all-pervasive in nineteenth-century literature by women" and that "works in this tradition generally begin by using houses as primary symbols of female imprisonment" (85). It seems that this motif is equally present in literature by men but what seems of primary importance here is the ease with which the home can come to function as a prison for women.

10. See Nenadic for a discussion on the use of the asylum as prison and the increasing presence of women in the statistics of the mad (150) and Miller who, in her discussion of the madwoman, identifies a category of madness for the woman who lies "ever in wait to 'cover'—account for or occlude—whatever behaviors, desires, or tendencies might be considered socially deviant, undesirable, or dangerous" (200).

11. Helena Michie discusses the motif of sisterhood in the works of Rossetti and Collins and the ways in which fallen women "are frequently recoupable through their sisters' efforts in a way forbidden to other Victorian women" ("Sister" 404). Michie does not comment specifically on *Man and Wife* but the obvious choice of the pure sister for Anne would be Blanche. This chapter argues that it is Hester who functions as a type of demon sister to Anne and who enables her to resume living. The implications of this are crucial. Hester's functioning as a sister for Anne is not just a case of simple ironic reversal but implies that badness and madness for women have to be located somewhere in the culture.

12. Barickman, MacDonald, and Stark point out that the ending "both represents and exposes Victorian sexual values" and that we are confronted with "a continuous text whose contradictions form a coherent design" (4, 18).

13. The ambiguities of Collins's social criticism are commented upon by a number of his critics. Allison Milbank finds in the "seemingly conservative writers" (of which Collins is one) an "unsettling and 'redemptive' dissatisfaction with the patriarchy they seem to defend" (2); Barickman, MacDonald, and Stark state that although one may find in a writer such as Collins what appears to be only a "passive reflection of prevailing masculine attitudes," these same novelists do "in a multitude of ways, draw attentions to their processes of distortion, so that we become aware of the stereotyped attitudes as well as of the stereotypes themselves" (3); Bourne Taylor states that be-

cause Collins deals "so openly" in *Man and Wife* with "class and sexuality," he is "forced into covering his tracks as he goes along." Thus, although he implies, on the one hand, that powerlessness is completely the "product of the codes of a dominant social structure," he ends up, on the other hand, "reinforcing the split between purity and danger" (213). Patricia Frick points out that Collins' "happy endings . . . suggest a certain degree of ambivalence, for in restoring his fallen heroines to the traditional refuges of marriage and respectability, Collins simultaneously strips them of much of their power, independence and magnetism" (349).

CONCLUSION

1. See also Elizabeth Ermath who discusses the liminal status of those objects that are not part of the consensus achieved by realism: "In a realistic novel . . . any term that challenges the prevailing formal consensus is a contradiction in terms; by definition it can have no ontological status at all" ("Fictional Consensus" 9).

Works Cited

Abraham, Nicholas, and Maria Torok. *The Shell and the Kernel*. Ed. and Trans. Nicholas T. Rand. Vol. 1. Chicago: U of Chicago P, 1994.

Armstrong, Nancy. *Desire and Domestic Fiction: A Political History of the Novel*. New York: Oxford UP, 1987.

Armstrong, Nancy, and Leonard Tennenhouse. *The Violence of Representation: Literature and the History of Violence*. Ed. Nancy Armstrong and Leonard Tennenhouse. New York: Routledge, 1989.

Arner, Robert D. "The Legend of Pygmalion in 'The Birthmark.'" *American Transcendental Quarterly* 14 (1971): 168–71.

Auerbach, Erich. *Mimesis: The Representation of Reality in Western Literature*. Princeton: Princeton UP, 1953.

Auerbach, Nina. *Woman and the Demon: The Life of a Victorian Myth*. Cambridge: Harvard UP, 1982.

Balibar, Étienne. "The Elements of the Structure and their History." *Reading Capital*. Ed. Louis Althusser and Étienne Balibar. London: New Left Books, 1975. 225–53.

Barber, C. L. *Shakespeare's Festive Comedies: A Study of Dramatic Form and its Relation to Social Custom*. Princeton: Princeton UP, 1979.

Barickman, Richard, Susan MacDonald, and Myra Stark. *Corrupt Relations: Dickens, Thackeray, Trollope, Collins, and the Victorian Social System*. New York: Columbia UP, 1982.

Barrett Browning, Elizabeth. *Aurora Leigh*. Ed. Kerry McSweeney. Oxford: Oxford UP, 1993.

———. *The Letters of Robert Browning and Elizabeth Barrett Browning, 1845–1846*. Ed. Elvan Kintner. 2 vols. Cambridge: Belknap-Harvard UP, 1969.

Barrett, Dorothea. *Vocation and Desire: George Eliot's Heroines*. London: Routledge, 1991.

Beer, Gillian. *The Romance*. London: Methuen, 1970.

Bennett, J. W. "The Apprenticeship of George Eliot: Characterization as Case Study in 'Janet's Repentance.'" *Literature and Medicine* 9 (1990): 50–68.

Bonaparte, Felicia. *The Gypsy-Bachelor of Manchester: The Life of Mrs Gaskell's Demon*. Charlottesville: U of Virginia P, 1992.

Bourne Taylor, Jenny. *In the Secret Theatre of Home: Wilkie Collins, Sensation Narrative, and Nineteenth Century Psychology*. New York: Routledge, 1988.

Bowie, Malcolm. *Lacan*. London: Fontana, 1991.

Brady, Kristin. *George Eliot*. Women Writers Ser. London: Macmillan, 1992.

Bronfen, Elisabeth. *Over Her Dead Body: Death, Femininity, and the Aesthetic*. New York: Routledge, 1992.

Brontë, Anne. *Tenant of Wildfell Hall*. Ed. G. D. Hargreaves. London: Penguin, 1979.

Brontë, Charlotte. *Jane Eyre*. Ed. Q. D. Leavis. Harmondsworth: Penguin, 1966.

Brooks, Cleanth, and Austin Warren. *Understanding Fiction*. New York: F. S. Crofts, 1944.

Brooks, Peter. *Body Work: Objects of Desire in Modern Narrative*. Cambridge: Harvard UP, 1993.

Brown, Wendy. *States of Injury: Power and Freedom in Late Modernity*. Princeton: Princeton UP, 1995.

Burgar, Sheila. "A Woman's Best Career: Choices for Women in Selected Novels by Anthony Trollope." *Critical Mass* 4:1 (1994): 37–54.

Caird, Mona. "Marriage." 1888. *"Criminals, Idiots, Women, and Minors": Nineteenth-Century Writing by Women on Women*. Ed. Susan Hamilton. Peterborough, ON: Broadview, 1995. 271–86.

Carroll, David. *George Eliot and the Conflict of Interpretations: A Reading of the Novels*. Cambridge: Cambridge UP, 1992.

Caruth, Cathy. *Trauma: Explorations in Memory*. Baltimore: Johns Hopkins UP, 1995.

———. *Unclaimed Experience: Trauma, Narrative, and History*. Baltimore: Johns Hopkins UP, 1996.

Case, Alison. "Gender and Narration in Aurora Leigh." *Victorian Poetry* 29:1 (1991): 17–32.

Chase, Richard. *The American Novel and Its Tradition*. Baltimore: Johns Hopkins UP, 1957.

Cixous, Hélène, and Catherine Clément. *The Newly Born Woman*. Trans. Betsy Wing. Minneapolis: U of Minnesota P, 1986.

Cobbe, Frances Power. "Wife-torture in England." 1878. *Criminals, Idiots, Women, and Minors: Nineteenth-Century Writing by Women on Women*. Ed. Susan Hamilton. Peterborough, ON: Broadview, 1995. 108–70.

Cohen, William A. *Sex Scandal: The Private Parts of Victorian Fiction*. Durham: Duke UP, 1996.

Collins, Wilkie. *Man and Wife*. Oxford: Oxford UP, 1995.

Cooper, Helen. *Elizabeth Barrett Browning, Woman and Artist*. Chapel Hill: U of North Carolina P, 1988.

Copjec, Joan. *Read My Desire: Lacan Against the Historicists*. Cambridge: MIT P, 1994.

Cornell, Drucilla. *Beyond Accommodation: Ethical Feminism, Deconstruction, and the Law*. New York and London: Routledge, 1991.

Crews, Frederick. *The Sins of the Fathers: Hawthorne's Psychological Themes*. New York: Oxford UP, 1966.

Davis, Lennard J. "Nude Venuses, Medusa's Body, and Phantom Limbs: Disability and Visuality." *The Body and Physical Difference: Discourses of Disability*. Ed. David T. Mitchell and Sharon L. Snyder. Ann Arbor: U of Michigan P, 1997. 51–70.

"Delirium." *Diagnostic and Statistical Manual of Mental Disorders*. 3rd ed., rev. 1987.

de Man, Paul. *Allegories of Reading: Figural Language in Rousseau, Nietzsche, Rilke, and Proust*. New Haven: Yale UP, 1979.

Demetrakopoulos, Stephanie. "George Eliot's 'Janet's Repentance': The First Literary Portrait of a Woman Addict and Her Recovery." *Midwest Quarterly* 35 (1993): 95–108.

Dickens, Charles. "An Appeal to Fallen Women." 28 October 1847. Rpt. in *Oliver Twist*. Ed. Fred Kaplan. New York: Norton, 1993. 381–83.

———. *Great Expectations*. Ed. Angus Calder. London: Penguin, 1965.

———. *Oliver Twist*. Ed. Kathleen Tillotson. World's Classics. Oxford: Oxford UP, 1982.

Dickerson, Vanessa D. *Keeping the Victorian House: A Collection of Essays*. New York: Garland, 1995.

Doggett, Maeve E. *Marriage, Wife-beating, and the Law in Victorian England: sub virga viri*. London: Weidenfeld and Nicolson, 1992.

Dowling, Andrew. "'The Other Side of Silence': Matrimonial Conflict and the Divorce Court in George Eliot's Fiction." *Nineteenth Century Literature* 52:2 (1995): 322–36.

Dworkin, Andrea. *Pornography: Men Possessing Women*. New York: Plume, 1989.

Eckstein, Barbara. "Hawthorne's 'The Birthmark': Science and Romance as Belief." *Studies in Short Fiction* 26 (1989): 511–19.

Edwards, P. D. *Anthony Trollope: His Art and Scope*. St. Lucia: Queensland UP, 1977.

Egan, Susanna. "Glad Rags for Lady Godiva: Woman's Story as Womanstance in Elizabeth Barrett Browning's *Aurora Leigh*. *English Studies in Canada* 20:3 (1994): 283–300.

Eliot, George. *The George Eliot Letters*. Ed. Gordon S. Haight. 7 vols. New Haven: Yale UP, 1954–1955.

———. *Middlemarch*. Ed. David Carroll. World's Classics. Oxford: Oxford UP, 1988.

———. *Scenes of Clerical Life*. Ed. Thomas A. Noble. World's Classics. Oxford: Oxford UP, 1988.

———. *Selected Critical Writing*. Ed. Rosemary Ashton. Oxford: Oxford UP, 1992.

Ellis, Kate Ferguson. *The Contested Castle: Gothic Novels and the Subversion of Domestic Ideology*. Urbana: U of Illinois P, 1989.

Ermarth, Elizabeth. *The English Novel in History: 1840–1895*. London: Routledge, 1997.

———. "Fictional Consensus and Female Casualties." *The Representation of Women in Fiction*. Ed. Carolyn Heilbrun and Margaret Higonet. Baltimore: Johns Hopkins UP, 1981. 1–18.

Felman, Shoshana. *Jacques Lacan and the Adventure of Insight: Psychoanalysis in Contemporary Culture*. Cambridge: Harvard UP, 1987.

———. *What Does a Woman Want?: Reading and Sexual Difference*. Baltimore: Johns Hopkins UP, 1993.

Felman, Shoshana, and Dori Laub. *Testimony: Crises of Witnessing in Literature, Psychoanalysis, and History*. New York: Routledge, 1992.

Fenves, Peter. "Exiling the Encyclopedia: The Individual in 'Janet's Repentance.'" *Nineteenth-Century Literature* 41 (1987): 419–44.

Ferraro, Kathleen J. "The Dance of Dependency: A Genealogy of Domestic Violence Discourse." *Hypatia* 11:4 (1996): 77–91.

Fetterley, Judith. *The Resisting Reader: A Feminist Approach to American Fiction*. Bloomington: Indiana UP, 1978.

Fogle, Richard Harter. *Hawthorne's Fiction: The Light and the Dark*. Norman: U of Oklahoma P, 1964.

Foucault, Michel. *Discipline and Punish: The Birth of the Prison*. Trans. Allan Sheridan. New York: Random House, 1979.

———. *The History of Sexuality: Volume I: An Introduction*. Trans. Robert Hurley. New York: Vintage, 1978.

———. *Power/Knowledge: Selected Interviews and Other Writings, 1972–1977*. Ed. Colin Gordon. New York: Pantheon, 1980.

Freud, Sigmund. "The 'Uncanny.'" *Art and Literature*. Trans. James Strachey. Ed. Albert Dickson. Pelican Freud Library. Harmondsworth: Penguin, 1985. 14: 335–76.

Frick, Patricia. "The Fallen Angels of Wilkie Collins." *International Journal of Women's Studies* 7:4 (1984): 343–51.

Friedman, Susan Stanford. "Gender and Genre Anxiety: Elizabeth Barrett Browning and H.D. as Epic Poets." *Tulsa Studies in Women's Literature* 5:2 (1986): 202–28.

Frye, Northrop. *Anatomy of Criticism: Four Essays*. Princeton: Princeton UP, 1957.

Gaskell, Elizabeth. *Cousin Phillis and Other Tales*. Ed. Angus Easson. Oxford: Oxford UP, 1981.

———. *The Letters of Mrs Gaskell*. Ed. J. A. V. Chapple and A. Pollard. Manchester: U of Manchester P, 1966.

———. "The Poor Clare." *My Lady Ludlow and Other Stories*. Ed. Edgar Wright. World's Classics. Oxford: Oxford UP, 1989. 271–333.

Gay, Peter. *The Cultivation of Hatred: The Bourgeois Experience: Victoria to Freud*. New York: Norton, 1993.

Gérin, Winifred. *Elizabeth Gaskell: A Biography*. Oxford: Oxford UP, 1976.

Gilbert, Sandra M., and Susan Gubar. *The Madwoman in the Attic: The Woman Writer and the Nineteenth-Century Literary Imagination*. New Haven: Yale UP, 1979.

Girard, René. *Violence and the Sacred.* Trans. Patrick Gregory. Baltimore: Johns Hopkins UP, 1977.

Gottlieb, Stacey. "'And God Will Teach Her': Consciousness and Character in *Ruth* and *Aurora Leigh.*" *Victorians-Institute-Journal* 24 (1996): 57–85.

Graver, Suzanne. *George Eliot and Community: A Study in Social Theory and Fictional Form.* Berkeley: U of California P, 1984.

Haight, Gordon S. *George Eliot: A Biography.* Harmondsworth: Penguin, 1968.

———. *George Eliot's Originals and Contemporaries: Essays in Victorian History and Biography.* Ed. Hugh Witemeyer. Ann Arbor: U of Michigan P, 1992.

Hammerton, James A. *Cruelty and Companionship: Conflict in Nineteenth-Century Married Life.* London: Routledge, 1992.

———. "Victorian Marriage and the Law of Matrimonial Cruelty." *Victorian Studies* 33 (1990): 269–92.

Harman, Barbara Leah. *The Feminine Political Novel in Victorian England.* Charlottesville: UP of Virginia, 1998.

Hawthorne, Nathaniel. *The American Notebooks.* Ed. Claude W. Simpson. Columbus: Ohio State UP, 1972.

———. "The Birthmark." *The Centenary Edition of the Works of Nathaniel Hawthorne.* Ed. William Charvat. Columbus: Ohio State UP, 1974. 10: 36–56.

———. *Hawthorne's Lost Notebook: 1835–1841.* University Park, PA: Pennsylvania State UP, 1978.

———. Preface. *The House of the Seven Gables.* Columbus: Ohio State UP, 1965.

Heilman, Robert. "Hawthorne's 'The Birthmark': Science as Religion." *South Atlantic Quarterly* 48 (1949): 575–83.

Helsinger, Elizabeth K., Robin Lauterbach, and William Veeder. *The Woman Question: Society and Literature in Britain and America, 1837–1883.* 3 vols. Chicago: U of Chicago P, 1983.

Herbert, Christopher. *Trollope and Comic Pleasure.* Chicago: U of Chicago P, 1987.

Higgins, Lynn A., and Brenda R. Silver, eds. *Rape and Representation.* New York : Columbia UP, 1991.

Hirsch, Marian. *The Mother/Daughter Plot: Narrative, Psychoanalysis, Feminism.* Bloomington: Indiana UP, 1989.

Holcombe, Lee. *Wives and Property: Reform of the Married Women's Property Act in Nineteenth-Century England.* Toronto: U of Toronto P, 1982.

Homans, Margaret. *Bearing the Word: Language and Female Experience in Nineteenth-Century Women's Writing.* Chicago: U of Chicago P, 1986.

Houston, Gail Turley. "Gender Construction and the Kunstlerroman: *David Copperfield* and *Aurora Leigh.*" *Philological Quarterly* 72:2 (1993): 213–36.

Hudd, Louise. "The Politics of a Feminist Poetics: 'Armgart' and George Eliot's Critical Response to *Aurora Leigh.*" *Essays and Studies* 49 (1966): 62–83.

Huskey, Melynda. "*No Name*: Embodying the Sensation Heroine." *Victorian Newsletter* 82 (1992): 5–13.

Irigaray, Luce. *Speculum of the Other Woman.* Trans. Gillian C. Gill. Ithaca: Cornell UP, 1985.

Jacobus, Mary. "The Difference of View." *Women Writing and Writing About Women.* Ed. Mary Jacobus. London: Croom Helm, 1979. 10–21.

———. *First Things: The Maternal Imaginary in Literature, Art, and Psychoanalysis.* New York: Routledge, 1995.

James, Henry. "Anthony Trollope." *Nation* 13 July 1865: 51–52. Rpt. in *Trollope: The Barsetshire Novels: A Casebook.* Ed. T. Bareham. London: Macmillan, 1983. 44–46.

———. "Anthony Trollope." *Century Magazine* 4 July 1883: 385–95. Rpt. in *Trollope: The Barsetshire Novels: A Casebook.* Ed. T. Bareham. London: Macmillan, 1983. 54–65.

———. Preface. *The American.* New York: Scribner's, 1907.

Johnson, Barbara. "Is Female to Male as Ground Is to Figure?" *Feminism and Psychoanalysis.* Ed. Richard Feldstein and Judith Roof. Ithaca: Cornell UP, 1989. 255–268

Kaplan, Cora, ed. *Aurora Leigh and Other Poems.* London: Women's P, 1978.

Kaye, J. W. "Outrages on Women." *North British Review* 25:49 (1856): 233–56.

Kincaid, James R. *The Novels of Anthony Trollope.* Oxford: Clarendon, 1977.

Knoepflmacher, U. C. *George Eliot's Early Novels: The Limits of Realism.* Berkeley: U of California P, 1968.

———. *Laughter and Despair: Reading of Ten Novels of the Victorian Era.* Berkeley: U of California P, 1971.

Kristeva, Julia. *Powers of Horror: An Essay on Abjection*. Trans. Leon S. Roudiez. New York: Columbia UP, 1982.

Lacan, Jacques. *Feminine Sexuality: Jacques Lacan and the* école freudienne. Ed. Juliet Mitchell and Jacqueline Rose. New York: Norton, 1985.

———. *The Seminar. Book VII. The Ethics of Psychoanalysis*. Trans. Dennis Porter. London: Routledge, 1992.

———. *The Seminar of Jacques Lacan: On Feminine Sexuality, The Limits of Love and Knowledge, Book XX. Encore: 1972–1973*. Ed. Jacques-Alain Miller. Trans. Bruce Fink. New York: Norton, 1998.

LaCom, Cindy. "It Is More than Lame: Physical Disability, Sexuality, and the Maternal in the Nineteenth Century Novel." *The Body and Physical Difference: Discourses of Disability*. Ed. David T. Mitchell and Sharon L. Snyder. Ann Arbor: U of Michigan P, 1997. 189–201.

Langland, Elizabeth. *Nobody's Angels: Middle-Class Women and Domestic Ideology in Victorian Culture*. Ithaca: Cornell UP, 1995.

Lechte, John. *Julia Kristeva*. London: Routledge, 1990.

Leps, Marie-Christine. *Apprehending the Criminal: The Production of Deviance in Nineteenth Century Discourse*. Durham: Duke UP, 1992.

Lesser, Simon O. *Fiction and the Unconscious*. Chicago: U of Chicago P, 1957.

Lewis, Linda. "Rape and Resurrection in *Aurora Leigh*." *Studies in Browning and His Circle* 19 (1991): 56–65.

Loesberg, Jonathan. "The Ideology of Narrative Form in Sensation Fiction." *representations* 13 (1986): 115–38.

Loraux, Nicole. *Tragic Ways of Killing a Woman*. Trans. Anthony Forster. Cambridge: Harvard UP, 1987.

Lynn, Andrew B. "Bondage, Acquiescence and Blessedness: Spinoza's Three Kinds of Knowledge and *Scenes of Clerical Life*." *George Eliot—George Henry Lewes Studies* (1996): 30–47.

Lyotard, Jean-François. *The Differend: Phrases in Dispute*. Trans. Georges Van Den Abbeele. Minneapolis: U of Minnesota P, 1988.

MacKinnon, Catherine A. *Feminism Unmodified: Discourses on Life and Law*. Cambridge: Harvard UP, 1987.

———. *Only Words*. Cambridge: Harvard UP, 1993.

Manheimer, Joan. "Murderous Mothers: The Problem of Parenting in the Victorian Novel." *Feminist Studies* 5:3 (1979): 530–46.

Marcus, Steven. "Freud and Dora: Story, History, Case History." *Freud: A Collection of Critical Essays*. New Jersey: Prentice-Hall, 1981. 183–210.

Martin, Carol A. "Gaskell's Ghosts: Truths in Disguise." *Studies in the Novel* 21:1 (1989): 27–40.

Mason, Mary G. "The Other Voice: Autobiographies of Women Writers." *Autobiography: Essays Theoretical and Critical*. Ed. James Olney. Princeton: Princeton UP, 1980. 207–35.

Massé, Michelle. *In the Name of Love: Women, Masochism, and the Gothic*. Ithaca: Cornell UP, 1992.

McSweeney, Kerry. *George Eliot (Marian Evans): A Literary Life*. London: Macmillan, 1991.

Meredith, George. "Modern Love." *Poems, Volume 1. The Works of George Meredith*. Vol. 29. Westminster: Archibald Constable, 1898. 7–56.

Michie, Helena. *The Flesh Made Word: Female Figures and Women's Bodies*. New York: Oxford UP, 1987.

———. "'There is No Friend Like a Sister': Sisterhood as Sexual Difference." *English Literary History* 56:2 (1989): 401–19.

———. "'Who Is This in Pain?': Scarring, Disfigurement, and Female Identity in *Bleak House* and *Our Mutual Friend*." *Novel* 22 (1989): 199–212.

Milbank, Alison. *Daughters of the House Modes of the Gothic in Victorian Fiction*. London: Macmillan, 1992.

Mill, John Stuart. "The Case of William Burn." *Newspaper Writings*. Ed. John M. Robson and Anne P. Robson. Toronto: U of Toronto P, 1986. 24. 952–54. Vols. 22–25 of *The Collected Works of John Stuart Mill*. 33 vols. 1963–1986.

Miller D. A. "*Cage aux folles*: Sensation and Gender in Wilkie Collins's *The Woman in White*." *Speaking of Gender*. Ed. Elaine Showalter. New York: Routledge, 1989. 187–215.

Millington, Richard H. *Practising Romance: Narrative Form and Cultural Engagement in Hawthorne's Fiction*. Princeton: Princeton UP, 1992.

Murphy, Patricia. "Reconceiving the Mother: Deconstructing the Madonna in *Aurora Leigh*." *Victorian Newsletter* 91 (1997): 21–27.

Nardin, Jane. *He Knew She Was Right: The Independent Woman in the Novels of Anthony Trollope*. Carbondale: Southern Illinois UP, 1989.

Nenadic, Stana. "Illegitimacy, Insanity, and Insolvency: Wilkie Collins and the Victorian Nightmares." *The Arts, Literature, and Society*. Ed. Arthure Mawick. London: Routledge, 1990. 133–62.

Noble, Thomas A. *George Eliot's* Scenes of Clerical Life. New Haven: Yale UP, 1965.

Nord, Deborah Epstein. *Walking the Victorian Streets: Women, Representation, and the City*. Ithaca: Cornell UP, 1995.

Norton, Caroline. "Review of the Divorce Bill of 1856." *The Wives: The Rights of Married Women*. London: Routledge, 1994. Vol. 3 of *Perspectives on the History of British Feminism*. Ed. Marie Mulvey Roberts and Tamae Mizuta. 6 vols. 1994.

Ovid. *The Metamorphoses of Ovid*. Trans. Mary M. Innes. Harmondsworth: Penguin, 1955.

Patmore, Coventry. "The Angel in the House." *The Broadview Anthology of Victorian Poetry and Poetic Theory*. Ed. Thomas J. Collins and Vivienne J. Rundle. Peterborough, ON: Broadview, 1999. 739–60.

Perkin, Joan. *Women and Marriage in Nineteenth-Century England*. Chicago: Lyceum Books, 1989.

Polhemus, Robert M. "Trollope's *Barchester Towers*: Comic Reformation." *Anthony Trollope's* Barchester Towers *and* The Warden. Ed. Harold Bloom. New York: Chelsea House, 1988.

Quinn, James, and Ross Baldessarini. "'The Birth-Mark': A Deathmark." *University of Hartford Studies in Literature: A Journal of Interdisciplinary Criticism* 13.2 (1981): 91–98.

Rand, Nicholas. Introduction. *The Shell and the Kernel*. Vol. 1. Chicago: U of Chicago P, 1994. 1–22.

Rashkin, Esther. *Family Secrets and the Psychoanalysis of Narrative*. Princeton: Princeton UP, 1992.

Reddy, Maureen T. "Female Sexuality in 'The Poor Clare': The Demon in the House." *Studies in Short Fiction* 21 (1984): 259–65.

Reich, Wilhelm. *Reich Speaks of Freud. Conversations with Kurt Eissler*. Ed. Mary Higgins and C. M. Raphael. New York: Farrar, Straus, and Giroux, 1967.

Restuccia, Frances L. "Literary Representations of Battered Women: Spectacular Domestic Punishment." *Bodies of Writing, Bodies in Performance*. Ed. Thomas Foster, Carol Seigel, and Elaine E. Berry. New York: New York UP, 1996. 42–71.

Reynolds, Margaret. "*Aurora Leigh*: 'Writing her story for her better self.'" *Browning Society Notes* 17:1–3 (1987–1988): 5–11.

Rich, Adrienne. *On Lies, Secrets, and Silence: Selected Prose 1966–1978.* New York: Norton, 1979.

Rooney, Ellen. "'A Little More than Persuading': Tess and the Subject of Sexual Violence." *Rape and Representation.* Ed. Lynn A. Higgins and Brenda R. Silver. New York: Columbia, 1991. 87–114.

Rose, Jacqueline. Introduction II. *Feminine Sexuality: Jacques Lacan and the* école freudienne. Ed. Juliet Mitchell and Jacqueline Rose. New York: Norton, 1985. 27–57.

———. "Where Does the Misery Come From?: Psychoanalysis, Feminism, and the Event." *Feminism and Psychoanalysis.* Ed. Richard Feldstein and Judith Roof. Ithaca: Cornell UP, 1989. 25–39.

Rosenblum, Dolores. "Face to Face: Elizabeth Barrett Browning's *Aurora Leigh* and Nineteenth-Century Poetry." *Victorian Studies* 26:3 (1983): 321–38.

Schor, Hilary. *Breaking the Chain: Women, Theory, and French Realist Fiction.* New York: Columbia UP, 1985.

———. *Scheherezade in the Marketplace: Elizabeth Gaskell and the Victorian Novel.* New York: Oxford UP, 1992.

Semmel, Bernard. *George Eliot and the Politics of National Inheritance.* New York: Oxford UP, 1994.

Shanley, Mary Lyndon. *Feminism, Marriage, and the Law in Victorian England, 1850–1895.* Princeton: Princeton UP, 1989.

Shaw, Sheila. "The Female Alcoholic in Victorian Fiction: George Eliot's Unpoetic Heroine." *Nineteenth-Century Women Writers of the English Speaking World.* Ed. Rhoda B. Nathan. New York: Greenwood, 1986. 171–79.

Shelston, Alan. "The Supernatural in the Stories of Elizabeth Gaskell." *Exhibited by Candlelight: Sources and Developments in the Gothic Tradition.* Ed. Valeria Tinkler-Villani and Peter Davidson. Amsterdam: Editions Rodopi, 1995. 137–46.

Shuttleworth, Sally. *George Eliot and Nineteenth-Century Science: The Make-Believe of a Beginning.* New York: Cambridge UP, 1987.

Simons, Jon. *Foucault and the Political.* London: Routledge, 1995.

Smith, Allan Gardner Lloyd. *Eve Tempted: Writing and Sexuality in Hawthorne's Fiction.* Totowa, NJ: Barnes & Noble, 1983.

Steinmetz, Virginia. "Images of 'Mother-Want' in Elizabeth Barrett Browning's *Aurora Leigh*." *Victorian Poetry* 21:4 (1983): 351–67.

Stone, Marjorie. "Genre Subversion and Gender Inversion: *The Princess* and *Aurora Leigh*." *Victorian Poetry* 25:2 (1987): 101–27.

Stoneman, Patsy. *Elizabeth Gaskell*. Bloomington: U of Indiana P, 1987.

Surridge, Lisa. "Dogs'/Bodies, Women's Bodies: Wives as Pets in Mid-Nineteenth-Century Narratives of Domestic Violence." *Victorian Review* 20:1 (1994): 1–34.

Tanner, Laura. *Intimate Violence: Reading Rape and Torture in Twentieth-Century Fiction*. Bloomington: U of Indiana P, 1994.

Taylor, Harriet. "The Enfranchisement of Women." *The Disenfranchised: The Fight for Suffrage*. London: Routledge, 1993. 1–37. Vol 3. of *Sources of British Feminism*. Ed. Marie Mulvey Roberts and Tamae Mizuta. 6 vols. 1993.

Thackeray, W. M. *Vanity Fair*. Ed. John Sutherland. World's Classics. New York: Oxford UP, 1983.

Thaden, Barbara Z. *The Maternal Voice in Victorian Fiction: Rewriting the Patriarchal Family*. New York: Garland, 1997.

Thompson, Nicola. "'Something Both More and Less Than Manliness': Gender and the Literary Reception of Anthony Trollope." *Victorian Literature and Culture*. Ed. John Maynard and Adrienne Auslande Munich. Vol. 22. New York: AMS, 1994. 151–71.

Tolstoy, Leo. *War and Peace*. Trans. Rosemary Edmonds. New York : Viking Penguin, 1957.

Trollope, Anthony. *Barchester Towers*. Ed. Robin Gilmour. Harmondsworth: Penguin, 1982.

———. *He Knew He Was Right*. Ed. David Skilton. London: Everyman, 1993.

Turner, Arlin. *Nathaniel Hawthorne: A Biography*. New York: Oxford UP, 1980.

Walkowitz, Judith R. *City of Dreadful Delight*. Chicago: U of Chicago P, 1992.

West, Robin. "The Difference in Women's Hedonic Lives: A Phenomenological Critique of Feminist Legal Theory." *Wisconsin Women's Law Journal* 3 (1987): 81–140.

Williams, Anne. *Art of Darkness: A Poetics of Gothic*. Chicago: U of Chicago P, 1995.

Woolf, Virginia. "Professions for Women." *The Death of the Moth and Other Essays*. New York: Harcourt, Brace, 1942.

———. *A Room of One's Own and Three Guineas*. Ed. Morag Shiach. World's Classics. Oxford: Oxford UP, 1992.

Youra, Steven. "'The Fatal Hand': A Sign of Confusion in Hawthorne's 'The Birth-Mark.'" *American Transcendental Quarterly* 60 (1986): 43–51.

Zanger, Jules. "Speaking of the Unspeakable: Hawthorne's 'The Birthmark.'" *Modern Philology* 80:4 (1983): 364–71.

Žižek, Slavoj. *The Metastases of Enjoyment : Six Essays on Woman and Causality*. London: Verso, 1994.

———. *The Plague of Fantasies*. London: Verso, 1997.

Zonana, Joyce. "The Embodied Muse: Elizabeth Barrett Browning's *Aurora Leigh* and Feminist Poetics." *Tulsa Studies in Women's Literature* 8:2 (1989): 241–62.

Index